KENTUCKY/TENNESSEE
TRAVEL ✦ SMART®

D0863732

Great Smoky Mountains National Park, Tennessee

KENTUCKY TENNESSEE

TRAVEL ✦ SMART®

Second Edition

Susan Williams Knowles

John Muir Publications
Santa Fe, New Mexico

Dedicated to my mother, Margaret Anderson Williams, who grew up on the border of Kentucky and Tennessee and gave me an appreciation for both nature and culture, and to my father, Lawrence H. Williams, who gave me the love of travel

The author wishes to thank Lynne Bachleda, Robert Cheatham, Roby Cogswell, Mark Fraley, Dan Holton, Patty Bladon Lawrence, Andrew Saftel, Donna Tauscher, and Jane Harris Woodside for their invaluable assistance.

John Muir Publications, P.O. Box 613, Santa Fe, New Mexico 87504

Printed in the United States of America
Second edition. First printing February 1999.

ISSN: 1099-9906
ISBN: 1-56261-470-3

Editors: Peg Goldstein, Chris Hayhurst
Graphics Editor: Tom Gaukel
Production: Rebecca Cook
Design: Janine Lehmann and Linda Braun
Cover Design: Janine Lehmann
Typesetting: Linda Harper
Map Illustration: American Custom Maps—Albuquerque, NM USA
Map Style Development: American Custom Maps—Albuquerque, NM USA
Printer: Publishers Press
Front cover photo: Leo de Wys Inc./Viadpans
Front cover inset photo: © Chad Ehlers/Photo Network
Back cover photo: Tennessee Photo Services

Distributed to the book trade by
Publishers Group West
Berkeley, California

While every effort has been made to provide accurate, up-to-date information, the author and publisher accept no responsibility for loss, injury, or inconvenience sustained by any person using this book.

HOW TO USE THIS BOOK

Kentucky/Tennessee Travel•Smart is organized in 15 destination chapters, each covering the best sights and activities, restaurants, and lodging available in that specific destination. Thanks to thorough research and experience, the author is able to bring you only the best options, saving you time and money in your travels. The chapters are presented in geographic sequence so you can follow an easy route from one to the next. If you were to visit each destination in chapter order, you'd enjoy a complete tour of the best of Kentucky and Tennessee.

Each chapter contains:

- User-friendly maps of the area, showing all recommended sights, restaurants, and accommodations.
- "A Perfect Day" description—how the author would spend her time if she had just one day in that destination.
- Sightseeing highlights, each rated by degree of importance: ✸✸✸ Don't miss; ✸✸ Try hard to see; ✸ See if you have time; and No stars—Worth knowing about.
- Selected restaurant, lodging, and camping recommendations to suit a variety of budgets.
- Helpful hints, fitness and recreation ideas, insights, and random tidbits of information to enhance your trip.

The Importance of Planning. Developing an itinerary is the best way to get the most satisfaction from your travels, and this guidebook makes it easy. First, read through the book and choose the places you'd most like to visit. Then, study the color map on the inside cover flap and the mileage chart (page 12) to determine which you can realistically see in the time you have available and at the travel pace you prefer. Using the Planning Map (pages 10–11), map out your route. Finally, use the lodging recommendations to determine your accommodations.

Some Suggested Itineraries. To get you started, six itineraries of varying lengths and based on specific interests follow. Mix and match according to your interests and time constraints, or follow a given itinerary from start to finish. The possibilities are endless. *Happy travels!*

SUGGESTED ITINERARIES

With *Kentucky/Tennessee Travel•Smart* you can plan a trip of any length—a one-day excursion, a getaway weekend, or a three-week vacation—around any special interest. To get you started, the following pages contain six suggested itineraries geared toward a variety of interests. For more information, refer to the chapters listed—chapter names are bolded and chapter numbers appear inside black bullets. You can follow a suggested itinerary in its entirety, or shorten, lengthen, or combine parts of each, depending on your starting and ending points.

Discuss alternative routes and schedules with your travel companions—it's a great way to have fun, even before you leave home. And remember: Don't hesitate to change your itinerary once you're on the road. Careful study and planning ahead of time will help you make informed decisions as you go, but spontaneity is the extra ingredient that will make your trip memorable.

Rugby, Tennessee

Best of Kentucky and Tennessee Tour

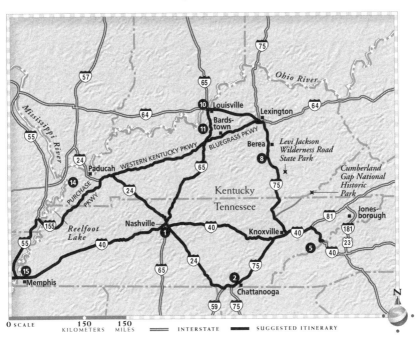

Follow this itinerary for a "greatest hits" tour of Kentucky and Tennessee.

❶ Nashville
❷ Chattanooga
❺ Great Smoky Mountains
❽ Cumberland Gap and Berea
❿ Louisville
⓫ Bardstown and Historic Central Kentucky ("My Old Kentucky
   Home," whiskey distilleries, Shaker Village at Pleasant Hill, Fort
   Harrod)
⓮ Western Waterlands
⓯ Memphis

Time needed: two weeks

Nature Lovers' Tour

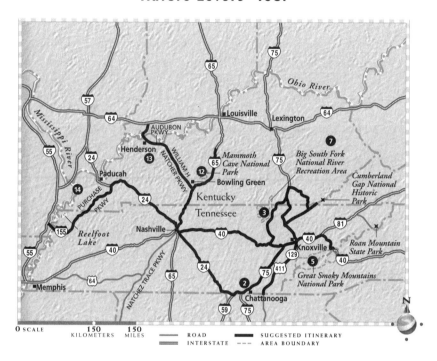

Mountains, rivers, caves—follow this tour and bask in the region's natural splendor.

- **❷ Chattanooga** (South Cumberland State Recreation Area)
- **❸ Rugby and the Big South Fork** (Big South Fork National Recreation Area, Daniel Boone National Forest, Obed Wild and Scenic River)
- **❺ Great Smoky Mountains**
- **❼ Eastern Kentucky**
- **⓬ Bowling Green and Mammoth Cave** (Mammoth Cave National Park)
- **⓭ Henderson and Owensboro** (John J. Audubon Park and Museum, Ohio River)
- **⓮ Western Waterlands**

Time needed: 10 days

Family Fun Tour

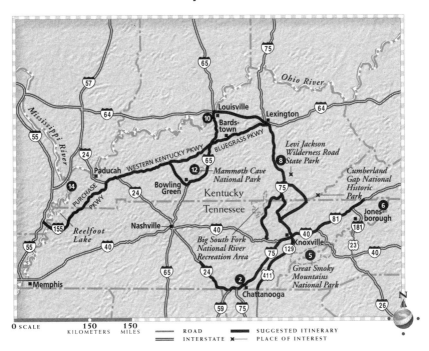

From river rafting to storytelling, there are treats here for travelers of all ages.

- **②** **Chattanooga** (Tennessee Aquarium, Creative Discovery Museum, Ocoee river rafting, Scenic Route 127)
- **⑤** **Great Smoky Mountains**
- **⑥** **Northeast Tennessee** (Jonesborough Storytelling Festival, Nolichucky river rafting, *The Wataugans* outdoor drama)
- **⑧** **Cumberland Gap and Berea**
- **⑩** **Louisville** (Kentucky Derby Museum, Louisville Science Center, *Belle of Louisville*)
- **⑫** **Bowling Green and Mammoth Cave** (Mammoth Cave, Shaker Museum)
- **⑭** **Western Waterlands**

Time needed: two weeks

America's Music Tour

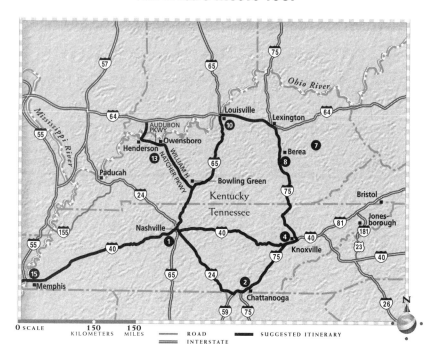

Kentucky and Tennessee offer bluegrass, jazz, blues, and country music at their best.

❶ Nashville (Grand Ole Opry, live music clubs, Nashville Chamber Orchestra, Blair School of Music)

❷ Chattanooga (Riverbend Festival, Bessie Smith Music Hall)

❹ Knoxville (bluegrass, jazz)

❼ Eastern Kentucky (Mountain Arts Center)

❽ Cumberland Gap and Berea (Berea Crafts Festival, Traditional Music Festival)

❿ Louisville (Kentucky Center for the Arts)

⓭ Henderson and Owensboro (W. C. Handy Blues Fest, International Bluegrass Festival)

⓯ Memphis (Opera Memphis, Germantown Performing Arts Center, blues and jazz)

Time needed: 10–14 days

Traditional Arts and Folk Culture Tour

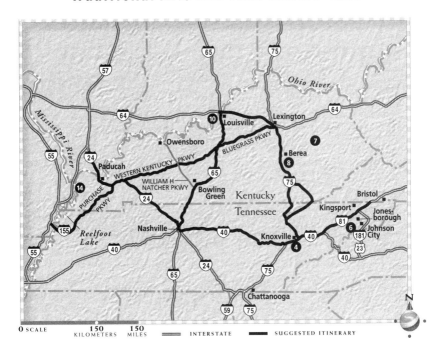

America's folk heritage is alive and thriving in this region.

- **Knoxville** (Museum of Appalachia, Norris)
- **Northeast Tennessee** (National Storytelling Headquarters, Carroll Reece Museum, Archives of Appalachia, Down Home Music Club, Birthplace of Country Music Alliance)
- **Eastern Kentucky** (Mountain Crafts Trail)
- **Cumberland Gap and Berea** (Appalachian heritage, crafts, music)
- **Louisville** (folk art, crafts, storytelling, local history)
- **Western Waterlands** (river culture, Museum of the American Quiltmakers Society)

Time needed: two weeks

Pondering the Past Tour

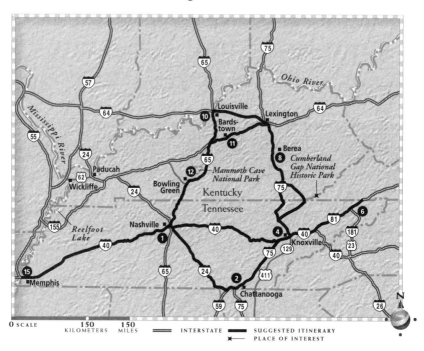

Visit these destinations for a fascinating historical tour.

❶ Nashville (The Hermitage, Tennessee State Museum)

❷ Chattanooga (African American Museum, Civil War battlefields)

❹ Knoxville (Museum of East Tennessee History, McClung Museum, scenic Highway 411)

❻ Northeast Tennessee (Jonesborough, Sycamore Shoals State Historic Area, Center for Appalachian Studies and Services)

❽ Cumberland Gap and Berea

❿ Louisville (Falls of the Ohio, historical museums)

⓫ Bardstown and Historic Central Kentucky (Old Fort Harrod State Park, Shaker Village at Pleasant Hill, Perryville)

⓬ Bowling Green and Mammoth Cave (Mammoth Cave, Shaker Museum at South Union)

⓯ Memphis (Chucalissa, Slavehaven, National Civil Rights Museum)

Time needed: three weeks

USING THE PLANNING MAP

Two major aspects of itinerary planning are determining your mode of transportation and determining the route you will follow as you travel between destinations. The Planning Map on the following pages will enable you to do just that.

First read through the destination chapters carefully and note the sights that intrigue you. Then photocopy the Planning Map so you can study the different routes that will take you to these destinations. (The mileage chart that follows will help you to calculate your travel distances.) Decide where you will be starting your tour of Kentucky and Tennessee. Will you fly into Nashville, Louisville, or Knoxville; or will you start from somewhere in between? Will you be driving from place to place, or flying into major transportation hubs and renting a car for day trips? The answers to these questions will form the basis for your route design.

Once you have a firm idea of where your travels will take you, copy your route onto the additional Planning Map in the appendix. You won't have to worry about where your map is, and the information you need on each destination will always be close at hand.

© David N. Davis/Photo Network

Tobacco barn, Kentucky

Planning Map: Kentucky/Tennessee

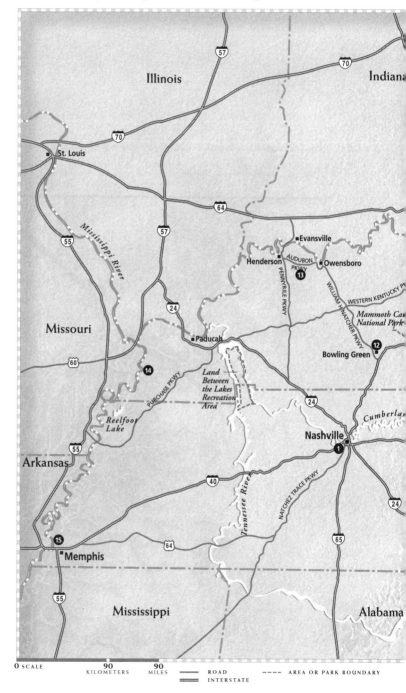

Illinois

Indiana

57

70

70

St. Louis

64

57

55

Mississippi River

Evansville

Henderson   AUDUBON   Owensboro
             PKWY
                          13

PENNYRILE PKWY

WILLIAM H NATCHER PKWY

WESTERN KENTUCKY PW

Mammoth Ca
National Park

24

Missouri

Paducah

Bowling Green   12

60

14

PURCHASE PKWY

*Land
Between
the Lakes
Recreation
Area*

Cumberla

24

*Reelfoo
Lake*

Nashville

1

Arkansas

55

40

65

Tennessee River

NATCHEZ TRACE PKWY

24

15

64

65

Memphis

55

Mississippi

Alabama

0 SCALE   90   90
           KILOMETERS   MILES   ■■■■ ROAD   ---- AREA OR PARK BOUNDARY
                                    ■■■■ INTERSTATE

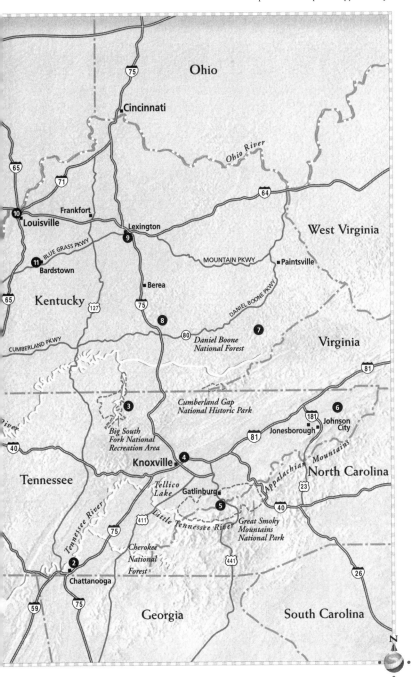

	Memphis, TN	Nashville, TN	Knoxville, TN	Chattanooga, TN	Jonesborough, TN	Paducah, KY	Henderson, KY	Owensboro, KY	Bowling Green, KY	Bardstown, KY	Louisville, KY	Frankfort, KY	Lexington, KY	Berea, KY	Cumberland Gap, TN	Rugby, TN
Nashville, TN	208															
Knoxville, TN	385	177														
Chattanooga, TN	315	140	107													
Jonesborough, TN	477	269	92	199												
Paducah, KY	168	136	313	276	455											
Henderson, KY	279	156	333	296	475	100										
Owensboro, KY	287	125	302	265	444	131	31									
Bowling Green, KY	267	59	236	199	378	151	97	66								
Bardstown, KY	359	151	209	291	274	210	147	116	92							
Louisville, KY	381	180	241	320	317	230	121	108	114	43						
Frankfort, KY	420	212	192	299	257	264	171	158	153	61	50					
Lexington, KY	414	206	170	277	235	266	202	171	147	56	71	22				
Cumberland Gap, TN	440	232	55	162	97	358	304	273	207	177	220	160	138	98		
Rugby, TN	391	183	71	119	163	293	239	208	142	207	250	190	168	128	84	
Gatlinburg, TN	425	217	40	147	94	373	342	276	249	292	232	210	170	90	111	

WHY VISIT KENTUCKY AND TENNESSEE?

Kentucky and Tennessee, located virtually in the middle of the United States, are as much a part of the early history of this country as they are of our contemporary culture. They may seem in a way familiar—even to those who have never set foot here. Perhaps your relatives came through on their way west or south; perhaps you raise horses, or have taken up quilting, or are a connoisseur of fine whiskey or pipe tobacco. Perhaps you own antique furniture, baskets, or pottery made by Tennessee or Kentucky artisans. Perhaps you have followed the paths of Daniel Boone, Sequoyah, Davy Crockett, Lewis and Clark, Abraham Lincoln, Ida B. Wells, or Alex Haley in your mind's eye so that their surroundings became visible to you long before you had the opportunity to see them for yourself. Coming to these lands in person will add richness to your understanding of our country's history and provide insights into the character of its early peoples. Seeing Mark Twain's *Huckleberry Finn* performed by the nationally prominent cast at Louisville's Actor's Playhouse just a few blocks from the Ohio River pulled me all the more deeply into the story and its contemporary relevance. Mark Twain, whose parents came from Tennessee, was incredibly clever at lambasting racial injustice, the pomposity and foolishness of political and religious leaders, and the fallacy of the conventional wisdom, all the while promoting the value of plain common sense.

Aside from fascinating history and rich culture, you'll also find incredible natural beauty here. From the mountainous eastern regions, to the grasslands and rolling hills at the heart of each state, to the western flatlands of the Mississippi River, both states are home to a surprising diversity of outdoor environments. One of the best things about exploring this wonderland of nature is that you can look down into a vast mountain valley or carefully pick your way along a scarcely trodden forest path, like a pioneer or one of the first Indians to inhabit this land. Yet even in the midst of seeming wilderness, state and national park facilities crisscross these states, providing technical resources, interpretive displays, guided activities, and a wide assortment of lodging.

Denizens of both states display not only a reverence for history but also a passion for tradition. Following the leads in this book, you'll encounter authentic customs and folkways—concerning everything from farming to folk art to food—that have been passed down from generation to generation. Driving the scenic routes, stopping at small out-of-the-way towns and historic homes, standing where your ancestors stood, tasting the local cuisine at every opportunity, and spending the night in places that remind you of where you are the minute you awaken, will grant you the fullest experience of Kentucky and Tennessee. Once you know what to look for, you can find many specifics of the region reflected in the larger cities—in the architectural details, in the street names and commemorative sites, in the old institutions and neighborhoods, and in the regional specialties on many menus.

HISTORY

The geologic history of the region spans a vast period of time. Fossil remains from the Devonian period of 400 million years ago—when the whole region was covered by tropical seas— can be found today along the Ohio River at Louisville, near its historically unnavigable shoals.

The formation of the river valley during the last two glacial epochs scraped the land back to the level of the formerly undersea fossils. The presence in both Kentucky and Tennessee of mammoths and mastodons and the prehistoric humans who hunted them 10,000 years ago is scientific fact. Strata of minerals, veins of igneous stone, and deposits of sedimentary rock have been exposed in jutting rocky hillsides and deep gorges that can be read like a book to reveal the story of this land.

The first peoples to inhabit the area spread through the region following the wide network of navigable waterways. The Archaic Indians and their successors inhabited caves, left traces of their ceremonies, and blazed hunting trails through both states. Before the arrival of the first white settlers, Mississippian Indians had established a few large cities and a number of ceremonial sites along the Tennessee and Mississippi Rivers. In a few instances the Cherokee (in the east) and the Chickasaw (in the west) took over the sites. At Mammoth Cave, Pinson Mounds, Chucalissa, and Wickliffe Mounds, and in farmers' fields in both states, traces of these peoples remain. Their history is still being written. Artifacts that now reside in many local and state museum collections are parts of a puzzle that is only very slowly being fitted together. It is clear that trade with Gulf Coast tribes, and possibly with the pre-Columbian peoples of Mexico, had been established by the most ancient Indians.

Ceremonial ball games somewhat similar to those of the ancient Maya were still being played by the East Tennessee Cherokee when French King Louis Philippe made his visit to the United States in 1797. Many fascinating found and excavated objects have never been fully studied. Sadly, some of the critical evidence needed for this research may have been destroyed in the aftermath of the Indian removal of 1838 or by the Tennessee Valley Authority's reengineering of the land and water of East Tennessee, which contained important Cherokee homelands.

In the second half of the eighteenth century, pioneer settlers (mostly English, Scottish, and Scots-Irish—Irish who settled in Scotland for a period before making the journey across the Atlantic) came down from Virginia into Tennessee. After the Treaty of Sycamore Shoals in 1775, many continued on through the Cumberland Gap into Kentucky, following the trail created by Daniel Boone and a group of 30 men working for Richard Henderson's Transylvania Land Company. Both in eastern Tennessee and along the Wilderness Road in Kentucky, you can find frontier life interpreted at museums such as the Bays Mountain Farmstead Museum, the Museum of Appalachia, and the Mountain Homeplace; at "living history" homes such as Rocky Mount and White Hall; at reconstructed fortified settlements such as Fort Boonesborough and Fort Harrod; and in homesteads that have remained almost fully preserved such as Hensley settlement at Cumberland Gap and Cades Cove in Great Smoky Mountains National Park.

Since both states were formed in the 20-year period following the American Revolution, many of the original landowners, the founders of cities and towns, and the first public officials in Kentucky and Tennessee were Revolutionary War heroes. Clarksville, Indiana (just across the river from Louisville), and Clarksville, Tennessee, were named for Louisville's founder George Rogers Clark. His younger brother William founded Paducah, Kentucky, after returning from his famous expedition with Meriwether Lewis. Knoxville was named after George Washington's secretary of war. The names of the region's major rivers—Kentucky, Tennessee, Ohio, and Mississippi—all derive from American Indian designations. Many other place-names, such as Cumberland, Kingsport, Lexington, Richmond, Bristol, and

Elizabethton, reflect the heritage of the English settlers who arrived before statehood.

The architectural history of this country is well illustrated in the buildings in both states that have been carefully preserved or lovingly restored. While the homes of prosperous eighteenth-century Tennesseans tended toward the rustic (they were, after all, built by frontiersmen, hunters, and farmers), the earliest fine homes in Kentucky belonged to the very wealthy. In the Kentucky capital of Frankfort, palatial Federal-style brick homes, built in the late 1790s for some of the state's first legislators, stand just as they did then in a quiet neighborhood right next to the river. Visitors will find the commanding "centre houses" of two early nineteenth–century Shaker settlements convincing proof of the superiority of shared economy during the beginning years of this country, when most Tennesseans and many Kentuckians were living in little more than log cabins. The prosperity in both states before and after the Civil War ensures that almost every one of the popular architectural styles of the nineteenth and early twentieth centuries are well represented. Louisville, Nashville, and smaller towns like Henderson, Paducah, and Clarksville were thriving river and railroad towns with large brick warehouses for the safe storage of goods and multistoried Victorian homes for prosperous merchants. Many towns in East Tennessee grew up along the railroad lines built to connect Richmond to Knoxville and Atlanta.

On the eve of the Civil War, Knoxville was poised to become a major industrial center, with a network of train tracks serving the mining and timbering operations of the Cumberland Mountains and freight links to the south and east. Memphis was the gateway marketplace for the cotton plantations of the Delta, and Nashville and Chattanooga were vital transportation centers for the movement of goods around the South. Kentucky, with its important trade ports at strategic points along the Ohio and Mississippi Rivers and the huge land holdings of gentlemen farmers and horsemen in its fertile center, formed the northern border of the slave states. Both Kentucky and Tennessee were split by divided loyalties during the Civil War, and their historic battlefields—Chickamauga, Shiloh, and Perryville—are saturated by the blood of native sons. This most painful period of our history seems very close at hand when one passes a Confederate monument in either state.

There is a lot to be learned about this country's economic development simply by observing physical reminders of the historical demography of these two states. Early transportation and trade routes into a scarcely populated land; the confusing settlement patterns and allegiances of British, French, Indians, and American frontiersmen during the Revolutionary War era; the brash arrogance of homesteaders plunging into what they supposed were uninhabited territories; the blind cruelty of many early leaders toward anything and anyone who stood in their way; the wholesale export and exploitation of natural resources; the spread of shipping and railroad commerce; the growth of a major agricultural infrastructure; the rise of manufacturing after the Civil War; the impact of freed African Americans and women on the work force; the rise of organized labor; and, finally, the postindustrial aftermath, all have left instructive marks here. Across both states there can be found memorial markers for the Trail of Tears, monuments to the region's first entrepreneurs, lands wasted by mining and manufacturing, well-built railroad depots, riverside shipping warehouses and factories (most no longer in use), and nostalgic reminders of a once-dominant agricultural system.

TRADITIONAL ARTS AND FOLK CULTURE

We can learn a great deal about the character of those who settled these lands by studying cultural expressions such as language, handicrafts, and customs. In many pockets of rural society, and in preserved historical colonies such as Kentucky's two Shaker villages, one can experience folkways that date back to the late eighteenth and early nineteenth centuries. The fact is that traditional ways of doing things, like farming, quilting, woodcarving, and cooking, can be found in full practice around both states. Folk tradition is not only emulated, but also respectfully reinterpreted by contemporary craftspeople. This is one of the country's most active craft-producing areas. The physical environment—the mountains, grasslands, rivers, and general patterns of nature—serves as inspiration for folk artists working in isolated areas, as well as for ever-increasing numbers of urban and rural craft artists. Crafts fairs, storytelling festivals, and traditional music celebrations are an important part of community life in both states. The Tennessee Crafts Fair, held in early May in Nashville; and similar fairs in Bell Buckle, Monteagle, Gatlinburg, and Memphis show off Tennessee's wealth of craft production. The Kentucky Art and Craft Foundation maintains permanent exhibit spaces around the state to keep the works of Kentucky artisans before the public at all times.

Berea, Kentucky, home to a dense population of craft shops, holds several annual traditional crafts and music events.

Bluegrass music, whose locus of development forms a triangle around eastern Tennessee, eastern Kentucky, and southwest Virginia, is widely performed all around the region. Summer bluegrass festivals and fiddling contests are annual events in cities like Owensboro and Henderson, Kentucky; and in Clarksville, Smithville, and Murfreesboro, Tennessee. Many take place in more rural locations like Renfro Valley and Rough River Dam, Kentucky; and Cosby, Bolivar, Woodbury, and Nine Mile, Tennessee. A brochure put out by the Folk Arts Program of the Tennessee Arts Commission a few years back listed more than 30 annual fiddling contests in Tennessee. Held in farmers' barns, local schools, or community centers, these events often last several days as fans sit around campfires trying out new licks, RVs are pulled into circles like covered wagons, and outdoor country kitchens dispense beans, barbecue, and cornbread.

While strains of the musical heritage of the British Isles can be heard within the bluegrass idiom, there are also many practitioners of traditional Irish, English, and Scottish music and dance throughout the Appalachian region. English contra-dancing is popular in Berea, Kentucky, and at several venues around Knoxville and Nashville, Tennessee; and you can find both mountain and hammered dulcimers being played during the annual dulcimer contest in Pineville, Kentucky. Small music clubs from Cincinnati to Knoxville, Whitesburg to Bowling Green, and Johnson City to Nashville feature acoustic musicians on guitar, dulcimer, fiddle, and pennywhistle playing the sprightly jigs and mournful ballads of their forefathers who settled this area.

Celebrations of culture—like the revival of the street game "dainty" in Louisville's Germantown; the annual "Roley Hole Marble" tournament at Tennessee's Standing Stone State Park; the National Storytelling Festival in Jonesborough, Tennessee; Seedtime on the Cumberland in Whitesburg, Kentucky; and folk medicine festivals at Red Boiling Springs, Tennessee, and Wickliffe Mounds, Kentucky— can be found here in abundance. Harvest festivals for tobacco, pumpkins, cotton, apples, and peaches are widely held in both states. Wildflower walks begin as early as April, and strawberries are honored during the month of May in numerous locations, but the most unusual springtime offering is probably the Ramp (a cousin of the onion) Festival, whose queen is crowned in Cosby, Tennessee. As you make your way across the rural landscape, hand-lettered signs on the back roads point you to the workshops of birdhouse-, basket-, and willow furniture–makers; while Kentucky parkway and interstate highway signs list antique shops and historic districts alongside places for food, gas, and lodging.

FINE ARTS

Contemporary classical musicians, visual artists, and creative writers are, as anywhere in the United States, to be found clustered around the major universities' music, art, and literature departments. Both Tennessee and Kentucky have several large state universities and a number of fine private universities and colleges that attract top artists to teaching positions. In both states, however, it is primarily in the major cities—Louisville, Memphis, Nashville, Lexington, Knoxville, and Chattanooga—that one finds the symphonies, opera companies, art museums, commercial galleries and nonprofit art spaces, and the literary events. An exception to this rule is Kentucky's strong network of professional theater companies which are headquartered not only in Louisville and Lexington, but also in Bowling Green, Horse Cave, and Paducah. Some smaller cities, such as Kingsport and Oak Ridge, Tennessee; and Owensboro, Kentucky, also have symphony orchestras. Artists following the national trend of moving away from the omnipotent artistic centers are also arriving here to swell the ranks of painters and sculptors in Louisville, Memphis, and Nashville. The rapid growth of Nashville's music industry is attracting untold numbers of musicians, music producers, screenwriters, and design and film professionals. And every year at Nashville's Southern Festival of Books, there are more and more "locals" among the nationally recognized coterie of writers.

CUISINE

Southern cooking is made up of a variety of types and styles of food. Just like the language of Southern speakers, it has been formed not only from the traditional culinary vocabulary of England, Ireland, and Scotland, but also from the African vernacular recipes. Its basic syntax comes from Native American food preparation, and its idiomatic expressions derive from the many pockets of ethnic German, Swiss, Italian, and Greek immigrants who settled in the region. Of course, any cuisine is dependent upon the availability of ingredients, and regional innovations often arise out of substitutions made from necessity.

Kentucky and Tennessee are as bountiful in foodstuffs as the other Southern states. The growing season is long and summertime harvests yield a wide variety of vegetables and fruits. Sweet corn, perfectly ripe red tomatoes, cucumbers, strawberries, blackberries, blueberries, beans, squash, and okra are commonly found on menus in both the humblest of plate-lunch diners and the fanciest of restaurants during the summer months. When you drive out into the countryside you'll see long, low chicken houses and muddy pig yards on rural farms; as well as fields full of grazing cattle and, occasionally, sheep and goats. The cold mountain streams harbor trout, and catfish are plentiful in rivers and lakes. Apples, nuts, and berries grow in the wild, but their widespread cultivation ensures their availability for apple and pecan pies, strawberry jam, and blueberry pancakes.

Wherever you find down-home food—at lunch counters and small local restaurants—you'll find seasonal specialties like fried green tomatoes (after the first frost), fresh mustard greens, sliced tomatoes, blackberry cobbler, cucumbers, and onions. Winter menus in these same sorts of inexpensive restaurants rely on soup beans (dried beans cooked slowly in water with ham hock), chowchow pickle relishes, stewed fruits and vegetables, grits, hominy, potatoes, and cornbread. Bacon, pork chops, and barbecued pork shoulder are likely to be on the menu, as are fried catfish and chicken. Establishments such as these reflect local culinary custom, availability of food in the community, and sometimes the origin of the community founders. Okra, yams, and stewed greens, all staples of the African diet, grow well in Southern soil. Their presence on Southern tables indicates the influence of African slaves who moved from one wealthy landowner's kitchen to another, spreading cooking lore and practice from one generation of cooks to the next. Corn, dried beans, potatoes, tomatoes, squash, and other native fruits, nuts, and vegetables are American Indian contributions.

Soul food restaurants offer all of the above, but usually with the addition of what were once the cheapest meats—gizzards, livers, hearts, brains, intestines (chitlins)—often fried or in unusual preparations that many have grown to enjoy. Other regional favorites, such as dishes that combine game with vegetables and other meats—like Kentucky Burgoo and Virginia Brunswick Stew—may also have arisen out of the same sort of "make-do" spirit. These may have had their origins with the early settlers who were trying to mask the taste of poorly dressed meats. Barbecuing, a method of smoking meat with or without sauce, can also be used to disguise the taste of meats often thought to be inedible, like mutton or groundhog. A standard Southern cooking method with numerous variants, barbecue is thought to have its origins either in the Mexican *barbacoa* (pit cooking) or the French method of roasting a whole pig *barbe a queue* (from beard to tail)—according to John Egerton, author of *Southern Food*. Barbecuing is something of an institution in Southern cooking—much has been written about it, everyone has their own opinion about what is "real" barbecue, and at least two cities in Tennessee and Kentucky claim to be the barbecue capital of the world. If you are interested in the folklore of food, barbecue makes for an endless topic of conversation and there is no limit to the hours one can spend in field research. I frequently turn off the road on just a whiff from a smoking barbecue pit. With the exception of Memphis, where you're as likely to find crusty barbecued spareribs in thick, sweet sauce as a chopped pork sandwich; and northern Kentucky, where mutton is cooked in a spicy tomato sauce, most of the barbecue places in both states serve pit-cooked, pulled pork or half chickens with a vinegar, tomato, and hot-pepper sauce.

An Old South Sunday dinner at home or a meal at one of the many fine regional restaurants will feature traditional dishes calling for once highly prized ingredients such as thinly sliced aged salt-cured ham, breast meat of chicken or turkey, white flour, aged cheese, chocolate, refined sugar, choice fruits, and nuts. These recipes originated at the bountiful tables of Kentucky and Tennessee's privileged citizens. Country ham and beaten biscuits are still considered something special and can be found on silver trays at cocktail parties and occasionally on restaurant menus. The famous Kentucky Derby pie is a rich concoction that features pecans, chocolate, butter, sugar, and lots of eggs. Bourbon candy, a dark chocolate coating over a cream filling containing bourbon and pecans, was invented in Frankfort during Prohibition. The delicious Kentucky Hot Brown, which had its origins as a luncheon specialty at Louisville's Brown Hotel, is composed of sliced roast turkey, sometimes with the addition of country ham, a béchamel sauce, sliced tomato, aged white cheddar, and a strip of bacon baked on top of toast points. Chicken salad, made with white meat only, often includes pecans, grapes, raisins, almonds, or other delicacies in addition to the usual mayonnaise and celery. Iced tea, a variation on the customary British beverage that was, doubtless, invented to suit the warm Southern summer weather, is consumed year-round, with a sprig of fresh mint added in summer. Traditional British fare such as roasts of beef, pork, and lamb with accompanying jellies and condiments are usually served with some sort of potatoes and have always been found on the tables of prosperous Southerners. Fried chicken and fresh-caught fish are frequent additions and have been known to appear on Southern plates as early as breakfast time.

While Italian and Greek restaurants and the occasional authentic Jewish deli can be found relatively intact in locations where they were established decades ago in both states, the cuisine of newer immigrant groups like Mexicans, Middle Easterners, and Thais has only recently become readily available here. There are many excellent family-owned restaurants in small and large cities alike where you will find both the specialties and the prices a pleasant surprise. Because of the strong presence of Japanese industry in the region, there are also a number of fine sushi restaurants—some with house specialties written only in Japanese.

FLORA AND FAUNA

The diverse terrain of Kentucky and Tennessee—from mountainous regions and high plateaus to riverbanks, acres of flat or rolling farmland, and swampy wetlands—is home to a variety of plants and animals. Extreme variations of geography in one location, such as the South Cumberland wilderness area of Tennessee, can encompass as wide a variety of plant life as is found in certain parts of Canada. The same can be said of bird populations, which vary not only according to terrain but also according to altitude. The Great Smoky Mountains National Park, whose highest peaks rise to over 6,500 feet and whose lowest valleys sink to under 2,500 feet, attracts three distinct categories of birds. Many of those in the highlands, above 4,000 feet, are Canadian species. Waterfowl are abundant in both states because of the vast network of rivers and streams in the east and the wetlands areas and large lakes in the west.

The park naturalists at Mammoth Cave, Kentucky, have published a checklist of some 250 birds that have been sighted in the park in recent years. This list could be used as a bird-watching guide for the middle territories of both states, far away from both the mountains and the low-lying waterlands.

The streams, rivers, and lakes of both states offer a wide variety of freshwater fish—from the cold-water mountain, brown, and rainbow trout and smallmouth and red-eye bass, to lake fish such as largemouth bass, brim, crappie, and catfish. Crawfish, turtles, and mussels are also found in the rivers. Mussel fishing was once a thriving industry along the Tennessee River in West Tennessee, for mussel-shell buttons were much in demand until plastic buttons began to be manufactured in the first quarter of the twentieth century.

Domesticated animals—cattle, horse, hogs, sheep, goats, chickens, even ostriches and emus—are visible in fenced fields throughout both states. Chipmunks, squirrels, groundhogs, and rabbits are as commonly spotted in neighborhood yards as they are in the rural areas. Out in the country you'll come upon wildlife out in the open, especially near lakes and rivers. White-tailed deer, wild turkeys, ducks, geese, quail, and pheasants are often seen. Visitors to both states who venture away from the busy roads and city centers to camp in the wild are likely to hear bobcats, raccoons, possums, and skunks prowling about under cover of darkness. Coyotes can sometimes be heard yelping in the distance, especially where there are livestock farms nearby.

In the Great Smoky Mountains, where black bears and red wolves are protected species, visitors are asked to keep food locked away and to make sure that even the charred remains of meats cooked on outdoor grills do not find their way into the wild-animal food chain. Bears like densely wooded areas and open thickets where they can easily find the wild nuts and berries that are their primary sources of food. In recent years park naturalists have begun a program of relocating bears and wolves to prior native habitats, such as the Big South Fork, in order to restore the normal balance of animal life.

Human interference in the natural order of things, especially the wholesale logging of the past and the voracious trapping and hunting that took place in the early years of this country, has taken its toll on the native animal population. Certain species of birds have all but vanished, and the change in air quality has affected many types of plants. The industrial pollution of air and water in this century has created some problems in Tennessee that are only now being recognized and addressed. Reforestation has been taking place for some years now and some previously endangered species are beginning to be restored. Nonnative animals such as the wild boar and the rainbow trout are being systematically hunted and fished-out in the Great Smoky Mountains.

Visitors should be aware that poisonous flora and fauna, which could put a damper on any vacation, are present in these parts, if only in a few forms. As avid hikers know, in the woods and lowlands of this area there are a wide variety of snakes. Copperheads and timber rattlesnakes in fields and forests as well as water moccasins and cotton-mouth near the edges of rivers and lakes are the poisonous ones. Most snakes will scurry for cover long before you see them, but sunny days will find them basking in the sun on rocks or logs—so look before you step. Yellow jackets and other forms of wasp can give a nasty sting to which many people are highly allergic. Standing water and stilled breezes make good breeding grounds for mosquitoes, especially in late summer. In recent years ticks have become more of a problem, especially the almost invisible seed ticks. When walking in high grass or dense forest during the summer months, it is advisable to wear socks covered with some sort of insect repellent. Those who are susceptible to poison ivy will find it growing here in abundance, so stay away from three-leaved vines climbing on tree trunks.

In the eastern parts of both states, a wide variety of wildflowers and wild flowering trees and shrubs—such as azalea, mountain laurel, rhodo-dendron, dogwood, and redbud—make the spring and summer months particularly beautiful. Because of the range of elevations in the region, you can find the same plant species blooming in different locales from April to July. The most delicate wildflowers grow deep in the woods and in shady spots on park hillsides. At least seven varieties of trillium—a three-leaved relative of the lily that has a central white, pink, or yellow flower—grow in the higher elevations. Varieties of the wild orchid, with descriptive names like lady's slipper and jack-in-the-pulpit, will delight a child's imagination. And the wild versions of garden flowers, such as the tiny Dutch iris, lily of the valley, and the primrose, can be found along-side pipsissewa, May apple, and Indian pipe. Many woodland plants were used by the Indians and early settlers for medicinal purposes. Some, like the bark and root of ginseng, are thought to have aphrodisia-cal powers and still bring a good price on today's market.

Many parts of both states remain heavily wooded, and deciduous trees mixed with evergreens create a spectacular fall display. Fall col-ors—the yellows of poplars, beeches, and birch trees; and the reds of maple, sweet gum, and red oak—appear first in the higher elevations, sometimes as early as the beginning of October near the Cumberland Gap, Roan Mountain, and the Smokies.

Virgin forest can still be found deep in the protected areas of both states. In the 1930s the Civilian Conservation Corps replanted many acres of logged timberland with evergreens, so in many locations today's visitor will encounter luxuriant stands of pine where there once stood hardwood forests.

LAY OF THE LAND

The high ridges of the Appalachian chain run north-south through the eastern portion of both states, with their western watershed draining into both Tennessee and Kentucky. The Clinch, Holston, Nolichucky, Tellico, and Hiwassee Rivers all join ultimately at the Tennessee River. Kentucky's Cumberland, Red, and Kentucky Rivers feed into the Ohio. The Tennessee and the Ohio are two of the major source rivers of the massive Mississippi River, while numerous other tributaries run through both states. The Great Smoky Mountains include the two highest peaks in the eastern United States: Mount Mitchell, in North Carolina, which is 6,684 feet above sea level; and Mount LeConte, in Tennessee, which stands at 6,643 feet. Kentucky's mountainous east is less lofty. Its highest point is Black Mountain, 4,145 feet above sea level, located near the Virginia border between Harlan and Whitesburg.

The geographical descent from the Appalachian Mountains takes place in stages from foothills to plateau then down into great wide valleys punctuated by occasional clusters of hills and bowl-like lakes. The Cumberland Plateau, which stretches from Kentucky down through Tennessee and into northern Alabama and the northeastern tip of Mississippi, is the last vestige of the Appalachian chain. The plateau's geography includes jagged limestone outcroppings, dramatic rock gorges, deep riverbeds, and spreading finger lakes as it levels off into the rolling hills and open grasslands of central Kentucky and Tennessee. The eastern edge of the Appalachian Mountains, with its abrupt peaks and drops, is much more dramatic. The long Sequatchie Valley, which traverses Tennessee from north to south, was once a single rock ridge that split into a relatively narrow rift with 800-foot walls on either side.

The Kentucky bluegrass region and the Cumberland Basin of Tennessee contain some of the richest farmland in the country. Fields boast tobacco, corn, soybeans, and wheat; cattle and horses graze peacefully in lush pastures. Around the edges of the basin, where the land begins to rise toward the plateau, sheep and goats straddle limestone boulders as they crop the grass. In Kentucky the western portion of this area is pockmarked with lakes and underground caves. Seams of coal and other minerals, once heavily mined here, are still a source of income for many Kentuckians. As it rolls west, the land grows flatter and begins to descend toward the Mississippi. Crossing the wide

Tennessee River or gazing out at the Ohio as it passes by Henderson and Owensboro seems somehow to take you back in time, to an age when everything depended on the river in one way or another. Riverboats still ply these waters and barges carry coal, lumber, and manufactured goods from the heartlands of these two states to outside markets.

The western portions of both states contain flat, open fields good for high-yield farming and lots of rich river-bottom land. Southwest Kentucky and northwest Tennessee are joined by the Land Between the Lakes, a recreation area located at the confluence of the Tennessee and Cumberland Rivers, which were dammed by the Tennessee Valley Authority to create Kentucky Lake and Lake Barkley. In southwestern Tennessee, where the fields must be irrigated and the sun beats down relentlessly in the summer, cotton was, and still is, the primary crop. The mighty Mississippi River flows along the western edge of both states. Kentuckians and Tennesseans of the past could either follow this fast-moving route to New Orleans—for many years the center of Southern commerce and culture—or cross over into the rough-edged civilization of the western frontier states of Missouri, Arkansas, and Texas.

OUTDOOR RECREATION

Nearly every type of outdoor sport can be undertaken in Kentucky and Tennessee. In fact, the only thing lacking is the ocean—scuba divers are forced to qualify for certification in lakes formed within abandoned rock quarries.

While one can walk the portion of the Appalachian Trail that passes through northeast Tennessee in a few days, and the Sheltowee Trace in several weeks' time, the mountainous areas of both states provide so many hiking routes that it is not possible to take on all of them in one lifetime. The serious rock climber will find challenging locales throughout the Appalachian chain, including Kentucky's Red River Gorge, the Wild and Scenic Obed River, the escarpment of the Cumberland Plateau, and Lookout Mountain in Tennessee. White-water lovers will enjoy the rapids of Big South Fork, Nolichucky Gorge, and the Ocoee River, site of the 1996 Olympic white-water events.

These two states are an angler's paradise—whether you wade into small cold streams using a fly or spin rod, troll from a bass boat, or go in for sportfishing in the deep lakes and swift rivers. In most cases, either a Tennessee or Kentucky fishing license is required and a trout stamp is necessary. The Kentucky Department of Fish and Wildlife (502/564-4336) can provide Kentucky fishing information and a list of licensed fishing guides. Check the listings in Tennessee's free vacation guide (800/G02-TENN) for optimum seasons and locations across the state, or call the Tennessee Wildlife Resources Agency (800/262-6704) and request a current fishing guide. They are available wherever fishing licenses are sold, often at convenience stores or at large retail establishments like K-Mart and Wal-Mart. TWRA also oversees hunting and boating activities throughout the state. The many recreational lakes created by the Tennessee Valley Authority (TVA) are perfect for water sports like swimming, boating, and waterskiing; while canoeists and kayakers will find both quiet and rushing waters on the many rivers.

Biking and running are popular activities in both states, as much of the land is gently rolling and the climate is temperate. The Tennessee Department of Transportation (615/742-5310) has mapped five bicycle routes. The Kentucky Bike Tour features six routes; for information write to P.O. Box 2011, Frankfort, KY 40602. The Tennessee State Park System (888/867-2757) has sponsored a series of Saturday running events called the Annual Running Tour. The races take place during the fall and winter months at different parks around the state and vary in length from five to thirteen miles. Many cities have running clubs that offer weekly or monthly group events. Check with outdoor outfitters for details.

Southeastern Tennessee calls itself the hang-gliding capital of the East. Chattanooga's Lookout Mountain is the home of several training facilities, and the lower Sequatchie Valley town of Dunlap is the site of regular club activities and nationally recognized hang-gliding events.

PLANNING YOUR TRIP

HOW MUCH WILL IT COST?

If you are prepared to spend $135 to $180 per day while traveling through these two states, and follow many of the suggestions in this book, you can enjoy lovely and unusual accommodations, visit memorable destinations, and taste the best local cuisine, with some luxury touches and a few splurges thrown in. A true bargain hunter who is not given to indulging costly whims in food, lodging, or mementos could do this trip for as little as $90 a day; campers might manage on about $20 less. My advice is to avoid summertime and special event rates in Nashville, Memphis, Louisville, and Lexington; be wary of autumn "leaf season," when the mountains are heavily touristed; and call ahead for cabin reservations at the state parks, for they are moderately priced and a stay in a rustic setting will add immeasurably to your visit.

Accommodations located on the major east-west and north-south interstate routes remain pretty consistent in price with the major hotel rates across the country, often making them more expensive than one might expect for an isolated location. While I have included them in the reference materials for some destinations, I choose these only out of necessity. They're good for when you arrive late at night, if everything else is booked, or for when a bed-and-breakfast host answers the door looking like Count Dracula.

Generally speaking, you should allow an average of $70 to $80 per hotel room night. Many bed-and-breakfasts will cost a bit more, but keep in mind that they often include breakfast for two in the total price. Some small family-owned motels charge as little as $40 for a double room, but you'll make up for it by paying $90 to $130 per night in Louisville, Lexington, Nashville, Chattanooga, or Memphis. Of course, sharing a room with your traveling companion will reduce your costs considerably, and if you don't mind carrying gear, an occasional camp-out will save you money as well. There are many clean and well-maintained camping spots in state and national parks where a site goes for less than $15, and sleeping under the stars may provide just the right change of pace from a hectic touring schedule.

A simple breakfast should cost somewhere from $6 to $8. I often manage for half that by carrying my own fruit and picking up a bagel or muffin and coffee at the best coffee place in town. Lunches can also be toted, for wherever you go you'll find roadside picnic tables or scenic spots for alfresco eating beside rivers and streams or at high mountain overlooks. Lunches at local diners will generally cost you no more than $6 for a "meat and three," or a vegetable plate with biscuits or cornbread. A barbecue sandwich heaped with coleslaw will tide me over any day—maximum cost $5. For a sit-down lunch in a nice restaurant, expect to pay anywhere from $10 to $18 including tip. Dinners range in price depending upon whether you like wine or beer with your meal and the extent to which you have decided to indulge yourself. It would be easy to spend $100 or more for two people eating out at one of the better restaurants in Louisville, Nashville, Memphis, Lexington, Chattanooga, or Knoxville; but a nice meal with a glass of wine or beer can be found in all of these cities for $30 or less per person, as can a no-frills but delicious and healthful dinner for as little as $10.

Incidental costs, such as gasoline, admission prices, film, bottled water, and snacks can be held to an average of $25 a day if you are vigilant. As a tourist, my weaknesses are books, unusual food items, and anything handmade. Kentucky and Tennessee crafts are not cheap, but this is the place to purchase them, for their markets in the rest of the country will price them higher than at home and you might be passing up the chance to see the artist at work. My advice is to set aside several traveler's checks early in the trip just in case you happen to find the handmade Shaker-style rocker you've always wanted in Berea, Kentucky, or Jonesborough, Tennessee.

WHEN TO GO

April, May, September, and October are the nicest months. Spring flowers and autumn colors are both spectacular, the days are warm and dry, and the nights fresh and cool. June can be very pleasant; though sometimes hot, it is almost always sunny and usually drier than July and August, which are guaranteed to be hot and humid.

Horse-racing season begins as early as April in Kentucky, so secure a room in or around Lexington ahead of time if you plan to go. Of course, staying in a Louisville or Lexington hotel during the Kentucky Derby festivities of early May would put a strain on anyone's wallet.

Summer is tourist season everywhere, but it is especially so in Nashville. Hotel prices are at peak level, country-music fans come out in droves, and long lines of people gather outside the Hard Rock Café for their chance to eat lunch. Memphis is just plain sweltering in July and August and, unless you are a native of New Orleans or Houston, you will probably find it unpleasant.

In the fall, college football weekends in Nashville, Knoxville, and Memphis can make it difficult to find a reasonably priced room. University of Kentucky basketball in Lexington draws huge crowds that fill most of the downtown hotels near the arena. The Great Smoky Mountains National Park, Big South Fork, Daniel Boone National Park, and the state parks in the eastern portion of both states are crowded during peak leaf season (mid-October, usually); and the small motels, bed-and-breakfasts, and country inns on their periphery often increase their prices accordingly.

I find traveling during the off-season quite rewarding. You don't have to keep to a schedule of hotel reservations, and you get a glimpse of the routines of "real-life" people in the region. Like a kid out of school, I have always taken pleasure in being off when everyone else was at work. One word of warning: Avoid traveling in January when many historic sites are closed and you are likely to encounter the heaviest snows of the season.

CLIMATE

The region's daytime spring and fall temperatures stay in the 60- to 80-degree range with relatively low humidity, while nights tend to drop into the 40s and 50s. Summer months can be quite sunny, humid, and hot, with temperatures remaining in the 90s for weeks at a time in July and August. The days are long, and with ample rainfall the flowers, fruits, and vegetables generally thrive. You'll find flowers blooming in sunny spots as early as mid-February, and the months of March through May offer both wildflowers and garden flowers galore. Many gardeners plant a second crop of lettuce and garden peas in the fall, hoping that frost will not come until after Halloween. Strawberries are ripe by Memorial Day while corn on the cob and homegrown tomatoes are ready by July Fourth. Once in a while Tennessee Thanksgiving tables will feature sliced tomatoes just off the vine.

December is likely to be cold and wet. Most snow falls in January, but yearly accumulations average little more than a foot. March comes in like a lion, often with howling winds and driving rains that can quickly become tornado weather. April and May are more likely to be sunny than showery, with temperatures ranging from the 70s to the high 80s.

KENTUCKY/TENNESSEE CLIMATE

Average daily high and low temperatures in degrees Fahrenheit

	Nashville	Great Smoky Mountains	Louisville	Memphis
Jan.	46/28	35/19	41/24	48/30
Mar.	60/38	39/24	55/32	63/43
May	79/57	57/43	76/55	81/61
July	90/69	65/53	87/68	92/72
Sept.	83/61	60/47	81/59	83/64
Nov.	54/38	42/28	56/37	62/42

TIME ZONES AND AREA CODES

The eastern portion of both states, which includes the cities of Lexington, Knoxville, and Chattanooga, is in the Eastern Time Zone; the dividing line runs roughly just outside the easternmost ridge of the Cumberland Mountains. Louisville, Nashville, and Memphis are on the leading edge of the central time zone, which includes most of the Midwest and Texas. In the summertime this means that daylight stretches past 9 p.m. in the eastern time zone, so in Lexington, Knoxville, Chattanooga, the Cumberland Gap, and the Great Smoky Mountains it is easy for travelers to set up camp late in the day or to take a scenic drive after supper.

Because of the high demand for internet access, and the increasing population in Tennessee, several new area codes have been added over the past few years. If a telephone number is no longer valid, the problem may be merely that the area code has changed. In addition, where once the time zone/area code delineations seemed to run nearly parallel, so that one could assume a certain area code was in the eastern time zone, some of the new area codes, such as 931 and 423 in Tennessee, cross two zones, so it is wise to verify arrival and departure times with your destination when traveling.

TRANSPORTATION

The region is served by a number of airports, cross-country buses pass through its major cities, and major north-south and east-west interstate highways crisscross both states. Kentucky and Tennessee are centrally located, and driving from home may not be as prohibitive in time or mileage as you might think. One full day of driving from Nashville will get you as far as Washington, D.C., Dallas, New Orleans, Kansas City, or Chicago. Railroad passenger service here is all but nonexistent now, although the freight lines are still active. Memphis is served by a north-south Amtrak route connecting it to New Orleans and Chicago; and both Cincinnati and Atlanta also have Amtrak passenger service. Amtrak has a toll-free reservation and information phone line: 800/872-7245.

If you plan on flying to the area, Nashville International Airport has the best airline connections, with nonstop flights to many cities on American, Delta, Southwest, U.S. Air, United, TWA, Continental, AmericaWest, and others. Louisville, Memphis International, and Knoxville are also served by many of the major airlines. Lexington and Chattanooga have good airports that support both nonstop and commuter flights. Cincinnati's international airport is actually located in northern Kentucky; and the huge Atlanta airport, also international, is just two hours south of Chattanooga.

Car rentals are available at all of the airports. If you are arriving in Nashville, it is best to reserve ahead and look for discounts (AAA, airline frequent flyer, travel promotion) because most travelers through the region are either on business or are tourists and prices tend to remain high and availability low for weekday rentals. Besides Avis, Hertz, National, Budget, Alamo, Thrifty, and Dollar—all of which can be reached toll-free and are generally located in the major airports— Sears and Enterprise are national companies that serve many cities without airports, and they often do so with lower rates.

All of the destinations, itineraries, and scenic routes in this book can be reached by a regular passenger vehicle, except on rare winter occasions when even the major highways become impassable for a day or so in the higher elevations. (Should you encounter bad weather while traveling, both states have road-condition hot lines that provide a very welcome service. Call 800/4KY-ROAD in Kentucky and 800/858-6349 in Tennessee.) For the adventuresome traveler, a bicycle trip across these two states could be plotted with information from the

Tennessee Department of Transportation, the Tennessee State Parks, and the Kentucky Bike Tour organization. Listed throughout this book are a number of outdoor outfitters in the region who not only sell but also rent camping equipment. If you are interested in horseback travel, the Tennessee Equine Trail Guide (Tennessee Department of Agriculture, 615/837-5160) lists city, state, and national riding trails, as well as a surprising number of camping and bed-and-breakfast accommodations that cater to horse owners. The guide also lists outfitters who can rent you a mount for day or overnight rides.

CAMPING, LODGING, AND DINING

If you intend to camp your way across Kentucky and Tennessee, begin by gathering information from both state park systems (Kentucky Department of Parks: 502/564-2172; Tennessee State Parks: 888/867-2757). Both provide a wide selection of cheap, clean, well-maintained campgrounds that are open year-round. The national parks (Great Smoky Mountains, Mammoth Cave, Big South Fork, Cumberland Gap) are listed in appropriate chapters of this book. When you arrive, check in at one of the local outdoor outfitters to purchase useful items you might have forgotten and to inquire about other good camping spots, white-water outfitters, bike routes, out-of-the-way hiking trails, rock-climbing venues, or other points of local interest. Often the folks who work at these shops are devoted sportspeople who are both friendly and knowledgeable.

I've included bed-and-breakfasts among my recommended lodgings for three reasons: First, a B&B, likely to be housed in a historic home, is often the nicest place to stay in a small town; second, you might learn something about the town's culture from your hosts; and third, a home-cooked breakfast is a nice way to start a day of touring—it gets you up and out. I have tried to include small locally owned hotels whenever possible, for in my experience they are often in safer, more attractive locations; are better maintained; and are at least as cheap as their national counterparts, which tend to be placed alongside the exits of interstate highways or near large shopping centers. Some campgrounds and motel courts include small, separate cabins; usually without television or telephone, these are often considered "budget" accommodations, but I prefer them for their privacy and rustic charm.

In the moderately priced category, I recommend the wonderful old cabins in the state parks, most of which rent for $50 to $60. This price includes linens, a small kitchen, one or two bedrooms, and a fireplace or screened porch. The modern state park lodges offer rooms in the same price range but with more standard accommodations. Many bed-and-breakfasts fall into this same price range if you add $10 to $20 for the price of breakfast for two. For the same cost you should be able to find a room at the nicest motel in any small town, some of the old historic hotels, or any national chain motel located in a rural area or along a major highway.

The outstanding historic inns and luxury B&B destinations charge upwards of $80 for a double room. The contemporary resort cabins at the state parks also fall into this price range, and so do most downtown hotels in large cities. The most expensive hotel rooms you'll find in the region are historic hotels that have been restored to their former glory in the major cities; and new luxury resort inns, where a room for two without breakfast can cost anywhere from $110 to $150 or more. Many of these hotels offer weekend packages, state and federal employee rates, and all manner of discounts when their occupancy falls below a certain percentile. Don't be afraid to bargain with them as evening draws near, for a night of pampered slumber is good for the soul.

I love to eat. I love the taste of fresh foods in season, and I love learning the culinary customs of places and people. I believe that one of the best ways to get to know a locale is to experience its characteristic cuisine. Accordingly, this guidebook recommends many simple eateries that visitors might not even consider at first glance. The budget category (usually well under $10) includes local diners, old-fashioned soda fountains, storefront ethnic restaurants, the new wave of upscale coffeehouses that serve a limited but often very good menu, and places that serve regional specialties (some for carryout only). Moderately priced ($10 to $25) recommendations include health food restaurants, restaurants located at historic sites, and restaurants that serve regional specialties in an aesthetic environment with good service. In the fine restaurant (that is, expensive) category I have tried to point out the one-of-a-kind historic sites—places that can function as a kind of touchstone for the traditional cuisine of a region. Once some parameters have been established, you can begin to judge the creative chefs and young innovators for yourself as you visit the popular restaurants in Louisville, Lexington, Knoxville, Memphis, Chattanooga, and Nashville. Such gourmet moments will probably make a dent in your travel budget; but Southern hospitality is most fully experienced at the dining table, so I hope you will make several fine restaurant outings a priority no matter what your itinerary. While some of the newest immigrants to the area are just starting out with budget-level dining rooms, you will also find excellent French, Italian, and Mediterranean cuisine in the upscale dining establishments of these cities. I have not listed those here, for although many are quite good, they also tend to be expensive. Instead—in hopes that visitors will come away with a lasting sense of where they have been—I have tried to point out those restaurants that feature an interesting local ambiance or interpret the local cuisine.

RECOMMENDED READING AND VIEWING

This region wears its stereotypes like burrs on a dog's coat—impossible to get rid of and so numerous that, in the aggregate, no particular one seems to be more harmful than any other. To better understand their sources, read about them in the words of some of the finest writers to depict the people and places of Tennessee and Kentucky. Robert Penn Warren, Peter Taylor, and Caroline Gordon hailed from northern Tennessee and the south-central Kentucky area near Nashville; Bobbie Ann Mason and Wendell Berry are still writing from central Kentucky; and Mary Lee Settle and James Still keep the words coming from Kentucky's Appalachian region. The works of James Agee and Cormac McCarthy capture the tragic humor of the environs of Knoxville and the mountains of East Tennessee, and Nikki Giovanni's own humor and toughness reflect her Knoxville upbringing. Wilma Dykeman, noted author of many books about the East Tennessee region, as well as the original WPA guide to Tennessee, still hosts a radio program in conjunction with Knoxville symphony performances on WUOT, 91.9.

In *The Scots-Irish in the Hills of Tennessee* (1995), Billy Kennedy—an Ulsterman and a newspaper reporter—traces the origins of the Northern Irish emigration into the Appalachian regions of Tennessee. This migrant group was composed primarily of Scottish Presbyterians who settled first in Northern Ireland before coming across the Atlantic.

In *Exploring the Big South Fork* (1994), Russ Manning directs hikers, bikers, climbers, and white-water enthusiasts to both popular and out of the way places. He also provides a good orientation to the whole area. Manning's *The Historic Cumberland Plateau: An Explorer's Guide* (University of Tennessee Press, 1993) covers a wide swath of land through both states—from Red River Gorge in the north to Chattanooga in the south; from Cumberland Gap in the east to the Obed River in the west.

Piercing the Heartland: A History and Tour Guide of the Fort Donelson, Shiloh, and Perryville Campaigns by Jim Miles (1991) is a good driving guide to the areas around these battlefields and contains fascinating battle narratives by a Civil War buff.

Vicki Rozema's *Footsteps of the Cherokees: A Guide to the Eastern Homelands of the Cherokee Nation* (1995) offers a summary of historical events leading to the 1838 removal of the Cherokee and discusses 19 geographic areas, about half of which are in Tennessee and North Carolina and the rest in Georgia and Alabama.

Appalachian Whitewater, Volume I: The Southern Mountains by Bob Sehlinger (1994) is an excellent guide that not only explains the geography and stream dynamics of the area but also provides a primer on basic paddling. Detailed descriptions of particular stretches of white water, with directions for finding them, make up the bulk of the book. Sehlinger's *Canoeing and Kayaking Guide to the Streams of Kentucky* (1994) is based on more than a year of field research by the author.

Laura Thornborough's *The Great Smoky Mountains* (1937) is a charming volume that was written during the first years of the national park's formation. Although now long out of print, the book is valuable not only for its historical perspective but also for the author's well-expressed environmental stance.

Independent filmmaker Ross Spears has produced excellent documentaries on James Agee and the TVA. Especially insightful is his *Long Shadows*, a study of the aftermath of the Civil War. Films like *Coal Miner's Daughter* and *Nashville* will give viewers a caustic glance back at the now-powerful country-music establishment; and, more recently, *The Firm*, a novel by John Grisham, presents an accurate portrait of Memphis and a cynical view of the contemporary South. *In Country*, written by Bobbie Ann Mason and filmed in and around Paducah, reflects both the rural culture of the area and the plight of many returning Vietnam vets to this patriotic region. Appalshop (606/633-0185), a nonprofit creative workshop cooperative in Whitesburg, Kentucky, in the far eastern part of the state, produces documentary films, art exhibits, books, and records honoring the rich culture of Appalachia. From their Mountain Community Radio Station (88.7) comes excellent Kentucky Public Radio programming featuring interviews, cultural news, and regional music. Similarly, the Center for Southern Folklore (901/525-3655), located on Beale Street in Memphis, collects regional cultural expressions on documentary film, audio tape, and in a series of publications.

RESOURCES

It used to be that a traveler could scan the local daily newspaper to take the pulse of the next town on his or her itinerary. In these days of national newspaper syndicates and sensationalist front-page stories, this is, unfortunately, no longer true. However, many cities have thriving alternative papers that come out weekly, biweekly, or even monthly that will prove more helpful to visitors seeking to put a finger on the cultural scene. These papers are usually free, and popular budget breakfast places, coffee houses, and music venues will normally have dispenser racks out front. By the same token, public radio stations, many of which are run by the state universities in Kentucky and Tennessee, have assumed the role of community bulletin boards for cultural happenings, so tune to the low end of the FM dial as you approach any sizable city in either state. Louisville, Lexington, Richmond, and Bowling Green in Kentucky; and Johnson City, Knoxville, Chattanooga, Nashville, and Memphis in Tennessee all have National, American, or Public Radio International affiliate stations.

For general travel information, a calendar listing of special events and festivals, and a free state map, request a vacation guide booklet from either state (Tennessee: 800/GO2-TENN; Kentucky: 800/225-TRIP). Both states have tourism Web sites as well: www.state.tn.us/tourdev (Tennessee); www.kentuckytourism.com (Kentucky).

There are several bed-and-breakfast associations that might be able to send you advance literature on member B&Bs. Others merely serve as reservation services or handle establishments that may not advertise elsewhere. The Kentucky Bed-and-Breakfast Association (800/292-2632) publishes an extensive, free, map/guide brochure. Bluegrass B&B Reservations (606/873-3208) serves the central Kentucky region around Lexington and Frankfort, and offers bookings at inns that do not appear in published guides. B&B of Lexington (800/526-9801) coordinates bookings for four lodgings in private homes in Lexington. The Tennessee B&B Innkeepers Association (800/820-8144) lists only B&Bs that have passed their inspection process; and the Natchez Trace B&B Reservation Service (931/285-2777 or 800/377-2770) has 10 Tennessee inns in their registry. Explore B&B listings on the internet at www.bbonline.com; the site includes photos of most houses, and lists entries by state.

Civil War: Both Tennessee and Kentucky have created Civil War "Heritage Trails" to assist visitors in identifying and finding sites of important Civil War activities. The history of this cataclysmic event is still being rewritten, as both scholars and the public seek to come to terms with its legacy. A welcome irony here is that neighboring states to the north and west are joining in to create unified Civil War trails, telling the history of both sides, that are being used for cooperative tourism across state lines. You can obtain these helpful booklets by calling the Kentucky Department of Travel Development (800/255 TRIP) and the Tennessee Department of Tourism (888/243-9769).

1
NASHVILLE

Nashville, located in the gently rolling hills of north-central Tennessee, has a metropolitan area population of nearly one million and is rapidly becoming the state's largest city. Three interstate highways cross here, a fact that partly accounts for the popularity of country music among truck drivers. Nashville's greatest fame rests upon the booming business of country music. Although widely known as the country music capital of the world, musicians of all stripes can be heard in Nashville's music venues, from its smoky barrooms to its balconied concert halls.

The historic buildings of downtown Nashville are undergoing tremendous renovation and restoration. Ryman Auditorium, home to the original Grand Ole Opry (which moved to a contemporary auditorium at suburban Opryland in the 1970s), has been restored to its former glory. The honky-tonks of lower Broadway, considered eyesores until just a few years ago, managed to escape the wrecking ball and are finally receiving their due from music-oriented visitors and historians of early country music. Just down the street, the four-story, one-block-deep brick structures of the riverfront warehouse district and the late-nineteenth-century limestone Customs House (a half mile up Broadway, the main east-west artery of Nashville) bear witness to Nashville's early history as a center of river trade. ◣

NASHVILLE

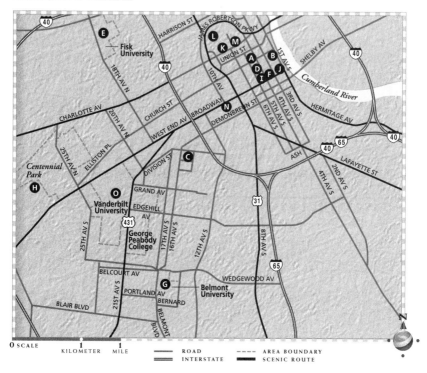

Sights

- **A** The Arcade
- **B** City Walk
- **C** Country Music Hall of Fame and Museum
- **D** Downtown Presbyterian Church
- **E** Fisk University
- **F** Hatch Show Print
- **G** Historic Belmont
- **A** Life and Casualty Tower
- **H** The Parthenon

- **I** Ryman Auditorium and Lower Broadway
- **J** Tennessee Fox Trot Carousel
- **K** Tennessee Performing Arts Center (TPAC)
- **L** Tennessee State Capitol
- **M** Tennessee State Museum
- **N** Union Station
- **O** Vanderbilt University and George Peabody College

Note: Items with the same letter are located in the same place.

A PERFECT DAY IN MUSIC CITY

Nashville's temperate climate almost always permits outdoor exercise early in the morning. Jog around Centennial Park or, for a surprisingly "North Woods" experience, hike one of the loop trails at Radnor Lake. After coffee and a freshly baked fruit scone at Provence, visit the Country Music Hall of Fame up the street, whose exhibits are unfailingly good; and Hatch Show Print, still a going business on lower Broadway, where you can see who is having a traditional block-print poster done for their next Nashville appearance. Peek inside the Parthenon at the gigantic statue of Athena and walk across Centennial Park to Hog Heaven, a great barbecue stand that even serves a smoked turkey sandwich. Spend the rest of the afternoon at Elder's Books on Elliston Place and at White Way Antique Mall. Nashville music events can get crowded quickly, so call ahead for reservations after you've chosen which musical genre you'd like to indulge. Have a nightcap at Merchant's Restaurant on lower Broadway, or enjoy music-making until well after midnight in any of the honky-tonks down the street.

MORE NASHVILLE FACTS

Nashville, Tennessee's capital, was founded in 1779 by James Robertson and John Donelson, whose Fort Nashborough has been reconstructed on the west bank of the Cumberland River, now First Avenue. During the Civil War, Nashville, a city of Confederate sympathies, was occupied by Federal troops because of its strategic location. Nashville is still a crossroads of the upper South and a current center of economic growth, as its recently built downtown skyscrapers attest. While it is home to Truckstops of America and Peterbilt, Nashville has also traditionally been a printing and publishing center, and in recent years it has become a mecca for the rapid rise of private hospital care companies, such as Columbia/ HCA and Healthtrust. Nashville prides itself on its nickname "the Athens of the South," and it is a matter of debate whether that name has its origin in that fact that the city is home to so many universities or that Centennial Park contains a full-scale replica of the Parthenon.

SIGHTSEEING HIGHLIGHTS

★★★ **City Walk**—The Metro Historical Commission's marked walking trail through downtown is a great way to get a feel for the early history of Nashville. Look for the teal blue stripe on the sidewalk and historical markers bearing silhouetted figures. The walk begins at Fort Nashborough (170 First Ave. N. between Church and Broadway; 615/255-8192) and passes through Nashville's historic riverfront. First and Second Avenues from Broadway to the County Courthouse are lined by deep brick warehouses into which goods were once loaded from the Cumberland River. Even today, this is a lively commercial area. Check out Butler's Run, a covered passageway between the two streets; Market Street Brewery, Nashville's first brewpub; and the old Acme Feed and Seed, at the corner of First and Broadway, where you can find everything from spring plant starts to souvenirs. City Walk covers sites from Nashville's earliest history, the Civil War era, the suffrage movement, the civil rights era, and more. **Historic Nashville** offers a guided walking tour on Saturdays and by reservation for $5 per person.

Details: Metro Historical Commission, 615/862-7970; Historic Nashville, 615/244-7835. (1½ hours)

★★★ **Country Music Hall of Fame and Museum**—The Hall of Fame on Music Row is a terrific museum of country music history that traces its roots from traditional Scots-Irish to blues to bluegrass. The Hall of Fame is run by the Country Music Foundation, which houses a fine library and archives, has the best gift shop on Music Row, and runs historic Studio B. By the way, Music Row is 16th and 17th Avenues and Demonbruen Street, where you'll find record-label headquarters, music studios, talent agencies, and the souvenir shops and museums of various country singers.

Details: 16th Ave. S. and Division St., Nashville; 615/255-5333. Daily 9–5; summer 8–6. $10.75 adults, $4.75 ages 6–11. (1½ hours)

★★★ **Downtown Presbyterian Church**—This historic church building is one of Nashville's architectural wonders. Designed by William Strickland, architect of the state capitol, this rare example of Egyptian revival architecture, completed in 1851, has stained-glass windows featuring papyrus motifs and interior trompe l'oeil paintings of a columned courtyard.

Details: Church St. at Fifth Ave., Nashville; 615/254-7584. Daily 8–4; guided tours Mon and Fri. (15 minutes)

★★★ **The Hermitage**—One of the best interpreted and restored historic sites in the country, the Hermitage, which was the home of

Andrew Jackson, actually began as a two-story log cabin. The house was built in 1821 with a Greek Revival facade added after a fire in 1836. There is also an interpretive center.

Details: 4580 Rachel's Ln., Hermitage; 615/889-2941. Daily 9–5. $8 adults, $7 seniors, $4 ages 6–12. (2 hours)

★★★ **The Parthenon**—Built originally in 1897 as the Art Building for the Tennessee Centennial Exposition, the Parthenon was rebuilt in 1931. It now houses a permanent art collection, a 42-foot sculpture of Athena Parthenos by Tennessee sculptor Alan LeQuire, and reproductions of the Elgin marble friezes from the Athenian original.

Details: Centennial Park, 2500 West End Ave., Nashville; 615/862-8431. Tue–Sat 9–4:30; extended hours in summer. $2.50 adults, $1.25 seniors and ages 4–17. (1 hour)

★★★ **Ryman Auditorium and Lower Broadway**—Don't miss the high temple of country music, at Fifth Avenue between Broadway and Commerce. The beautifully remodeled Ryman hosts a variety of country, gospel, bluegrass, pop, and rock events, and occasional musical theater. Call for tickets. After the show, walk through the alley to the back door of Tootsie's Orchid Lounge, where legendary Opry performers came to grab a quick one between shows. Stroll down Broadway to Gruhn Guitars, the famous music store with museum quality instruments for sale and a widely knowledgeable staff. **Hatch Show Print**, one block further, between Third and Fourth Avenues, is a historic show poster shop where you can see woodblock printing in progress (615/256-2805). Pawn shops, honky-tonks, and record stores are all still in business and remain much as they were when the Opry was still downtown.

Details: 116 Fifth Ave. N., Nashville; 615/254-1445. Daily 8:30–4. $6 adults, $2.50 ages 12 and under. (1 hour)

★★ **Cheekwood**—Leslie Cheek, a wealthy wholesale grocery broker, built this English manor house on the eve of the Great Depression. The Georgian-style house sits on 55 acres and is now a fine and decorative arts museum. The grounds include botanical gardens and greenhouses, changing exhibits, seasonal botanical events, and educational programs.

Details: 1200 Forrest Park Dr., Nashville; 615/356-8000. Mon–Sat 9–5, Sun 11–5; extended hours in summer. $6 adults, $5 seniors and college students, $3 ages 6–17. (2 hours)

✯✯ **Fisk University**—This historic campus, built in 1866 and named after Union General Clinton B. Fisk, was one of the first black colleges. Park and walk around the campus. The most striking building is the Victorian Jubilee Hall, now a dormitory, where you can view the portrait of the famed Jubilee Singers, whose performances of Negro spirituals helped raise money for the university and took them to the court of Queen Victoria. Across campus, the university library houses important works of art, manuscript, and archival collections related to the Harlem Renaissance. In the campus center, the administration building contains wall murals by Harlem Renaissance artist Aaron Douglas. The Carl Van Vechten Gallery of Fine Art houses a collection of American modern art donated by Alfred Stieglitz and Georgia O'Keeffe as well as important works by African American artists of the first half of the twentieth century. Admission to the gallery is free, although a donation is requested. Closed Monday.

Details: D.B. Todd Blvd. at 17th Ave., Nashville; 615/329-8453. Tue–Fri 9–5, Sat and Sun 1–4. (1½ hours)

✯✯ **Tennessee Fox Trot Carousel**—Native son Red Grooms has created a circus of historical characters on an actual mechanized merry-go-round. The carousel is a joy-filled way to learn history, created by a master of pop art.

Details: First Ave. at Broadway (Riverfront Park), Nashville. Daily 10–dusk, summer until 9. $1.50 per ride. (30 minutes)

✯✯ **Tennessee State Capitol**—This elegant and stately building was designed by William Strickland around 1845, and was completed in 1859, five years after his death. His drawings and a model are on display at the Tennessee State Museum. The grounds contain monuments to historical Tennesseans and Capitol Hill affords a nice view west and north of the city. Guided tours are available through the Tennessee State Museum (number listed below).

Details: Charlotte Ave. at Seventh Ave., Nashville; 615/741-2692. Mon–Fri 9–4. Admission is free. (30 minutes)

✯✯ **Tennessee State Museum**—Located on the lower floors of the Tennessee Performing Arts Center, the museum traces the state's history through artifacts and imaginative re-creations. Dioramas include a Mississippian Indian village, a log grist mill, and a religious revival meeting. In the early Indian section, my favorite exhibits are a 30-foot poplar canoe, surprisingly large axe and spear points, and beautifully carved soapstone pipe bowls. A well-stocked museum shop offers a bonanza of souvenir and gift possibilities.

Details: 505 Deaderick St., Nashville; 615/741-2692. Tue–Sat 10–5, Sun 1–5. Admission is free. (1½ hours)

✸✸ **Travellers Rest**—This is my favorite historic house in Tennessee because it is off the main tourist routes and looks very much as it might have 200 years ago. The home of Judge John Overton (founder of Memphis), it was built in 1799 and is beautifully maintained and interpreted, with a number of Overton's possessions still in place in rooms throughout the house. Overton, Andrew Jackson's law partner, named his home after Jackson's favorite horse, Traveller.

Details: 636 Farrell Pkwy., Nashville; 615/832-8197. Tue–Sat 10–5, Sun noon–5. $6 adults, $3 ages 6–11, under 11 free. (1 hour)

✸ **The Arcade**—This collection of shops is one of the oldest enclosed shopping arcades in the country. Visit the P-Nut Shop (you'll smell the roasting nuts as soon as you enter) and walk around the upstairs balcony where the frosted glass door offices look like Humphrey Bogart's in *The Maltese Falcon.*

Details: Between Fourth and Fifth Aves. and Church and Union Sts., Nashville; 615/255-1034. Mon–Fri 6–6. (15 minutes)

✸ **Belle Meade Plantation**—This historic house and its grounds were once the home of William Gates Harding, whose stables were famous in the early years of Tennessee statehood when Andrew Jackson rode mounts from Belle Meade.

Details: 5025 Harding Rd., Nashville; 615/356-0501 or 800/270-3991. Mon–Sat 9–5, Sun 1–5. $8 adults, $7.50 seniors, $3 ages 6–12. (1 hour)

Historic Belmont—This 1850 antebellum mansion was built by Nashville's wealthiest woman, Adelicia Hayes Acklen. Now located on the campus of Belmont University, it is worth a stroll through grounds still defined by a Palladian villa landscape plan and iron garden statuary. The house itself is filled with the high-Victorian furniture and European decorative art collected by its mistress.

Details: 1900 Belmont Blvd., Nashville; 615/460-5459. Tue–Sat 10–4, Sun 2–5; open Mon in summer. $6 adults, $5.50 seniors, $2 ages 6–12. (1 hour)

Life and Casualty Tower—Nashville's first skyscraper, this late-1940s art deco building is a reminder of the city's historical prominence as an insurance center. L&C and National Life and Accident (now combined as American General) started in Nashville, as did American Express. Until the Bell South Tower was built several years ago, no Nashville building had been allowed to exceed its 27-story height.

Details: Fourth Ave. and Church St. Lobby open Mon–Fri during business hours. (15 minutes)

Sankofa African Heritage Museum—Housing more than 500 works of African sculpture in a new complex that includes the Sankofa Gardens restaurant, this museum was created in the old style: glass cases crowded with objects and a minimum of explanatory information, which allows viewers free reign to glean what they will from the combination of ceremonial, utilitarian, and artistic items presented. This museum, founded by Dr. James Peebles, owner of Winston-Derek Publishers, is the only one around devoted entirely to works from the African continent.

Details: 101 French Landing Dr. (MetroCenter), Nashville; 615/256-0201. Mon–Sat 10–6, Sun 1–5. $10 adults, $5 seniors, under 12 free. (1 hour)

Tennessee Performing Arts Center (TPAC)—This site is worth seeing only if the schedule of events is enticing. There are three theaters where you can find Broadway Shows and major musical performances in all genres, including the fine Nashville Symphony (615/255-5600), Nashville Ballet (615/244-7233), and Nashville Opera (615/292-5710). Look for performances by the outstanding American Negro Playwright Theater (615/871-4283), Tennessee Dance Theatre (615/248-3262), and Tennessee Repertory Theatre (615/244-4878) groups. Humanities Outreach Tennessee offers special daytime performances for Tennessee schoolchildren throughout the year, so if you are traveling with kids, you might want to check it out.

Details: 505 Deaderick St., Nashville; 615/782-4000 (general information) or 615/255-9600 (box office and Ticketmaster). Mon–Fri 8–4:30 and during weekend performances.

Union Station—Nashville's Romanesque Revival–style train station is now a hotel. The train shed behind it, which is in dire need of restoration, is listed in the *National Register of Historic Places* as one of the largest metal structures in the country.

Details: 1001 Broadway, Nashville; 615/726-1001. Open daily. Admission free. (30 minutes)

Vanderbilt University and George Peabody College—These two campuses are now part of the same university system. Stroll the tree-lined Vanderbilt University campus (the trees are labeled), whose oldest buildings date from 1873. Stop in at the Fine Arts Gallery, located in the Victorian gymnasium; the modern Sarratt Student Center; and the main library Special Collections room to see current exhibits. Check the desk at the Sarratt Student Center for film, concert, and Great Performances series events.

Details: West End and 21st Aves. S., Nashville; 615/322-7311 (Vanderbilt operator) or 615/322-2471 (Sarratt Student Center). Open daily. All campus buildings free. (1½ hours)

FITNESS AND RECREATION

Nashville has lots of parks for walking, jogging, and biking. The centrally located **Centennial Park** adjoins the **Centennial Sportsplex**,

© Chad Ehlers/Photo Network

Nashville riverfront

which features an indoor pool, outdoor tennis courts, and an ice rink. A nominal fee is charged for admission to the Sportsplex. For more information call 615/862-8480. **Edwin and Percy Warner Parks**, located in west Nashville about 10 miles from downtown, are open year-round for hiking, running, and biking. **Edwin Warner Nature Center** offers educational programs and guided hikes for children, (615/352-6299). **Radnor Lake Natural Area**, on Otter Creek Road between Franklin and Hillsboro Roads, was a gift from the L&N Railroad to the state of Tennessee. It offers extensive hiking trails and a scenic drive by the lake and is open from dawn to dusk. Contact the visitors center for information, 615/373-3467.

There is a large network of YMCAs in Nashville, and the downtown **YMCA** (615/254-0631) features a rooftop pool. The **Vanderbilt University Track** is open to the public. Check with **Cumberland Transit**, 615/321-4069; and **Bike Pedlar**, 615/329-2453, both on West End Avenue near Vanderbilt University, for information on local biking, rock climbing, and water sports in the area as well as indoor recreation venues that might be open for public use.

Nashville is also a center for such recreational healing arts as therapeutic massage and yoga; check the Nashville Scene for listings. **Yoga Source**, at Cummins Station, 615/254-9642, offers a full range of massage instruction; and the **Yoga Room**, 615/383-6197, is a longtime Nashville favorite. **Westside Athletic Club**, 615/352-8500, offers evening yoga classes on a pay-as-you-come basis.

FOOD

There are lots of options for interesting, moderately priced food in Nashville. The luxury restaurants can be easily duplicated or surpassed in other cities, so I would recommend saving your money for a nicer place to stay in the right part of town. Two exceptions are the **Capitol Grille** in the Westin Hermitage Hotel (downtown, 231 Sixth Ave. N.; 615/244-3121) and **F. Scott's** (greater Nashville, 2210 Crestmoor Rd.; 615/269-5861). The Capitol Grille, a cozy and elegant dining room located downstairs in a historic Beaux Arts building, has a menu featuring new American cuisine with a Southern touch. It's open for breakfast, lunch, and dinner at prices that seem more than reasonable given the quality of food and service. Don't let F. Scott's suburban location put you off—the seasonal menu by an award-winning chef, extensive wine list, and superb service are well worth the effort. Dinner only, seven nights a week.

The most famous breakfast in town is at the **Loveless Motel and Cafe**, about 15 miles out in the country (greater Nashville, 8400 Highway 100; 615/646-9700.) The Loveless, which now has mail-order country hams and preserves, specializes in hot biscuits, redeye gravy, country ham, homemade peach and blackberry preserves, and fried chicken. It's also open for lunch and dinner and is usually less crowded then, but it's always wise to call for reservations. Another weekend breakfast favorite is **Nathan's** (I-24 and Bell Rd. in the Ramada Inn; 615/731-5611), which, despite its Italian lunch and dinner menu, serves from-scratch fruit pancakes, homemade raisin bread, French toast, and country ham, grits, and biscuits. Nearer at hand in midtown Nashville are: the **Pancake Pantry** (1796 21st Ave. S., Hillsboro Village; 615/383-9333), where the Music Row power-elite eat and kids can enjoy "bears in the snow" (chocolate pancakes with powdered sugar); **Bongo Java** (2007 Belmont Boulevard, 615/385-5282), a funky coffeehouse with an innovative menu and carryout baked goods, and **Fido** (1812 21st Ave. S., Hillsboro Village; 615/385-7959), where they roast their own coffee and serve up oatmeal topped with bananas and brown sugar, egg dishes, and fully loaded bagels. **Provence** (1705 21st Ave. S., 615/386-0363), also in Hillsboro Village, has a sunny dining room, great coffee, French pastries and breads, and scrumptious sandwiches and salads.

Lunch options range from "meat and three" plate lunches to gourmet carryout to elegant power-lunch restaurants. In the inexpensive category try **Arnold's Country Kitchen** (downtown, 605 Eighth Ave. S., 615/256-4455); or, for an authentic down-home experience, **Sylvan Park** (midtown, 4502 Murphy Rd., 615/292-9275). You'll rub shoulders with some interesting folks and taste some real Southern cooking.

If you are in the mood, treat yourself to a civilized lunch at **Satsuma Tea Room** (417 Union, 615/256-0760), where the menu changes daily and features delicious 1950s specialties such as turkey à la king and congealed fruit salad, as well as the best yeast rolls in the world. It's usually very crowded, but sharing a table here can be part of the fun. Also downtown are two fine, moderately priced sushi restaurants serving rice and noodle dishes as well. **Koto** (137 Seventh Ave. N., 615/255-8122) and **Ichiban** (109 Second Ave. North, 615/254-7185) are both open for lunch and dinner. Wonderful downtown dinner options in the moderately expensive price range include **Café 123** (123 12th Ave. N., 615/255-2233) and **Royal Thai** (204 Commerce St., 615/255-0821).

NASHVILLE

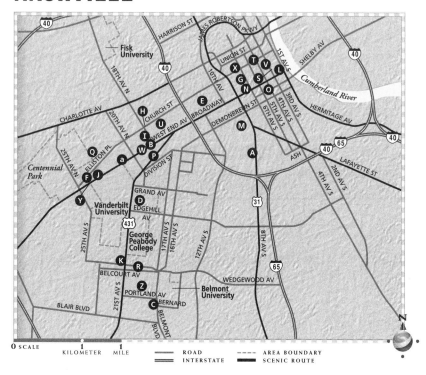

In Midtown Nashville near Vanderbilt University are inexpensive choices such as **Elliston Place Soda Shop** (2111 Elliston Pl., 615/327-1090) and **Vandyland** (2916 West End Ave., 615/327-3868), both of which are classic lunch counters. Vegetarians and adventuresome diners will like the moderate prices and innovative preparations at **Dancing Bear** (1805 Church St., 615/963-9900) and **Basante's** (1800 West End Ave., 615/320-0534). Both are open for dinner, when the lights are dimmed and both chefs put on extra-special menus that make these two of Nashville's finest up-and-coming restaurants. Moderately expensive but worth it are **Midtown Café** (102 19th Ave., 615/320-7176) and the **Sunset Grille** (2001 Belcourt Ave., 615/386-3663), which serve some of Nashville's best lunches to the city's best-known customers. Both are open for dinner. In this same price range but open only for dinner are **Cakewalk/Zola** (3001 West End Ave., 615/320-7778) and **Boundry,**(911 20th Ave. S., 615/321-3043). Less expensive and less formal, but still great dinner choices in midtown are **Sitar**, (116 21st Ave. N., 615/321-8889),

Food

- Ⓐ Arnold's Country Kitchen
- Ⓑ Basante's
- Ⓒ Bongo Java
- Ⓓ Boundry
- Ⓔ Café 123
- Ⓕ Calypso Café
- Ⓖ Capitol Grille
- Ⓗ Dancing Bear
- Ⓘ DaVinci's Pizza
- Ⓙ Elliston Place Soda Shop
- Ⓚ Fido
- Ⓛ Ichiban
- Ⓜ Jody's Bar Car
- Ⓝ Koto
- Ⓞ Merchant's
- Ⓟ Midtown Café
- Ⓠ Mosko's Muncheonette
- Ⓡ Pancake Pantry
- Ⓡ Provence

Food (continued)

- Ⓢ Royal Thai
- Ⓣ Satsuma Tea Room
- Ⓤ Sitar
- Ⓡ Sunset Grille

Lodging

- Ⓡ Commodore Inn and Guest House
- Ⓥ Courtyard by Marriott—Downtown
- Ⓦ Courtyard by Marriott—West End
- Ⓧ Crowne Plaza
- Ⓑ Days Inn West End
- Ⓣ Doubletree
- Ⓨ Hampton Inn—Elliston Place
- Ⓥ Hampton Inn—West End
- Ⓩ Hillsboro House
- ⓐ Loew's Vanderbilt Plaza
- Ⓖ Westin Hermitage

Note: Items with the same letter are located in the same area.

serving Indian food; **DaVinci's Gourmet Pizza** (1812 Hayes St., 615/329-8098), which has many innovative vegetarian selections; and **Calypso Café** (2424 Elliston Pl., 615/321-3878).

On the run around town? Drive through or sit down for a quick lunch at: **Bar B Cutie** (5221 Nolensville Pike, 615/834-6556; or 501 Donelson Pike, 615/872-0207); **Mosko's Muncheonette** (midtown, 2204 Elliston Pl., 615/327-3562); **Clayton-Blackmon** (4117 Hillsboro Rd., Green Hills; 615/297-7855); **Bread & Company** (4105 Hillsboro

Rd., Green Hills; 615/292-7323; and 106 Page Rd., 615/352-7323); or the **Corner Market** (6051 Hwy. 100, 615/352-6772).

At the end of the day, or after an evening of music, try **Jody's Bar Car** (209 10th Ave. S., 615/259-4875) for a sunset cocktail or a night-cap. Featuring pool tables and a view out over the railroad tracks, Jody's restaurant serves a late-night menu on weekends. **Merchant's** (401 Broadway, 615/254-1892), located in a historic lower-Broadway drugstore, features live jazz on weekend nights.

LODGING

The midtown area, around Vanderbilt University and Music Row, is—because of the many close-by restaurants in the area—the most desirable location for lodgings away from the tourist attractions. Two B&Bs near Hillsboro Village are **Commodore Inn and Guest House** (1614 19th Ave. S., 615/269-3850) and **Hillsboro House** (1933 20th Ave. S., 615/292-5501), both of which are close enough to town to allow visitors to stroll out in the evening to a movie at the nearby Belcourt Cinema or to find a sit-outside restaurant for morning coffee or late-night libations. There are a number of acceptable larger hotels in this area including the luxurious **Loew's Vanderbilt Plaza** (2100 West End Ave., 615/336-3335). Inquire about corporate rates and weekend specials at this elegant place, one of Nashville's finest. Other good choices in the moderate-to-expensive category are the newly remodeled **Vanderbilt Holiday Inn Select** (2613 West End Ave., 615/327-4707) and the **Courtyard by Marriott** (1901 West End Ave., 615/327-9900). Less pricey but adequate accommodations in this same convenient location include two **Hampton Inns** (1919 West End Ave., 615/329-1144; and 2300 Elliston Pl., 615/320-6060) and **Days Inn West End** (1800 West End Ave., 615/327-0922).

Recommended downtown choices include the **Westin Hermitage** (213 6th Ave. N., 615/244-3121 or 800/WESTIN-1), an all-suite hotel owned by Westin that guarantees a luxury stay (inquire about weekend specials and "bed-and-breakfast" rates); the **Crowne Plaza** (623 Union St., 615/259-2000), an efficient business hotel with a friendly attitude which has great views from its rooftop restaurant); and the **Doubletree** (315 Fourth Ave. N., 615/244-8200), a quiet and luxurious hotel tucked into a corner on the Nationsbank plaza.

In the Greater Nashville area, the best accommodations are in a group of hotels located off Elm Hill Pike and Donelson Pike near the airport. They includes the **Airport Marriott** (Briley Pkwy. and Elm Hill Pike, 615/889-9300); **Holiday Inn Express** (1111 Airport Center Dr., 615/883-1366); **Doubletree Guest Suites** (2424 Atrium Way, 615/889-8889), and **Holiday Inn Select** (2200 Elm Hill Pike, 615/883-9770).

For more luxurious lodgings in the same vicinity, try the **Opryland Hotel**, 615/883-2211, a colossal convention hotel with lots to offer but some of the highest prices in town; or the refined and elegant **Sheraton Music City** (777 McGavock Pike, 615/885-2200). The Sheraton's country-club atmosphere comes replete with outdoor tennis courts and pool, a fine-dining restaurant, and extensive, manicured grounds. A word of warning: Avoid the cheap motels along Murfreesboro Road, Nolensville Road, Dickerson Pike, and Eighth Avenue South; and exercise caution at any establishment located just off the interstate highways.

A new addition to the downtown hotel scene is **Courtyard by Marriott** (170 Fourth Ave. N; 615/256-0900 or 800/321-2211), located in a nicely remodeled bank. On the northern outskirts of downtown sits the **Regal Maxwell House Hotel** (2025 MetroCenter Blvd. at Eighth Ave.; 615/259-4343). The hotel is friendly and surprisingly luxurious for the money.

CAMPING

There are several large, easy-to-find campgrounds off Briley Parkway near Opryland. Here, your neighbors are likely to be country music aficionados. These places are huge, with 300 to 400 sites and full hookups, but campers must take their chances with cleanliness, noise, and crowded conditions. Another, more pleasant option is to stay near Percy Priest or Old Hickory Lakes, particularly during the summer. On Percy Priest Lake, in East Nashville, the U.S. Corps of Engineers runs three seasonal campgrounds: **Anderson Road Campground** (37 sites, no hookups; 615/361-1980), **Cook Campground** (57 sites, no electricity; 615/889-1096), and **Seven Points Campground** (60 sites, hookups; 615/889-5198). At Old Hickory Lake, to the north, the U.S. Corps of Engineers operates three additional seasonal campgrounds: **Cages Bend** (615/824-4989), **Cedar Creek Recreation Area** (60 sites, hookups, swimming area; 615/754-4947), and **Shutes Branch Public Use Area** (35 sites, electricity and water; 615/754-4847).

GREATER NASHVILLE

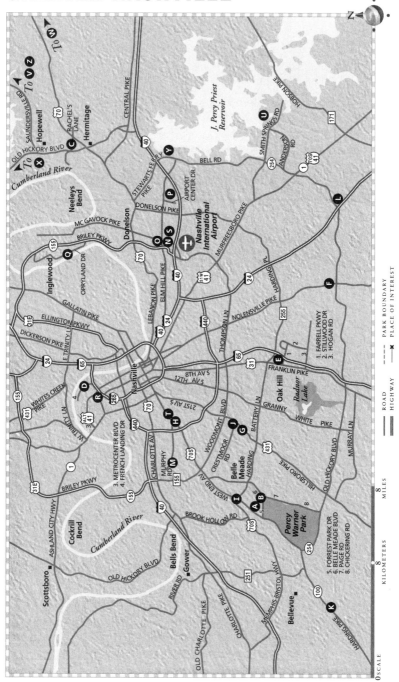

Sights

- **A** Belle Meade Plantation
- **B** Cheekwood
- **C** The Hermitage
- **D** Sankofa African Heritage Museum
- **E** Travellers Rest

Food

- **F** Bar B Cutie
- **G** Bread & Company
- **H** Cakewalk/Zola
- **G** Clayton-Blackmon
- **I** Corner Market
- **J** F. Scott's
- **K** Loveless Motel and Cafe
- **L** Nathan's
- **M** Sylvan Park
- **H** Vandyland

Lodging

- **N** Airport Marriott
- **O** Doubletree Guest Suites
- **P** Holiday Inn Express
- **O** Holiday Inn Select
- **Q** Opryland Hotel
- **R** Regal Maxwell House Hotel
- **S** Sheraton Music City
- **T** Vanderbilt Holiday Inn Select

Camping

- **U** Anderson Road Campground
- **V** Cages Bend
- **W** Cedar Creek Recreation Area
- **X** Cook Campground
- **Y** Seven Points Campground
- **Z** Shutes Branch Public Use Area

Note: Items with the same letter are located in the same area.

NIGHTLIFE

For music in Music City, the first thing you should do on arrival is check club listings in *The Tennessean*, *Nashville Scene*, and *Nashville CitySearch* (online: www.nashville.citysearch.com). If you don't see any names you know, decide on a musical genre and just go anyway; you'll be glad you did. Try the **Station Inn** (402 12th Ave. S., 615/255-3307) for bluegrass and traditional music; **Bluebird Cafe** (4104 Hillsboro, 615/383-1461) for singer-songwriter nights; and

Douglas Corner Café (2106 Eighth Ave. S., 615/298-1688) and **The Sutler** (1608 Franklin Rd., 615/297-9195) for singer-songwriter nights and small bands. Try **328 Performance Hall** (328 Fourth Ave. S., 615/259-3288), **12th and Porter Playroom** (114 12th Ave. N., 615/254-7326), **Exit/In** (2208 Elliston Pl., 615/321-4400), or **Ace of Clubs** (114 Second Ave. S., 615/254-ACES) for major acts in club venues.

Tickets to the **Grand Ole Opry**, which is still performed as a live radio show, can be obtained by calling 615/889-6611 or by stopping in at the **Ryman Auditorium** (116 5th Ave. N.; 615/254-1445 or, for tickets only, 615/889-6611). The Ryman's fine acoustics and almost sacred past make any performance there something special.

Multiplex theaters in and around Nashville show first-run Hollywood offerings. **Belcourt Cinema** (2101 Belcourt Ave., 615/742-8123) and **Sarratt Cinema** (24th Ave. S. at Vanderbilt Pl., 615/322-2471) show first-run foreign films along with avant-garde American films. **Franklin Cinema** (419 Main St., Franklin, 615/790-7122) does the same and serves beer. Nashville is also home to one of the oldest independent film festivals in the country, the Sinking Creek (now Nashville Independent) Film Festival, which holds forth for a week each June. Call 615/322-4234 to see if anything is playing while you are in town.

Sports options include the **Vanderbilt University Commodores** (both men's and women's basketball, 615/322-3544); AAA baseball with the **Nashville Sounds** at Greer Stadium (534 Chestnut, 615/242-4371); the **NHL Nashville Predators** (Nashville Arena, Fifth Ave. at Broadway, 615/770-2000). The **Tennessee Oilers**, after a season at Vanderbilt Stadium, will move to the NFL stadium on the east bank of the Cumberland River. For tickets, contact the ticket office at 1914 Church Street, 615/341-7627, or call Ticketmaster at 615/255-9600.

GALLERIES

The following galleries are worth noting: **Collector's Gallery**, 6602 Hwy. 100, 615/356-0699; **Cumberland Gallery**, 4107 Hillsboro Circle, 615/297-0296; **In the Gallery**, 624 A Jefferson, 615/255-0705; **Local Color Gallery**, 1912 Broadway, 615/321-3141; and **Zeitgeist Gallery**, 209 10th Ave. S., 615/256-4805. They form the Nashville Association of Art Dealers. Pick up a guide at any one of them or find a *Nashville Scene* for current exhibit listings. The

Tennessee Arts Commission Gallery and the Nashville International Airport, both nonprofit institutions, offer top-quality local and regional art exhibits as well.

SIDE TRIP: FRANKLIN AND COLUMBIA

A 20-mile drive out Franklin Road (Hwy. 31) or Hillsboro Road (Hwy. 431) leads through horse country. Historic **Franklin** (1799) is a beautiful walking town with many good antique shops. The 1830 **Carter House** (1140 Columbia Ave., 615/791-1861) and 1826 **Historic Carnton Plantation** (1345 Carnton Ln., 615/794-0403) were sites of the Civil War Battle of Franklin in November of 1864. A Tennessee Antebellum Trail brochure guarantees discount-admission to nine sites in the area (800/381-1865) including these two.

Continue on Highway 31 to **Spring Hill**, home to General Motors' Saturn car plant, a factory that is virtually hidden on former plantation land. **Rippa Villa** (5700 Main St., 931/486-9037), a museum and visitor's center, distributes both APTA (Association for the Preservation of Tennessee Antiquities) and Tennessee Antebellum Trail brochures. APTA markers designate many sites not open to the public. **Columbia**, which in 1850 was the third-largest city in Tennessee after Memphis and Nashville, has a historic district that includes the 1816 **James K. Polk Ancestral Home** (301 W. 7th St., 931/388-2354). **Mount Lebanon** was the site of the first Baptist Church (1843) for free blacks in Tennessee. The **Canaan** community, out Mt. Pleasant Pike, was settled by freed slaves after the Civil War ended.

HELPFUL HINTS

Nashville has two public radio stations that do a fine job advertising public events and cultural happenings—WPLN at 90.3 and WMOT at 89.5, a jazz-oriented station from Middle Tennessee State University in Murfreesboro. *Nashville Scene* (www.nashscene.com) is a weekly alternative paper that can be found free all over town—check it out for music, film, and gallery listings. The same sorts of things can be found in Nashville's online city guide **CitySearch** (www.nashville.citysearch.com).

Nashville Life is a bimonthly magazine with a lively informative tone that covers the cultural life of the city.

For a great souvenir of Nashville, pick up a six-pack of GooGoo Clusters—chocolate-covered mounds of caramel, marshmallow, and peanuts. The debate rages on over whether the acronym for this candy invented in 1912 actually stands for Grand Ole Opry, and **Standard Candy Company** isn't talking. Standard Candy also makes old-fashioned straight peppermint sticks that come packed in their famous blue metal King Leo can. Call them at 800/226-4340 to place an order.

Nashville also has a number of good bookstores. **Davis-Kidd Booksellers** (4007 Hillsboro Rd., 615/292-1404), with several stores in other Tennessee cities, started here. Check out **Elder's** (2115 Elliston Pl., 615/327-1867) and **Dad's Old Books** (4004 Hillsboro Rd., 615/298-5880) if you are in the market for antique books. The **Southern Festival of Books** and its companion, **Antiquarian Book Fair**, sponsored by the Tennessee Humanities Council, take place in early October on Legislative Plaza downtown. If you can plan your trip to include this wonderful free event—which brings authors and audiences together in intimate settings and promotes the love of reading for all ages—do it. For more information about the festival, call 615/320-7001 or look it up on the Web at www.TN-Humanities.org.

Scenic Route: Tennessee Backroads to Chattanooga

Southeast of Nashville, the land becomes gently rolling and lush. This is Tennessee's answer to the Kentucky Bluegrass. It is here you'll find Tennessee Walking Horses and Tennessee whiskey. Driving about thirty miles southeast of Nashville on I-24, you'll find the charming town of Murfreesboro. It has lovely old brick homes dating from the mid- to late-1800s (it was the state capital for a brief period). If you're hungry, stop in at the **City Cafe** on the main square for fried chicken, fresh vegetables, and homemade pie. Tune your radio to 89.5 as you leave Murfreesboro and lock in Middle Tennessee State University's fine public radio station, WMOT, for jazz.

From Murfreesboro, Highway 70S will take you to Woodbury, the white-oak basket capital of Tennessee. Stop in at the **Arts Center of Cannon County** (1424 John Bragg Hwy., 615/563-ARTS or 800/235-9073) to see an art exhibit, find out about upcoming plays or live music, and inquire about visiting craftpeople in the vicinity.

TENNESSEE BACKROADS

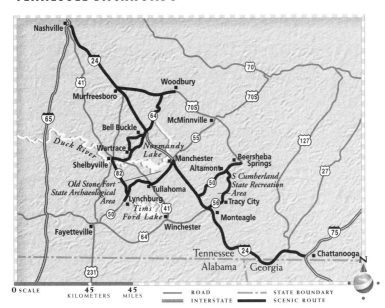

Fifteen miles south of Woodbury on Hwy 64, **Bell Buckle** sits along the railroad tracks. Stop in at the **Bell Buckle Cafe** (Railroad Square, 931/389-9693) for delicious smoked-out-back barbecue and live music on the weekends and **Bell Buckle Crafts** (Railroad Square, 931/389-9371) to see locally made wares.

Shelbyville, "the Walking Horse Capital of the World," is located another ten miles south, in the midst of gently rolling farmland. Shelbyville's classic town square dates from 1810. The very formal **Tennessee Walking Horse Celebration** is held here every year in late August. Inquire at the **Tennessee Walking Horse Museum** (721 Witthorne St., 931/684-0314) about tickets to the different events and about stable tours around Shelbyville. The Shelbyville Chamber of Commerce (100 Cannon Blvd, 931/684-3482 or 888/662-2525) will give you a guide to area horse farms.

Follow Highway 82 east to Highway 55 and **Lynchburg**. You'll have entered Jack Daniel country. The world-famous **Jack Daniel Distillery** (931/759-6180), founded in 1866 by Jasper Newton Daniel and visible from every angle of this one-horse town, offers free tours daily. But there's no tasting—this is a dry county. A visit to Lynchburg is not complete without a family-style lunch at **Miss Mary Bobo's Boarding House** (931/759-7394). Reservations are a must, and Miss Mary's is closed on Sunday. Not far up the road is "the other" Tennessee sour-mash whiskey distillery, **George Dickel Distillery** (1950 Cascade Hollow Rd., Tullahoma; 931/857-3124), founded in 1867. The distillery offers free tours Monday to Friday.

Highway 55 will take you back out to I-24. Twenty miles down the road is **Monteagle**, which got its start as the "Chautauqua of the South" in 1882. It houses one of four remaining Chautauqua programs in the country (the original, at Chautauqua, New York, began in 1874). Lodging is available year-round at the deluxe **Adams-Edgeworth Inn** (Monteagle Assembly, 931/924-4000) and the equally accommodating **North Gate Inn** (103 Monteagle Assembly; 931/924-2799).

Monteagle is adjacent to the **South Cumberland State Recreation Area** (Hwy. 41A, Tracy City; 931/924-2980) a 12,000-acre wilderness area that includes **Savage Gulf Canyon**, **Great Stone Door**, **South Cumberland State Park**, **Grundy Forest**, and **Foster Falls**. Tracy City is home to the friendly **Dutch Maid Bakery** (111 Main St., 931/592-3171), in business since 1902. ◪

2
CHATTANOOGA

Coca-Cola was first bottled in Chattanooga, Bessie Smith was born here, and the city's name was immortalized in popular song. Its name derives from Creek Indians, who described Lookout Mountain as a "rock coming to a point." Indians were familiar travelers of the Tennessee Valley long before Spanish explorer Hernando DeSoto "discovered" the area in 1540. By 1816 John and Lewis Ross had established a landing, warehouse, and ferry service downtown.

Chattanooga was a strategic supply-line location during the War Between the States and the site of such major battles as Chickamauga and Chattanooga in 1863. The Confederate loss at Chattanooga is considered a major turning point in opening the way for Union forces into the Deep South. Chattanooga's manufacturing economy attracted freedmen from all over the South after the war. Many African American entrepreneurs and professionals made their start here.

Decades of exploiting natural resources have taken their toll on Chattanooga, which has suffered from environmental pollution. For the past 10 years though, the city has been taking action to clean up its air and water. Part of Chattanooga's post-industrial economic resurgence is due to its development as an alluring tourist destination.

The Tennessee Aquarium, the first freshwater aquarium in existence, was built in 1992; a six-story IMAX theater was constructed several years later. Both are located in Ross's Landing Park and Plaza, designed as a microcosmic History Walk, combining public art and native plantings to tell the story of Chattanooga. ◣

CHATTANOOGA

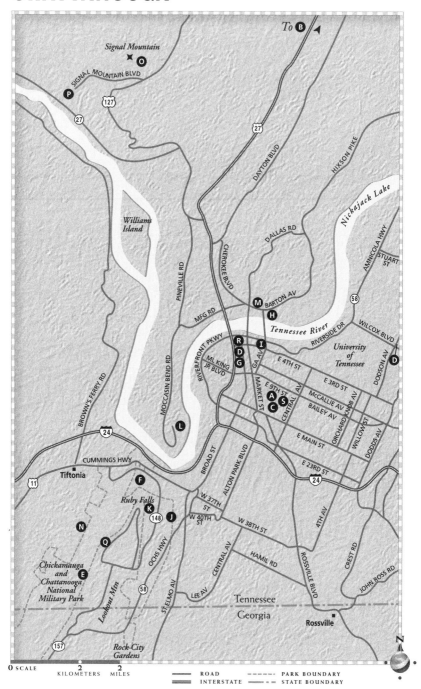

To **B**

Signal Mountain **O**

SIGNAL MOUNTAIN BLVD

P

127

27

Williams Island

DAYTON BLVD

HIXSON PIKE

Nickajack Lake

DALLAS RD

AMNICOLA HWY

STUART ST

PINEVILLE RD

CHEROKEE BLVD

MFG RD

BARTON AV

M

H

58

Tennessee River

RIVERSIDE DR

WILCOX BLVD

MOCCASIN BEND RD

RIVERFRONT PKWY

R

D

G

I

ML KING JR BLVD

GA AV

E 4TH ST

University of Tennessee

DODSON AV

D

BROWN'S FERRY RD

E 3RD ST

MARKET ST

CENTRAL AV

E 9TH ST

A

S

C

McCALLIE AV

BAILEY AV

ORCHARD KNOB AV

WILLOW ST

DODDS AV

L

E MAIN ST

24

CUMMINGS HWY

E 23RD ST

11

Tiftonia

BROAD ST

ALTON PARK BLVD

24

F

4TH AV

Ruby Falls

K

148

J

W 37TH ST

W 40TH ST

W 38TH ST

N

Q

OCHS HWY

CENTRAL AV

HAMIL RD

ROSSVILLE BLVD

CREST RD

JOHN ROSS RD

Chickamauga and Chattanooga National Military Park

E

58

ST ELMO AV

LEE AV

Tennessee
Georgia

Rossville

Lookout Mtn

157

Rock City Gardens

N

0 SCALE   2   2
   KILOMETERS MILES

—— ROAD   - - - - - PARK BOUNDARY
═══ INTERSTATE   ~~~~ STATE BOUNDARY

Sights

- **A** African American Museum and Bessie Smith Music Hall
- **B** Antiques Warehouses
- **C** Chattanooga Choo Choo
- **D** Chattanooga Regional History Museum
- **E** Chickamauga/Chattanooga National Military Park
- **F** Cravens' House
- **G** Creative Discovery Museum
- **H** Frazier Avenue
- **I** Hunter Museum of Art
- **J** Incline Railway
- **K** Lookout Mountain's Point Park
- **L** Moccasin Bend
- **M** North Shore Gallery
- **K** Ochs Museum at Point Park
- **N** Chattanooga Nature and Wildlife Rehabilitation Center
- **O** Signal Mountain
- **P** Signal Point Park
- **Q** Sunset Park
- **R** Tennessee Aquarium
- **S** Warehouse Row

Note: Items with the same letter are located in the same place.

A PERFECT DAY IN CHATTANOOGA

After coffee and a pastry at Rembrandt's Coffee House in the Bluff View Art District, visit the nearby public sculpture garden overlooking the Tennessee River. One long block back will take you to the Hunter Museum of American Art, with its fine Albert Paley iron gateway out front, its magnificent view of the river behind, and the finest collection of contemporary art in the state. The Back Inn Café across the street will serve you a gourmet luncheon on their outside patio or you might wish to cross the river to hip Frazier Avenue for a funky and healthy lunch at Mudpie's. The innovative and mesmerizing Tennessee Aquarium will take up most of the afternoon, but leave time for a stop at the Chattanooga African American Museum, just a couple blocks down from Warehouse Row, and the Chattanooga Choo Choo, both of which deserve a look. At the end of the day, drive up Lookout Mountain and watch the sunset from pretty little Sunset Park on the west side. Afterwards, enjoy a long, leisurely dinner at the Southside Grill.

SIGHTSEEING HIGHLIGHTS

✯✯✯ **Chattanooga African American Museum and Bessie Smith Music Hall**—Opened in February 1996, the museum and auditorium are located in a marvelous adaptive reuse building. The museum, which moved from smaller quarters, has both a collection of African art and a permanent display of Chattanooga's African American history with some fascinating artifacts. The music hall features concert performances, lectures, and special events.

Details: 200 E. Martin Luther King, Chattanooga. Museum: 423/267-1076. Mon–Fri 10–5, Sat noon–4. $5 adults, $3 seniors, $1.50 ages 6–12, under 5 free. Music Hall: 423/757-0020. Open same hours as above. Admission is free. (1 hour)

✯✯✯ **Chattanooga Choo Choo**—That famous old train station is now a Holiday Inn, with bunkerlike guest buildings hidden behind a landscaped railyard with trains. You can still see the grandeur of the station's central terminal in the hotel lobby, whose atriumlike dining area and large rest rooms testify to its original function. The hotel's gourmet restaurant and some of the guest rooms are actually in old dining cars. A word of warning, the well-known tune is played on the premises, and you may find yourself whistling the ditty hours later if you are not careful.

Details: 1400 Market St., Chattanooga; 423/266-5000. Open daily. Admission is free. (15 minutes)

✯✯✯ **Chickamauga/Chattanooga National Military Park**—The first and largest national military park established after the Civil War, the park commemorates the 1863 Battles of Chickamauga and Chattanooga. At Chickamauga, the Confederates, under General Braxton Bragg, tried to cut off the Union's supply lines and force surrender by pushing them into the city of Chattanooga. Just over two months later, at the Battle of Chattanooga, the Grant-led Federal forces were able to break the siege and ultimately achieve a strategic victory.

Details: Hwy. 27, Fort Oglethorpe, GA; 706/866-9241. Daily 8 a.m.–dark, visitors center closes at 4:45 p.m. Admission is free. (1½ hours)

✯✯✯ **Creative Discovery Museum**—Several blocks away from the Tennessee Aquarium, this museum for children of school-age and above provides in-depth, directed learning experiences in areas such as art,

music, technology, and history. Any one of these could intrigue a child for an hour or so, according to one parent. The museum provides hands-on docents who help children start on their own particular quest.
Details: 321 Chestnut St., Chattanooga; 423/756-2738. Tue–Sat 10–5, Sun noon–5. $7.75 adults, $4.75 ages 2–12. (2 hours)

⭐⭐⭐ **Hunter Museum of American Art**—When touring this museum, be sure to look for James Cameron's circa 1852 portrait of Colonel Whiteside and his family. It includes a Lookout Mountain landscape with Moccasin Bend below and is one of the earliest and best Tennessee landscapes in existence. The permanent collections here are outstanding, with fine examples from all periods of American art, including the contemporary period. A growing fine-art glass collection featuring examples from many well-known glassmakers is a particular highlight. Don't miss the museum's sculpture garden. The museum is in the Bluff View Art District, which also houses the River Gallery, a commercial gallery that features both fine art and crafts; and the public River Gallery sculpture garden (free admission), which contains works by regional and national artists arranged in a winding park overlooking the Tennessee River. Also in the district is the **Houston Museum of Decorative Art** (201 High St., Chattanooga; 423/267-7176) an old-fashioned museum containing an extensive collection of antique glass.
Details: 10 Bluff View, Chattanooga; 423/267-0968; Tue–Sat 10–4:30, Sun 1–4:30. $5 adults, $4 seniors, $3 students. (1½ hours)

⭐⭐⭐ **Lookout Mountain's Point Park**—From here you have a fine view of **Moccasin Bend**, always strategic for controlling river access to points north and south, even prior to the Civil War. On September 20, 1782, a group of militiamen commanded by John Sevier—later the first governor of Tennessee—defeated an Indian party led by Cherokee Chief Dragging Canoe—one of the dissenters in the 1775 Treaty at Sycamore Shoals—in one of the final battles of the Revolutionary War. Also on Lookout Mountain, the **Cravens' House**, built in 1854, served as a headquarters for both sides during the Civil War. The **Ochs Museum at Point Park** (founded by newspaper executive Adolph Ochs, who purchased the *New York Times* in 1896 and whose family still runs it) interprets the battles that took place here for visitors. The "classic" tourist destinations of Rock City (1400 Patten Rd., Lookout Mountain; 706/820-2531), which started as a private garden with unusual rocks and plantings and a great view in 1932; and Ruby Falls (1720 South Scenic Hwy., Lookout Mountain; 423/821-2544), named after the wife of its 1928 discoverer, are located on the east side of the mountain. You might want to go for the kitsch. Tiny **Sunset Park**, a public park with beautiful west-facing views, has become a major rock-climbing destination so don't be surprised to find small groups of intent climbers around the corner of a path.

At the base of the mountain is the **Incline Railway** (827 East Brow Rd., Chattanooga; 423/821-4224), another popular tourist site. If you want the distinction of having ridden one of the world's steepest cable cars, go for it. The railway, built in 1895, will let you off just three blocks from Point Park. *(2 hours)*

★★★ **Tennessee Aquarium and IMAX Theater**—Visitors learn about the history and ecosystem of the Tennessee River from its origins in the Appalachian Mountains to its commingling with the Mississippi River at the Gulf of Mexico. The aquarium features a fine folk art exhibit across from the gift shop at the rear—you can see it without going through the aquarium. The plaza outside contains built-in historical and interpretive information. Across the plaza is the IMAX 3-D Theater.

Incline Railway, Lookout Mountain

© Phyllis Picardi/Photo Network

Details: Ross's Landing Plaza, One Broad St.; 800/262-0695. Daily 10–6. Aquarium: $10.95 adults, $5.95 ages 3–12; IMAX Theater: $6.95 adults, $4.95 ages 3–12; combo tickets: $14.95 adults, $8.95 ages 3–12. (2½ hours)

✭✭ **Chattanooga Nature and Wildlife Rehabilitation Center**—The center is a 375-acre arboretum, botanical garden, and wildlife- and nature-viewing site that also includes Civil War battlefields and Indian paths and cabins. An environmental education center includes a wildlife hospital and recovery facility that aids the return of injured animals to the wild.

Details: 400 Garden Rd., Chattanooga; Chattanooga Nature Center: 423/821-1160; Reflection Riding: 423/821-9582. Mon–Sat 9–5, Sun 1–5. $3 adults, $2 seniors and ages 4–11. (1½ hour)

✭✭ **Chattanooga Regional History Museum**—This lively little museum is located in a historic building just across the street from the Creative Discovery Museum. Its focus is on interpreting the history of the area for generations to come; to that end the CRHM presents exhibits and publications designed to pique the curiosity of school-age children.

Details: 400 Chestnut St., Chattanooga; 423/265-3247. Mon–Fri 10–4:30,Sat and Sun 11–4:30. $2.50 adults, $1.75 seniors, $1.50 students ages 5–18. (1 hour)

✭✭ **Signal Mountain**—Across the river from downtown Chattanooga, this mountain served as a strategic Union signal point during the siege of Chattanooga, when supplies were scarce and troops had to decide whether to trust land or water routes into the city. Now primarily a residential area, Signal Mountain has several interesting pockets of shops and restaurants. Plum Nelly's craft shop and Waycrazy's BBQ are among the more colorful choices here. Seek out the Mountain Opry (Fairmount Rd., in the Walden Ridge Civic Center; 423/ 886-5897), for free traditional music on Friday nights beginning at eight. *(1 hour)*

✭ **Frazier Avenue**—Across the river from downtown are several blocks of shops, restaurants, and galleries. The ambitious strider can walk across Walnut Street Bridge and find: **Rock Creek Outfitters** (100 Tremont at Frazier Ave., 423/265-5969), gear-central for area climbers, canoeists, kayakers, hikers and campers; **North Shore Gallery**

(101 Frazier, 423/265-2760), a dealer in "outsider" or untrained artists; **Association for Visual Artists (AVA) Gallery** (30 Frazier, 423/265-4282); **Barrett & Company Bookstore** (16 Frazier, 423/267-2665); and **Mudpie Coffeehouse and Newsstand** (12 Frazier, 423/267-9043). *(1 hour)*

✸ **Warehouse Row**—Located near the Choo Choo, Warehouse Row is another innovative adaptive reuse of railroad storage buildings. It features the best brand-name shopping that I have encountered anywhere, including outlet stores for Coach, Ralph Lauren, Guess, and Sam & Libby.
   Details: 1110 Market St., Chattanooga; 423/267-1111. Mon–Sat 10–7, Sun noon–6, extended hours in summer. (1½ hour)

Antiques Warehouses—There are several large antiques warehouses located on Highway 153 north of town. These dealers hold estate sales in other cities and Saturday auctions in Chattanooga on a regular basis. Call Clements, Mickey's, or Northgate to see when the next scheduled auction might be.

FITNESS AND RECREATION

Chattanooga, where the Appalachian Mountains meet the Tennessee River, is an incredibly rich area for all manner of outdoor recreation. If you are going to be staying for several days, request the **Southeast Tennessee Outdoor Recreational Guide** from the Chattanooga Visitors Bureau, 800/322-3344. Outdoor sports enthusiasts should also check with local outfitters like **River City Biking**, 423/265-7176, and **Rock Creek Outfitters**, 423/265-5969, for advice. Bowater Inc. (multinational paper company) has made a number of its acres of timberland in the region available for public use, such as the **North Chickamauga Pocket Wilderness**, located approximately 10 miles north of the city.
   There are biking and walking trails all around the riverfront and one can cross from one side to the other over the 100-year-old downtown Walnut Street Bridge, which has been redesigned as a pedestrian bridge. The **Tennessee Riverpark**, 423/493-9244, includes children's play areas, interpretive historical sections, fishing docks, and bike trails. Sections of the Riverwalk are being gradually added, with the eventual goal being to have a greenway following the riverbends leading in,

through, and out of the city. There are completed bike paths along the Moccasin Bend loop road and along North Chickamauga Creek above the dam. Road biking is allowed in **Chickamauga National Battlefield** and **Prentice Cooper State Forest**. Both mountain bikes and road bikes can be used in the Ocoee Ranger District of **Cherokee National Forest**.

Rock climbing is a popular sport in this region. The **Tennessee Wall**, a well-known climbing destination, is accessed through Prentice Cooper State Forest, close to downtown; and **Sunset Park** on Lookout Mountain has good climbs for beginning and intermediate climbers.

The Chattanooga area is the hang-gliding capital of the East and **Lookout Mountain Flight Park and Training Center** (Hwy. 189 South, Rising Fawn, Georgia; 800/688-LMFP) is the largest hang-gliding school in the United States.

Water sports such as canoeing, kayaking, and white-water rafting are a big business on the Ocoee and Hiwassee Rivers. The summer Olympic events of 1996 were held on the Ocoee in Tennessee. There are officially designated outfitters from which to choose, so check the Southeast Tennessee Recreation Guide for information.

FOOD

There are several good downtown choices for lunch and dinner in the moderate price range. **Big River Grille** (222 Broad; 423/267-BREW) is a brewpub near the Tennessee Aquarium. Although it is sometimes noisy, it serves consistently good food and is lively enough to keep youngsters happy. You'll smell the smoke coming from **Hog Wild Barbeque** (500 Broad, 423/265-7595), and right down the block you'll see **Lupi's Pizza** (406A Broad; 423/266-5874) and next door **Grayfriar's Coffee House** (406B Broad; 423/267-0376). My favorite Chattanooga restaurant is **Southside Grill** (Cowart Ave., 423/266-9211) near the Choo Choo off Market Street. Southside serves terrific Southern cuisine (fried green tomatoes with smoked crawfish, for example), has good service, and is moderately priced ($20–$25 entrées) but worth every penny.

Just up the hill from downtown you'll find both the restaurants of the Bluff View Art District and those near UT Chattanooga. The **Back Inn Café** (High St. and Second, 423/ 757-0108), across the street from the Hunter Museum, has a view overlooking the river, a nice patio for sitting outside, and serves gourmet light lunches and dinners with

CHATTANOOGA

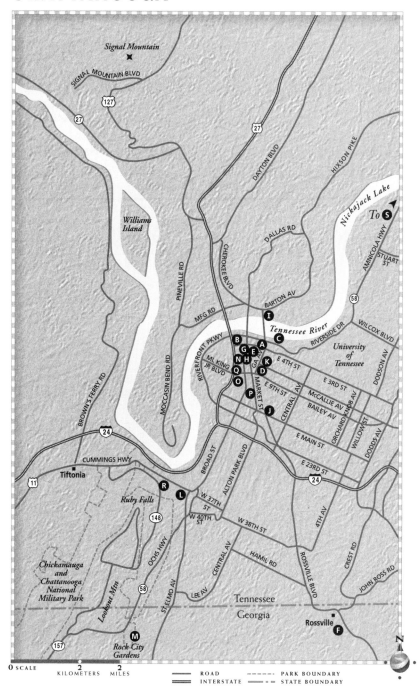

Signal Mountain

SIGNAL MOUNTAIN BLVD

127

27

Williams
Island

PINEVILLE RD

MFG RD

CHEROKEE BLVD

DAYTON BLVD

27

DALLAS RD

BARTON AV

HIXSON PIKE

Nickajack Lake

To S

AMNICOLA HWY

STUART ST

58

Tennessee River

RIVERSIDE DR

WILCOX BLVD

University of Tennessee

DODSON AV

MOCCASIN BEND RD

RIVERFRONT PKWY

ML KING JR BLVD

I

C

B
G
E
A
N H
Q
O
K
D
P
J

MARKET ST

E 4TH ST

E 3RD ST

CENTRAL AV

McCALLIE AV

BAILEY AV

E 9TH ST

ORCHARD KNOB AV

WILLOW ST

DODDS AV

E MAIN ST

E 23RD ST

24

BROWN'S FERRY RD

24

CUMMINGS HWY

11

Tiftonia

Ruby Falls

R

L

148

BROAD ST

ALTON PARK BLVD

W 37TH ST

W 40TH ST

W 38TH ST

4TH AV

OCHS HWY

58

Chickamauga
and
Chattanooga
National
Military Park

Lookout Mtn

ST ELMO AV

LEE AV

CENTRAL AV

HAMIL RD

ROSSVILLE BLVD

CREST RD

JOHN ROSS RD

Tennessee

Georgia

Rossville

F

157

M

Rock City
Gardens

N

0 SCALE

2
KILOMETERS

2
MILES

——— ROAD   - - - - - PARK BOUNDARY
═══ INTERSTATE - · - · STATE BOUNDARY

Food

- **Ⓐ** Back Inn Café
- **Ⓑ** Big River Grille
- **Ⓒ** Bluff View Inn
- **Ⓓ** Brass Register
- **Ⓔ** Chef's Underground Cafe
- **Ⓕ** Darr's Chow Time BBQ
- **Ⓖ** Grayfriar's Coffee House
- **Ⓗ** Hog Wild Barbeque
- **Ⓖ** Lupi's Pizza
- **Ⓘ** Mudpie's Coffeehouse
- **Ⓘ** Northside Lunch
- **Ⓐ** Rembrandt's Coffee House
- **Ⓙ** Southside Grill
- **Ⓚ** Vine Street Market

Lodging

- **Ⓚ** Adams Hilborne
- **Ⓛ** Alford House B&B
- **Ⓒ** Bluff View Inn
- **Ⓜ** Chanticleer Inn B&B
- **Ⓝ** Chattanooga Clarion
- **Ⓙ** Chattanooga Choo Choo/Holiday Inn
- **Ⓞ** Days Inn Rivergate
- **Ⓟ** Marriott
- **Ⓠ** Radisson Read House
- **Ⓡ** Sky Harbor Bavarian Inn

Camping

- **Ⓢ** Harrison Bay State Park

Note: Items with the same letter are located in the same area.

friendly service. Upstairs in the same building is the pricier **Bluff View Inn**. Around the corner is **Rembrandt's Coffee House** (corner of High and Second, 423/267-2451) which makes great sandwiches and has beautiful German-style pastries. Near UT Chattanooga is the **Vine Street Market** (414 Vine, 423/267-8165), a friendly, moderately priced restaurant that also has gourmet grocery items for sale in an adjacent room. Also near the university is **Chef's Underground Cafe** (720 Walnut St., 423/266-3142), a small upscale restaurant featuring Jamaican specialties. A few blocks closer to downtown is the **Brass Register** (618 Georgia Ave., 423/265-4121), a cozy fern bar that serves good food and drinks at moderate prices and has been around for at least 20 years.

For cheap eats across the river, try **Northside Lunch** (202 Frazier Ave., 423/756-9799). One of the original inhabitants of the now burgeoning Frazier Avenue District, Northside is a classic that looks like its been in business for at least 50 years. Its prices have stayed fixed for nearly as long. Breakfast costs around $3, a cheeseburger is $2, and a mug of cold draft beer $1. Down the street is **Mudpie's Coffeehouse** (12 Frazier, 423/267-9043), where the atmosphere is a cross between health-food store and slacker café. Baked goods and great specials, along with coffee drinks and imported beers, keep the steady clientele coming. Last but not least, located in the environs of Chattanooga, is **Darr's Chow Time BBQ** (801 McFarland Ave., a few miles south of town in Rossville, Georgia; 423/866-7770). The owners have run barbecue places in Chattanooga since the 1950s. The old Chow Time in Tiftonia, a '50s diner kind of place with a neon Chow Time clock, is now closed, but mourned by many. Darr's serves some of the best meat you'll ever eat. The smoked pork shoulder, pit-cooked over hickory coals for 12 hours, is never allowed to sit directly above the heat and is served with vinegar-based sauce on the side. Darr's also features a selection of five kinds of beans.

LODGING

Try to stay away from the motels bordering busy roads and highways. Downtown Chattanooga offers a number of options including the famous old **Read House Hotel** (Broad and Martin Luther King Aves., 423/266-4121 or 800/333-3333), now a **Radisson**. This elegant hotel, which was recently remodeled, went through some growing pains with the change of management but should have smoothed out by now. The **Chattanooga Choo Choo/Holiday Inn** (1400 Market, 423/266-5000 or 800/Track 29), also in the upper echelon price range for Chattanooga, seems a bit more family oriented. In both cases travelers should inquire about weekend specials to try and bring the price down. Within walking distance of the aquarium you'll find several nice hotels, including the **Chattanooga Clarion** (407 Chestnut, 423/756-5150) and the **Chattanooga Marriott** (Two Carter Plaza, 423/756-0002 or 800/228-9290).

   Day's Inn Rivergate (910 Carter Street; 423/266-7331), also convenient to downtown sights, is located just across Martin Luther King Boulevard from the Read House. Rooms are newly renovated, management is friendly, continental breakfast is included, and the price is right.

   If you want to try a fancy bed-and-breakfast inn, there are several around town in old neighborhoods. The **Bluff View Inn** (411 E. Second St., 423/265-5033) and **Adams Hilborne** (801 Vine St.,

423/265-5000) are both listed in the Tennessee Bed-and-Breakfast Association Directory and on the Net at www.bbonline.com.tbbia. On Lookout Mountain you might try the more moderately priced **Alford House B&B** (5515 Alford Hill Dr., Lookout Mountain, TN; 423/821-7625 or 800/817-7625); or the **Chanticleer Inn B&B** (1300 Mockingbird Lane, Lookout Mountain, GA; 706/820-2015), which is built of mountain stone. Also on Lookout Mountain is a charming motel built in 1938 called the **Sky Harbor Bavarian Inn** (1939 Old Wauhatchie Pike, Lookout Mountain, TN; 423/821-8619). It's old-fashioned, moderately priced, and comes with a view. Chattanooga has become quite a tourist destination in summer, so if you are having trouble finding a place to stay, stop by the Visitors Bureau (1001 Market, near the Tennessee Aquarium; 800/322-3344) for an accommodations guide.

CAMPING

Harrison Bay State Park (Hwy. 58, 423/344-6214) located 24 miles north of Chattanooga on Chickamauga Reservoir, offers lakefront campsites with hookups from April through October.

NIGHTLIFE

To find out about Chattanooga happenings, listen to public radio on the University of Tennessee Chattanooga's WUTC, 88.1 FM; or pick up the monthly alternative paper *Chug*. You can ring up the 24-hour "Arts Line" at 423/756-ARTS to find out about performances by the **Chattanooga Symphony and Opera Association**, the **Chattanooga Little Theatre**, or events at the **Tivoli Theater, Soldiers & Sailors Memorial Auditorium**, or **Bessie Smith Music Hall**. The ornate **Tivoli** (709 Broad, 423/757-5042), built in 1921, has been restored to its original brilliance. This 1,700-seat downtown venue features Broadway shows as well as dance, opera, and classical and popular music events. Downtown near the aquarium is a new multiplex cinema named the **Bijou** (423/265-5220), which also shows an art film series called **No. 2 at the Bijou**, sponsored by the Arts and Education Council. Brochures for the films can be found at coffeehouses and bookstores around town or by writing the council (P.O. Box 4203, Chattanooga, TN; 37405).

If you go for sports, check out the **UTC Mocs**. Chattanooga's minor league baseball team, the **Lookouts,** is one of the oldest in the country, chartered in 1885. Call 423/267-2208 to see if they're at home in the newly renovated 1929 Engel Stadium.

Several music clubs offer live blues and jazz. Look in the paper or call the WUTC radio station for information about music around town. On Friday nights you can get a taste of old-time bluegrass up on Signal Mountain at the **Mountain Opry.** The **Boiled Frog** (1259 Market St., 423/756-3764) has live jazz on Saturdays and pretty good New Orleans–style food.

FESTIVALS AND FREEBIES

Chattanooga hosts an annual music and arts festival called **Riverbend** (423/265-4112), which lasts for nine days in late June and features out-standing national and regional acts. The **Bessie Smith Jazz Fest** is held in May; call 423/267-0944 for information. To inquire about the **Southern Literature Festival** held every spring, call Allied Arts at 423/756-2787.

Miller Plaza in downtown Chattanooga features free musical per-formances and artists-in-residence year-round. If you are interested in this city's amazing downtown revival, stop by the **Chattanooga Downtown Planning and Design Center** in Miller Plaza and talk to the folks who are making it happen (423/266-5948).

Scenic Route: Highway 127

Highway 127 and Highway 27, about forty miles to the east, run parallel to I-75, the major north-south corridor from Atlanta to Cincinnati and beyond. Try the old roads if you like to see things as they used to be. Leaving Chattanooga, Highway 27 will take you over Walden Ridge to the four-lane Highway 30. As you drop into the **Sequatchie Valley**, the road descends over 800 feet into one of the most scenic landscapes in the region. You'll reach Highway 127 at Dunlap, which bills itself as "the Hang Gliding Capital of the Eastern United States." The valley, no wider than five miles at any point, runs along the Sequatchie River.

An hour or so up Highway 127 you'll find **Cumberland Mountain State Park** (931/484-6138), one of Tennessee's oldest and most beautiful parks. The native stone bridge over the lake as you enter was built by the Civilian Conservation Corps under the supervision of Alvin York in 1934. The park restaurant has won awards. The rustic cabins have screened porches and fireplaces. There's a pool for swimming, a lake for paddleboats, and hiking year-round. Near the park is the **Homestead Museum**, (931/456-9663), located in a cone-shaped stone water tower. The museum

HIGHWAY 127

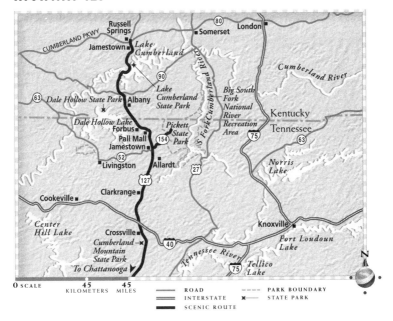

tells the story of **Cumberland Homesteads**, a model New Deal community of stone homes on 30-acre plots. Across the road is the **Cumberland Mountain General Store** (931/484-8481). **The Homestead B&B** (1165 Hwy. 68, 931/456-6355 or 888/782-9987) offers visitors a chance to see inside one of the well-built stone bungalows (the first homes in the area to have electricity).

In Crossville, call the **Cumberland County Playhouse** to see what they're staging (931/484-5000). The clean and quiet **Holiday Hills Resort** (Hwy. 70 E., 931/484-9566) is close to the playhouse. The **Donut Shoppe** a few miles away offers breakfast and lunch. Hours are 4:30 a.m. to 3:30 p.m.

Heading north on Hwy 127, you'll find the original **Cumberland Mountain General Store** (it has a nice soda fountain with good burgers and milkshakes) at Clarkrange. About five miles west you'll find the turnoff (Hwy. 62) for the **Muddy Pond Mennonite Community**. Stop at the **General Store** (931/445-7829) for a driving map. Some households here sell baked and canned goods and fresh produce at the front door. And don't miss the **Muddy Pond Backen Haus** (931/445-3875) about 10 miles down the road, where you can get wonderful cinnamon rolls and coffeecakes to go.

Continue north on 127 toward Allardt to find **Allardt Haus Antiques**, **Indianman Wooden Indians**, and the **Old Schoolhouse B&B**. **East Fork Stables** (P.O. Box 156, Allardt, 931/879-1176 or 800/97TRAIL) offers cabins, camping, and stable accommodations. The turn for Rugby is east on Highway 52, just north of Allardt, and for Big South Fork it's Highway 154 east, just south of Jamestown. At Pall Mall, just north of Jamestown, the **Alvin York Gristmill**, a beautiful red clapboard structure astride a stream on limestone piers, is the center of the **Sergeant Alvin C. York State Historic Park** (931/879-4026), commemorating one of Tennessee's best-loved World War I heroes.

Just before you cross into Kentucky, you'll see the landmark **Forbus General Store** on the right—better for souvenir photos than souvenirs. Now the road begins to climb over mountainous terrain.

Near Albany, Kentucky, home to the **Foothills Festival**, you'll pass the **Hopkins Rural School**, **Caney Gap Antiques**, and the tiny **Branham Motel** (606/387-6606). The area has small wooden cottages, craft shops, and hand-lettered signs advertising quilts, handmade furniture, and bluebird houses. Near Russell Springs, Kentucky, you'll pass **Bray's General Store** and the quaint **Pinehurst Motel** (502/343-4143), which has eight rooms and six cottages. ∎

3

RUGBY AND THE BIG SOUTH FORK

The Big South Fork, created by the U.S. Army Corps of Engineers from former mining and timbering lands beginning in the 1970s and turned over to the Park Service in 1990, is one of the best-kept secrets in Tennessee among white-water paddlers and backcountry campers. Rugby, Tennessee, a Victorian-era utopian community, is located in a rural area on the northern Cumberland Plateau about 25 miles south of the Kentucky border. Combining the two makes for an unusual and delightful vacation destination.

The Big South Fork, a national recreation area, is between Rugby and the Kentucky border. Its 110,000 acres of rugged, rocky gorge surround a fork of the Cumberland River flowing down from Kentucky and offer spectacular scenic views, challenging water recreation, miles of hiking and backpacking trails, and unrestricted backcountry camping. The area is bounded on the west by Pickett State Park, one of Tennessee's oldest; and on the south by Rugby, a charming village filled with Victorian architecture. A welcome respite from the rigors of nature, the Historic Rugby Preservation Association offers period lodging and dining in what feels for all the world like the middle of nowhere. ◼

THE BIG SOUTH FORK

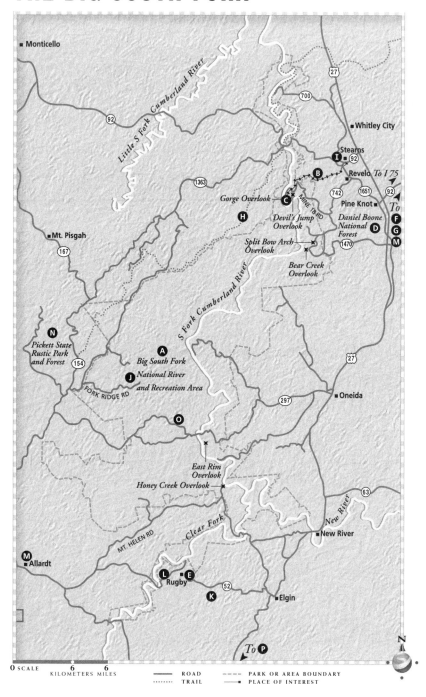

Monticello

Little S Fork Cumberland River

92

(700)

27

Whitley City

Stearns I 92

(1363) B Revelo *To I 75*

Gorge Overlook C 742 1651 92

MINE 18 RD Pine Knot *To* F

H Devil's Jump Overlook Daniel Boone National Forest D G

Mt. Pisgah Split Bow Arch Overlook M

167 Bear Creek Overlook 1470

S Fork Cumberland River

N 27

Pickett State Rustic Park and Forest A

154 Big South Fork J National River and Recreation Area

FORK RIDGE RD 297 Oneida

O

East Rim Overlook

Honey Creek Overlook 63

New River

M MT. HELEN RD Clear Fork New River

Allardt

L E

Rugby

K 52

Elgin

To P

N

Sights

- **A** Big South Fork National Recreation Area
- **B** Big South Fork Scenic Railway
- **C** Blue Heron Outdoor Historical Museum
- **D** Daniel Boone National Forest
- **E** Historic Rugby
- **F** Natural Bridge State Park
- **G** Red River Gorge
- **H** Sheltowee Trace National Recreation Trail
- **I** Stearns Museum

Food

- **E** Harrow Road Café

Lodging

- **E** 1880 Pioneer Cottage

Lodging (continued)

- **J** Charit Creek Lodge
- **K** Clear Fork Farm B&B
- **L** Grey Gables Bed & Breakfast Inn
- **E** Newbury House B&B
- **M** Old Allardt Schoolhouse
- **E** Percy Cottage
- **N** Pickett State Park

Camping

- **O** Bandy Creek Campground and Stables
- **A** Big South Fork
- **P** Frozen Head State Natural Area
- **N** Pickett State Park

Note: Items with the same letter are located in the same town or area.

A PERFECT DAY IN BIG SOUTH FORK COUNTRY

After breakfast pack a picnic and put on appropriate gear for a daylong fresh-air outing. In the morning tour the remains of mining operations by boarding the Big South Fork Scenic Railway at Stearns, Kentucky. It will take you along the routes of the coal trains that used to service the mine, to the Blue Heron Outdoor Historical Museum. Enter Big South Fork at the Bandy Creek headquarters and spend the day hiking, floating the river in a canoe, or joining a white-water rafting expedition for the afternoon. After a full day outdoors, drive to Rugby for dinner

at the Harrow Road Café and a quiet overnight at one of the Historic
Rugby lodgings. Spend the next morning walking in this surprisingly
civilized enclave as if it were your own neighborhood back in 1885.

SIGHTSEEING HIGHLIGHTS

✿✿✿ **Big South Fork National Recreation Area**—Named after the
southern fork of the Cumberland River, Big South Fork connects with
Kentucky's 670,000-acre Daniel Boone National Forest, cutting a
swath of protected timber across the eastern third of both states. The
Sheltowee Trace National Recreation Trail (a sort of miniature
Appalachian Trail, 257 miles in length) runs through the length of
Daniel Boone, across the top of Big South Fork, and ends at
Tennessee's Pickett State Park. "Sheltowee," which means turtle, is the
Shawnee name given to Boone by Chief Blackfish as he adopted the
captive Boone into the tribe. There is also a stretch of hiking trail
named for and mapped by John Muir.

At the northern end of **Daniel Boone National Forest**, about 50
miles east of Lexington, you'll find the spectacular **Red River Gorge**

Big South Fork National Recreation Area

Tennessee Tourist Development

and **Natural Bridge State Park** (Slade, KY; 606/663-2214) where you can see more than 80 natural sandstone arches.
Details: P.O. Drawer 630, Oneida, TN 37841; 931/879-3625.

✭✭✭ **Historic Rugby**—Founded in 1880 by English social reformer Thomas Hughes as a place where the second sons of the British landed gentry could "work like peasants and live like gentlemen," Rugby was an idealist's dream that failed within 10 years. At its height in 1885, the colony, sponsored as a commercial venture by the Board of Aid to Land Ownership, owned 75,000 acres of land and had as many as 450 members who built at least 75 structures. English, Scottish, and American colonists worked together, lived side-by-side, and enjoyed a somewhat esoteric lifestyle. They dressed for tea every afternoon at four, and spent most of their free time reading or playing at croquet, tennis, lawn bowling, and other pursuits of the British leisure class. It's no wonder Rugby's agriculture and home-grown industry efforts failed. Walking tours are available year round, except in January, when the school closes. Church services are still held every Sunday in the 1887 Episcopal church, and the library remains intact as one of the finest collections of Victoriana in the United States.
Details: Hwy. 52, 423/628-2441. Daily 9–5, last tour at 4:45. $4.25 adults, $3.75 seniors, $2.25 ages 6–17. (2 hours)

✭✭ **Blue Heron Outdoor Historical Museum**—The former Stearns Mine is now a very effectively interpreted coal mining and logging camp. It can be reached via Highway 92 from Stearns or by a ride on the **Big South Fork Scenic Railway**. Admission to the interpretive museum is free; for more information call the Kentucky Visitors Center at Stearns (606/376-5073).
Details: Hwy. 1651, Stearns; 606/376-5330 or 800/462-5664. Train runs May–Sept Wed–Fri at 10 a.m., Sat–Sun at 10 and 2; Oct Tue–Fri at 10 a.m., Sat–Sun at 10, 11:30, and 2. 11-mile train ride plus museum is $10 adults, $5 ages 3–13. (1½ hours)

✭✭ **Stearns Museum**—This small local museum, which offers a look at the history of the Stearns Coal and Lumber Company as it existed from 1902 to 1976, also covers the general history of McCreary County.
Details: Hwy. 1651 (just off Hwy. 27), Stearns; 606/376-5730. Tue–Sat 9–4, Sun noon–5. $2 adults, $1 students ages 6–12. (30 minutes)

FITNESS AND RECREATION

Big South Fork National Recreation Area, located between Highway 27 and Highway 127 at the border of Tennessee and Kentucky, offers backcountry hiking, camping, biking, horseback riding, and all forms of river sports. For information and a map of the area, write: National Park Service, Big South Fork, P.O. Drawer 630, Oneida, Tennessee, 37841. Stop by Bandy Creek Visitors Center (Rt. 297, 931/879-3625) for information about outfitters, horseback-riding stables, and other activities.

The **Daniel Boone National Forest** connects with the Big South Fork near Stearns, Kentucky. Not only does the forest contain all manner of scenic trails, hiking, and river-recreation opportunities, but the Red River Gorge, in the northern part of the park, is a well-known rock-climbing area. **Sheltowee Trace Outfitters** (800/541-RAFT) serves the Stearns area in the south with guided canoe and raft expeditions March through October. While you're in the area, stop by the Daniel Boone National Forest's southernmost visitors center (Hwy. 27, Whitley City, KT; 606/376-5323) so you can plan your trip to the rest of the forest.

Pickett State Park (Hwy. 154, Jamestown, TN; 931/879-5821) is adjacent to Big South Fork on the west side. It is known for its diversity of botanical growth (second only to that found in the Smokies), its rugged rock formations and natural bridges, and its wealth of hiking trails. Pickett also has some of the nicest rustic stone cabins of any of Tennessee's state parks (see Lodging).

At **Frozen Head State Natural Area** (Wartburg, TN; 423/346-3318), about 40 miles from Rugby in the Cumberland Mountains, you can hike in mountainous terrain that contains 14 peaks. Its namesake snow-covered mountain stands at 3,324 feet. This area was an Indian hunting ground, and there is evidence of a Woodland Indian trail over the mountains from the Clinch River Valley to the east down into the Cumberland River Valley. Frozen Head, with no less that 12 trails built by the Civilian Conservation Corps in the 1930s, provides a nice day of rugged hiking and spectacular views across the Cumberland Plateau.

The Wartburg visitors center provides directions to the **Obed Wild and Scenic River**, a National Park Service site co-managed by the Tennessee Wildlife Resources Agency. The Obed lives up to its name, offering impressive limestone gorges and clear rushing streams. Hiking, fishing, rafting, and canoeing (as well as swimming in a few quiet spots) are all available here in relative isolation. River put-ins and difficulty ratings are marked so that canoe expeditions can be planned for maximum enjoyment. The Obed encompasses the **Catoosa Wildlife Management Area**, which is a designated site for managed game hunting in the spring and fall. Call the National Park Service (423/346-6294) for more information.

FOOD

The **Harrow Road Café** (423/628-2441; Sun–Thu 8–6, Fri–Sat 8–9:30), operated by Historic Rugby, serves regional specialties with an old-fashioned air, such as spoon rolls, shepherd's pie, fried catfish, ham and biscuits, and bread pudding. Breakfast, lunch, and dinner are offered at reasonable prices. Otherwise, there are few eating establishments in the area. Pack picnic lunches and snacks. The accommodations listed below all offer dining or kitchen facilities, however.

LODGING

Charit Creek Lodge (423/429-5704) is situated within Big South Fork. This establishment, to which there is no road access, is located approximately 1.8 miles in by the shortest route. It stands at the site of a cabin built in 1817 in a pasture framed by bluffs. Both lodge accommodations and private cabins are available, with rates including dinner and breakfast. A horse stable is also available. This lodge is under the same management as the LeConte Lodge on top of Mount LeConte in Great Smoky Mountains National Park.

    Pickett State Park (931/879-5821) offers chalets, rustic stone cottages with fireplaces, and cabins. The cottages ($60–$100) are some of the best the Tennessee state parks have to offer.

    Historic Rugby, Inc. (423/628-2441) runs three lodging facilities in historic buildings: **Newbury House B&B**, the **1880 Pioneer Cottage** (where Thomas Hughes stayed when he first came to Rugby), and **Percy Cottage**.

    If you can't book a room in Rugby, there are several other nearby B&Bs. The **Grey Gables Bed-and-Breakfast Inn** (Hwy. 52, Rugby; 423/628-5252)—where a $115 double includes breakfast and dinner— is a contemporary rustic lodge with eight rooms and private baths. Horse boarding is available here and at **Clear Fork Farm B&B** (328 Shirley Ford Rd., Robbins, TN; 423/628-2967), a brick farmhouse with three rooms and private baths. To experience an ingenious historic rehabilitation, stay at the **Old Allardt Schoolhouse** (Hwy. 52, Allardt; 931/879-8056), built circa 1910. It has been remodeled into a two-bed, two-bath lodge with a shared kitchen. There is a porch on either end, and the entrances are separate. Located on Highway 52 west of Rugby at the intersection of Highway 296, the Schoolhouse is open year round, and discounted weekly rates are available.

CAMPING

Frozen Head State Natural Area (423/346-3318) in Tennessee offers both tent camping with facilities and backcountry camping. Like most Tennessee state parks, reservations are not accepted for campsites, but you can call for information. **Pickett State Park** (931/879-5821), also in Tennessee, offers camping and hookups. At **Big South Fork**, backcountry camping is allowed without permits year round. **Bandy Creek Campground and Stables** (931/879-4013) has tent and RV camping.

In the **Daniel Boone National Forest**, there are many camping areas for which information can be obtained at the closest of six ranger district offices.

SPECIAL EVENTS

Historic Rugby, Inc. sponsors a traditional **Spring Music and Crafts Festival** in early May and the **Rugby Annual Pilgrimage** the first week of October. Both events offer a fine opportunity to see Rugby come alive. Many of the privately owned homes are open for tours on festival days, and craftspeople and musicians from the surrounding areas come in to participate. Historic Rugby (P.O. Box 8, Rugby, TN 37733; 423/628-2441) will respond graciously to your inquiries.

4
KNOXVILLE

This hilly city, whose landmarks in the Old City bear witness to its former prominence as a railroad and manufacturing center, has a fine view of the Great Smoky Mountains and is home to the state's largest university community, the University of Tennessee. Knoxville was once an American frontier outpost. At the site where the confluence of the Holston and French Broad Rivers becomes the Tennessee River, pioneer James White built a fort in 1786. Visitors will find his 20-by-30-foot cabin, reconstructed from the original hand-hewn logs; plus the 1792 mansion of William Blount, first territorial governor of "the United States south of the River Ohio," right in downtown Knoxville. Blount christened the small town in honor of Major General Henry Knox, George Washington's secretary of war. Tennessee's constitution was drafted by Blount and Andrew Jackson in Blount's office, and in 1796, when Tennessee became the 16th state, Knoxville became its first capital.

Today's Knoxville is a city on the move. It boasts the largest and newest art museum in the state and a new Museum of East Tennessee History. Its highways are undergoing a needed expansion, while the watchful eyes of local environmental groups attempt to safeguard the fragile East Tennessee environment. Outdoor recreation abounds in the areas surrounding Knoxville—the Great Smoky Mountains National Park to the east; Big South Fork National Recreation Area to the north; the Cumberland Mountains of the Appalachian chain to the west; and the wide, flat Tennessee River Valley to the south. ◼

DOWNTOWN KNOXVILLE

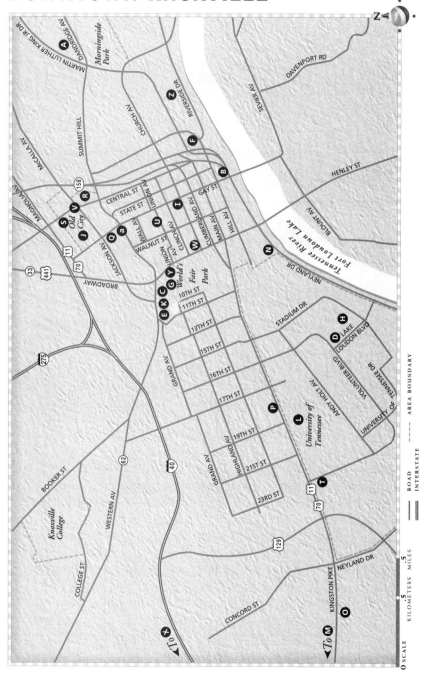

Sights

- Ⓐ Beck Cultural Exchange Center
- Ⓑ Blount Mansion
- Ⓒ Candy Factory
- Ⓓ Ewing Gallery of Art and Architecture
- Ⓔ Fort Kid
- Ⓕ James White Fort
- Ⓖ Knoxville Museum of Art
- Ⓗ McClung Museum of Natural History and Anthropology
- Ⓘ Museum of East Tennessee History
- Ⓙ Old City
- Ⓚ Sunsphere
- Ⓛ University of Tennessee

Food

- Ⓜ Bistro by the Tracks

Food (continued)

- Ⓝ Calhoun's
- Ⓞ Cappuccino's
- Ⓟ Copper Cellar
- Ⓠ Harold's Deli
- Ⓡ Java
- Ⓢ Lucille's
- Ⓜ Mango
- Ⓣ Stir Fry Cafe
- Ⓤ Tomatohead
- Ⓥ Tomo

Lodging

- Ⓦ Hilton
- Ⓧ Holiday Inn Papermill
- Ⓨ Holiday Inn Select
- Ⓩ Hyatt Regency
- ⓐ Radisson Summit Hill

Note: Items with the same letter are located in the same place.

A PERFECT DAY IN KNOXVILLE

Stop for coffee at Java in the Old City before heading uptown to the Museum of East Tennessee History, the James White Fort, and Blount Mansion. Look east from the high ground of downtown for a view of the Great Smoky Mountains. Next, the Knoxville Museum of Art will provide late-morning edification and a light lunch at the Artist's Palette Café. A few blocks west is the University of Tennessee (UT) campus. Find the Ewing Gallery in the Art and Architecture building for a glimpse into an enormous factory-like working art department. Ask at the gallery, which generally has excellent shows, for a guide to the UT Sculpture Tour, a changing exhibit of outdoor sculpture around the campus. While on campus visit the McClung Museum of Natural History and Anthropology for the latest research findings in Tennessee's Native American history. Take a late-afternoon walk in Cherokee Park to catch the sunset by the Tennessee River. After dinner, head to the Laurel Theater for the best in traditional acoustic music or, if you can get tickets, to a performance at the Tennessee or Bijou Theatres downtown.

SIGHTSEEING HIGHLIGHTS

★★★ **Blount Mansion**—The 1792 home of Governor William Blount, this frame house was called a mansion by early Knoxville dwellers because of its gracious scale. Typical of the period are the separate kitchen and office buildings behind the main dwelling. It was here in the governor's office, with the help of Andrew Jackson and several others, that the first state constitution was drafted. The furnishings are original Blount, who served as the first governor of the Southwest Territory (1790–1796) and first United States senator from Tennessee (1796–1798). The mansion also features period gardens and a visitor's center and museum shop in a building dating from 1818.
Details: 200 W. Hill Ave., Knoxville; 423/525-2375. Tue–Sat 9:30–5, Sun 2:30–5. $4 adults, $3.50 seniors, $2 ages 6–12. (1 hour)

★★★**James White Fort**—Knoxville's founder, James White, who arrived in Tennessee in 1786 to claim a land-grant award after the Revolutionary War, built a log home strategically near the confluence of the Holston and French Broad Rivers, which come together to form the Tennessee. As other settlers came, White harbored them in this complex, adding more buildings as needed. With the arrival of William Blount a few years later, Knoxville was set permanently on the site. Visitors can see the authentic and reconstructed log buildings in the company of period-clothed guides and view original artifacts in the museum, blacksmith shop, and loom house.
Details: 205 E. Hill Ave., Knoxville; 423/525-6514. Jan–Feb Mon–Sat 10–4; Mar–Dec 9:30–4:30. $4 adults, $3.50 seniors, $2 ages 6–12. (45 minutes)

★★★ **Knoxville Museum of Art**—Designed by Edward Larrabee Barnes, this museum features traveling exhibits and fine original shows of regional and national contemporary artists. There is also an exploratory gallery for students, a gift shop, and a restaurant. On

Friday evenings the museum is open late for "Alive after Five," a free local jazz performance before a live audience in the museum's great hall that is broadcast over WUOT radio (91.9). Weekend lectures and film series take place in the museum auditorium, often at additional charge.
Details: 410 10th St., Knoxville; 423/525-6101. Tue–Thu 10–5, Fri 10–9, Sat 10–5, Sun noon–5. Admission is free except for occasional traveling exhibits.(1 hour)

✯✯✯ **Museum of East Tennessee History**—This museum, sponsored by the East Tennessee Historical Society, has an excellent orientation film that will change the way you see the whole region. An important repository for the region, the museum contains collections of documents, genealogy materials, works of art, and artifacts that are vital to the history of the area. Genealogists and historians will be interested to know that housed upstairs in the same building are the Knox County Archives and the McClung Historical Collection.
Details: 600 Market St., Knoxville; 423/544-4318. Mon–Sat 10–4, Sun 1–5. Admission is free. (1 hour)

✯✯✯ **Old City**—A walk through this district will take you by brick warehouse buildings near the railroad tracks, the JFG coffee roasting plant, and several worthwhile antique stores. A walking-tour brochure is available at retail establishments in this four-block neighborhood filled with restaurants.
Details: Jackson and Central Aves., Knoxville. *(30 minutes)*

✯✯ **Marble Springs**—John Sevier, first governor of Tennessee, built this home when he came to Knoxville in 1796. Marble Springs, a smaller version of Blount's wooden house, was a gentleman's farm in the manner of many Tennessee country homes. It is located to the east of Knoxville on the way to the town of Sevierville, named for the governor. Sevier, a legendarily harsh foe of the Indians, served six terms as governor and two terms in Congress.
Details: 1220 West Governor John Sevier Hwy., Knoxville; 423/573-5508. Tue–Sat 10–5, Sun 2–5. $2 adults, $1 seniors and students, ages 5 and under free. (1 hour)

✯✯ **Ramsey House**—The first stone house built in Knoxville, Ramsey House dates from 1797 and was designed by English architect Thomas

Hope. It is made of cut limestone and the pink Tennessee marble that is quarried around the Knoxville area. Revolutionary War officer Colonel Francis Alexander Ramsey was noted in the census of 1800 as having the finest house in the state of Tennessee. The house is located to the east of Knoxville, on the way to the Great Smoky Mountains, and is worth a stop.

Details: 2614 Thorngrove Pike, six miles east of Knoxville (take exit 398 from I-40 East); 423/546-0745. Tue–Sat 10–4, Sun 1–4; closed Jan–Mar. $3.50 adults, $3 seniors, $1.50 students, ages 7 and under free. (1 hour)

✷✷ **University of Tennessee**—This scenic campus sprawls on either side of Cumberland Avenue just west of downtown Knoxville. Outstanding sites include the **Ewing Gallery of Art and Architecture**, where you can pick up a catalogue and walking map of the campus Sculpture Tour; and the **McClung Museum of Natural History and Anthropology**. The innovative Sculpture Tour enables the University to have a changing exhibit of large-scale sculpture on campus. Sculptors come to Knoxville from all over to leave a piece on site, since opportunities to display outdoor sculpture are rare. UT also purchases one piece every year for its permanent campus collection. The McClung Museum is one of the few resources in the state for the study of the Indian civilizations that preceded the white settlement of Tennessee. Here—and at the Tennessee State Museum in Nashville—you will see some incredible finds, including two 30-foot-long poplar canoes made from single straight trees. You'll also learn what researchers have interpreted from the implements and ornaments of the Cherokee and the Mississippian Indians, who built towns and ceremonial sites here; and the Woodland Indians, who wandered these lands and owned traded items from as far away as the Gulf of Mexico.

Details: 17th and Cumberland Aves., Knoxville. Ewing Gallery: 423/974-2000; McClung Museum: 423/974-2144. Ewing Gallery hours change during school year so call ahead; McClung Museum hours are Mon–Fri 9–5, Sat 10–3, Sun 2–5. Admission is free. (1 hour)

✷ **Beck Cultural Exchange Center**—This research facility is dedicated to the achievements of African Americans in Knoxville, which initially sided with the Union during the Civil War. Knoxville's African American heritage is a proud one that includes Red Summer (1919), during which black soldiers returning from World War I protested racial discrimination. The Beck Center provides art activities and changing exhibits at no charge.

Details: *1927 Dandridge Ave., Knoxville; 423/524-8461. Tue–Sat 10–6. Admission is free. (1 hour)*

✦ **Candy Factory**—Located next door to the Knoxville Museum of Art, the Candy Factory was built in 1919 by Littlefield and Steere, makers of Red Seal candy. You can take a tour of the current candy-maker occupant, The South's Finest Chocolate Factory, and purchase their wares on site. The building also houses the Knox County Visitors Information Center, the Knoxville Arts Council gallery, the Foothills Crafts Guild, and other nonprofit arts groups. Just a block away on 11th Street is the "artist's colony," where Victorian houses contain arts-and-crafts studios. Behind the Candy Factory building is the 1982 World's Fair site, home of the **Sunsphere** observation tower which offers a wonderful view of the mountains on a clear day. Across the street from the museum and Candy Factory is **Fort Kid**, an innovative playground that always seems to have kids in it, even on weekdays.

Details: *10th St., Knoxville. Candy Factory general information: 423/546-5707; Knox County Tourist Council: 423/523-7263; South's Finest Chocolate Factory: 423/522-2049; Knoxville Arts Council: 423/523-7543; Sunsphere: 423/523-4228. Candy Factory Building open Tue–Sat 10–5, Sun 1–5; Sunsphere Observation Tower open Mon–Sat 10–3. Admission is free. (1 hour)*

FITNESS AND RECREATION

Run, bike, or walk in **Cherokee Park** along the Tennessee River and you will see most of Knoxville's fitness devotees. The rest of them are at the YMCA downtown or at the UT climbing gym. The **Third Creek Bicycle Trail** winds around the town, and more greenways are under construction. There are tennis courts in public parks and on the UT campus (accessible in summer). For information about camping, hiking, and rock climbing in the area, or about organized canoeing and rowing activities, check with local stores such as **Blue Ridge Mountain Sports** (4417 Kingston Pike, 423/588-2638) and **River Sports Outfitters** (2918 Sutherland Ave., 423/523-0066). **Whittle Springs Golf Course** (3113 Valley View, 423/525-1022) and the **Knoxville Municipal Course** (3925 Schadd Rd., 423/691-7143) are both open to the public. The **Ijams Nature Center** (2915 Island Home Ave., 423/577-4717), an 80-acre environmental education center, offers perennial gardens and nature walks on a series of trails.

If you desire a rewarding half-day uphill hike in isolated woods without going to Great Smoky Mountains National Park, try **House Mountain State Park**, about 15 miles north of town on Rutledge Pike (Hwy. 11W, 423/933-6851).

For information about regional geology, flora, fauna, and local outdoor groups, check the bookshelves at the outdoor equipment stores, visit the excellent Lawson McGhee Public Library downtown (500 West Church, 423/544-5750), or try the Tennessee-based Davis-Kidd Booksellers (113 North Peters Rd., 423/690-0136).

FOOD

Downtown choices in the inexpensive price range include breakfast at either **Java** (South Central, 423/525-1600) in the Old City, which has excellent baked goods and is open early; or **Harold's Deli** (131 S. Gay St., 423/523-4315), which serves a classic lox, eggs, and bagel breakfast. Both also serve lunch. Budget-conscious travelers, strict vegetarians, and most everyone else will like the **Tomatohead** (12 Market Square, 423/637-4067), which serves great fresh vegetable pizzas, healthful daily specials, and home-baked treats for lunch and dinner. For a moderately priced supper downtown, try **Tomo** (112 South Central, 423/546-3308) for good sushi and udon dishes. A block away, **Lucille's** (104 North Central, 423/546-3742) has pricier food and live jazz. This is a Knoxville favorite, so call for reservations.

If a short outing suits your mood, a five-mile drive out Highway 441 (Chapman Hwy.) southeast toward the mountains will take you to the wonderful **Ye Olde Steakhouse** (Hwy. 441 S., 423/577-9328). They serve fine steaks and more at reasonable prices in a rustic log building. Drive a few miles north to the Fountain City area of town and you'll find **Litton's Market and Restaurant** (2803 Essary Dr., 423/688-0429), a historic neighborhood spot that serves delicious, filling meals at moderate prices; and has great old photographs of Knoxville lining the walls.

Around the University of Tennessee campus, just west of downtown on "the Strip," as Cumberland Avenue is known, is the original **Copper Cellar** (1807 Cumberland, 423/673-3411), a cozy dining room which specializes in hearty portions, prime beef, and seafood with some unusual touches; and quality guaranteed. On the outskirts of the UT campus, near the mammoth football stadium but with a nice

GREATER KNOXVILLE

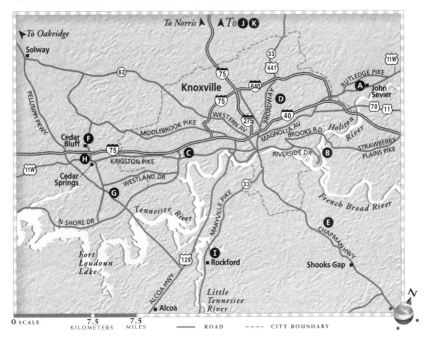

Sights

A Marble Springs

B Ramsey House

Food

C Fresh Market

D Litton's Market and Restaurant

E Ye Olde Steakhouse

Lodging

F Hampton Inn West

F Holiday Inn Select, Cedar Bluff

Lodging *(continued)*

G Maple Grove Inn

H Ramada

I Wayside Manor Bed and Breakfast

Camping

J Big Ridge State Park

K Norris Dam State Park

Note: Items with the same letter are located in the same town or area.

view of the Tennessee River, is **Calhoun's** (400 Neyland Dr., 423/673-3355), a fern bar–type restaurant specializing in barbecued ribs but also serving a good, complete menu.

On the west side of town, out Kingston Pike (Cumberland Ave. extended), are several of my favorites for a moderately priced supper. They include **Mango** (5803 Kingston Pike, 423/584-5053) and **Stir Fry Cafe** (7240 Kingston Pike, 423/588-2064), a hip spot in the corner of a shopping center that serves quick Thai-influenced dishes with a contemporary flair at moderate prices. If you'd like an exquisitely prepared meal and don't mind a small splurge, **Bistro by the Tracks** (130 Northshore Dr., 423/558-9500) is a tiny gourmet restaurant open for both lunch and dinner. Copper Cellar also has a westside location adjoining its upscale Italian restaurant **Cappuccino's** (7316 Kingston Pike, 423/673-4322). If you want to pack your own picnic, go to the **Fresh Market** (4475 Kingston Pike, 423/584-8699), a gourmet grocery store with carryout foods and a bakery.

LODGING

There are few, if any, bed-and-breakfast accommodations in Knoxville and visitors would be well-advised to use caution at inexpensive motels along major thoroughfares. Downtown Knoxville has several executive hotels, most of which offer weekend specials with the exception of convention bookings and during football season. You'll find the **Holiday Inn Select** (525 Henley, 423/522-2800), the **Radisson Summit Hill** (401 Summit Hill Dr., 423/522-2600), and the **Knoxville Hilton** (501 Church, 423/523-2300) all in the center of town. Just across the Tennessee River is the **Hyatt Regency** (500 Hill Southeast, 423/637-1234), Knoxville's largest and most elegant hotel.

Just to the west of downtown and the University of Tennessee campus, in a convenient location as long as you have a car, is the **Holiday Inn Papermill** (1315 Kirby Rd., 423/584-3911). In the outskirts of west Knoxville at the Cedar Bluff exit are **Hampton Inn West** at Cedar Bluff (9128 Executive Park Blvd., 423/693-1101), **Holiday Inn Select Cedar Bluff** (304 Cedar Bluff Rd., 423/693-1011), and the **Ramada Inn Knoxville** (323 Cedar Bluff, 423/693-7330). Also in the area is the **Maple Grove Inn** (8800 Westland Dr., 423/690-9565), a historic 1799 home that is now a resort and meeting place. If you are headed to the mountains or flying into Knoxville you might want to stay south of town on the way to the airport and the south entrance to Great Smoky Mountains National Park. The **Wayside Manor B&B** (4009 Old Knoxville Hwy. 33, Rockford; 423/970-4823 or 800/675-4823) is on eight acres and has four rooms in the main inn, a two-bedroom cabin, and a five-bedroom lodge.

CAMPING

Norris Dam State Park (423/632-1825), about 20 miles northwest of Knoxville, has nice rustic cabins and two campgrounds with hookups that are available on a first-come, first-served basis. **Big Ridge State Park** (423/992-5523), approximately 20 miles north, has tent-only and back-country campsites as well as a regular campground. There are many commercial campgrounds in and around Knoxville, but quality varies because this is such a heavily touristed area in summer. I would recommend relying on the state and national parks in the area for satisfactory camping arrangements. Call 888/TN-PARKS or visit their Web site at www.tnstateparks.com for information about all of the parks. The Tennessee Valley Authority maintains a number of large and small lakes in the Tennessee River watershed, some of which have camping facilities. The TVA trails coordinator is headquartered at Norris, Tennessee, and can be reached at 423/632-1600. The national parks in the area—Big South Fork National Wilderness Area, Great Smoky Mountains, and Cherokee National Forest—are covered in other chapters of this book.

NIGHTLIFE

Check out *Metro Pulse*, Knoxville's alternative weekly paper, for listings; or tune into WUOT public radio at 91.9 FM to find out what's happening while you're in Knoxville. Music offerings abound, starting with live acoustic music at the **Laurel Theater** (1538 Laurel Ave., 423/522-5851). Built as a church in 1898, Knoxville's beloved roots-music venue is located just north of the UT campus in the Fort Sanders historic neighborhood. Their programs focus on traditional music of the region, contra dancing, and live acoustic music of all kinds, from jazz to world music and more. The **Bijou Theater** (803 South Gay St., 423/522-0832) is a restored downtown vaudeville theater that offers the best in national and regional music, including jazz, bluegrass, contemporary country, rock, and pop acts; as well as classical music, ballet, and theater. The **Tennessee Theater** (604 Gay St., 423/522-1174), built in 1928 as a movie palace, is an ornate and stately auditorium that still shows occasional repertory cinema with a live organ prelude, but more often mounts top-notch big-name concerts. The acoustics and ambiance make hearing music here something extraordinary. The **University of Tennessee Department of Music** (423/974-3241) a nationally recognized music program, brings in prominent pop, rock, and jazz musicians for public concerts during the school year, and also presents classical and jazz performances by faculty and students. UT's **Theatre Department** (423/974-5161) operates both the **Clarence Brown** and **Carousel Theatres** on campus, and produces both musicals and dramatic performances. Check at the UT Student Center on Cumberland Avenue for information about the **University Film Series**, which is also excellent. Knoxville's **Symphony and Chamber Orchestra** (423/523-1178), as well as the **Knoxville Opera Company** (423/523-8712) and the **Knoxville City Ballet** (423/544-0495), offer annual concert series. You can find excellent local programming on **WUOT,** with the nightly *Improvisations*, a show on the history of jazz, at half past six; *Unhinged*, an eclectic new music show Friday nights at 10; and *Live at Laurel* Sunday evenings at half past five.

Nightlife in the Old City revolves around **Java** and **JFG Coffeehouses** and **Lucille's** outdoor jazz courtyard; while bars on "The Strip" are rowdy student scenes with occasional live music. One exception is **Barley and Hops** (1912 Cumberland, 423/546-0066), which features a full schedule of new music from nationally emerging bands. Want more? Call Knoxvoice (423/525-9900) for a recorded listing of happenings.

Knoxville is a mecca for sports lovers, with the nationally ranked **Lady Vols** basketball team and consistently strong **Tennessee Volunteers** football teams. The **Knoxville Smokies** play AA baseball for the Toronto Blue Jays at Bill Meyer Stadium (633 Jessamine St., 423/637-9494).

SIDE TRIPS: NORRIS AND OAK RIDGE

Since Knoxville is located at the juncture of two natural wonders—the Tennessee River and the Smoky Mountains—and in the midst of historical and present-day pockets of culture such as the Appalachian and Native American, it makes a good base from which to explore. I've listed several daylong itineraries that you might wish to try.

Located about 20 miles north of Knoxville, off I-75 on Highway 441, Norris, Tennessee, is situated in the foothills of the Cumberland

Mountains. This small community, established in 1934, was one of the first planned communities in the country. It is the home of **Norris Dam** (423/632-1825), the first dam built by the Tennessee Valley Authority (TVA). The Regional Library System in Tennessee, which still sends bookmobiles out over rural roads, started here as a book depository for the workers building the dam. The City Hall/Police/Fire Department has a map and brochure. You can tour the 1930s chrome-trimmed, deco-influenced power house (call ahead) and stay in the rustic cabins that are now part of **Norris Dam State Park** (1261 Norris Freeway, Lake City; 423/426-7461). This park also has beautiful wooded hiking trails. The **Lenoir Museum**, inside the park next to a working gristmill, has a collection of artifacts from Indian times to the Great Depression.

If you take Highway 61 to the park, you'll pass the highly recommended **Museum of Appalachia** (Hwy. 61, Norris; 423/494-0514), which consists of two large exhibit buildings with a 65-acre working Appalachian farm community attached. There are 30 authentic log outbuildings on the premises. Local resident John Rice Irwin, whose family was among the pioneer settlers in the area, has labored for many years to build his dream—a repository that celebrates the ingenuity of mountain folk. The museum collection, which in places is arranged almost like a flea market, contains many objects that may have never been seen by most people. Many of these objects are still in use at the working rural homesteads tucked back into the hills. There is a relatively new music museum, which celebrates those who come from the upper East Tennessee area in particular. Be sure to inquire about the famous October Homecoming Celebration if you'll be here in the fall.

Across the street from the museum is the **Appalachian Artisans Craft Shop** (Hwy. 61, Norris; 423/494-9854), the oldest crafts cooperative in the state, where you can purchase both traditional and not-so-traditional items made by artisans in the local area.

Oak Ridge, founded in an out-of-the-way location in 1942 to house the laboratories and reactors where the atomic bomb was being developed, is located about 25 miles west of Knoxville. Today one can visit the **Oak Ridge National Laboratory** grounds on a self-guided driving tour or make reservations for a guided bus tour through the visitors center. The **Oak Ridge Visitors Center** (302 S. Tulane Ave., 423/482-7821) and the **American Museum of Science** (300 S. Tulane Ave., 423/576-3200), which stand side by side, are both open daily. The Museum is science-based and interactive, so kids will enjoy the experience. Underneath the upbeat facade there is an undercurrent of defensiveness here, not surprising among folks who have dedicated their lives to something so controversial. Seeing the home of the atomic bomb from today's historical perspective will certainly prompt new insights into the endeavors of 50 years ago. Oak Ridge is an interesting community with an aging population of creative, quirky scientists who support cultural activities with a vengeance.

If you choose to stay overnight, check with the visitors center to see if the **Oak Ridge Symphony**, **Civic Ballet**, or **Community Playhouse** are performing; or to see if there is a special exhibit at the **Oak Ridge Art Center**. The **Garden Plaza Hotel** (215 South Illinois Ave., 423/481-2468), a modern facility with a spacious lobby and nice facilities, is located within sight of the museum and visitors center.

Scenic Route: Highway 411 from Knoxville to Cleveland

Highway 411 is the old main road from Knoxville to Atlanta whose path lay along the railroad route. This route, a total distance of 90 miles, could be followed round-trip from Knoxville or could be used to travel from Knoxville to Chattanooga or Atlanta. It passes through what was once the home of the "Overhill" Cherokee, those who chose to settle on the western side of the Great Smoky Mountains. Today the region includes monuments to the Cherokee who lived here before the Indian Removal of 1838. The Indians resided in cities such as Toqua, Citico, Tuskeegee, Chota, and Tanasi (from which the name Tennessee was derived), many of which were inundated when TVA's Tellico Dam project was completed in the late 1970s. Some of the flooded sites, such as Toqua, were pre-Cherokee cities built in the fifteenth century by Mississippian Indians. Head east out of Knoxville on Highway 129 for 17 miles to Alcoa, then south on Highway 411 until you come to the **Cherokee National Forest** (Tellico: 423/253-2520). Bounded on the north by the Tennessee River, the forest

HIGHWAY 411

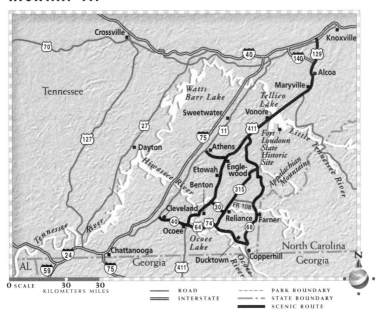

provides opportunities for hiking, horseback riding, and other outdoor recreation within a 625,000-acre area. At the far end of the forest and about 10 miles west is **Red Clay State Historic Park**, the Cherokee Council site where many important deliberations took place in the 1830s just prior to the forced departure on the Trail of Tears. In between, in Englewood, Athens, Etowah, and Ducktown, you'll see relics and reminders of the late-nineteenth- and early-twentieth-century industrialization of the rivers, mountainsides, and open pasturelands of the Tennessee River Valley.

Vonore, site of both the **Sequoyah Birthplace Museum** (Hwy. 360, Citico Rd., Vonore; 423/884-6246) and the reconstructed **Fort Loudoun** (Hwy. 30, Vonore; 423/884-6217), is located just off Highway 411 about 30 miles south of Alcoa. The Sequoyah Birthplace Museum is owned by an eastern band of Cherokee Indians and is dedicated to Sequoyah, who lived from 1776 to 1843. In 1821 Sequoyah introduced an 86-character alphabet based on the syllables of the Cherokee spoken language. The museum contains artifacts excavated in the Tennessee Valley that provide evidence of pre-Cherokee habitation as far back as 8,000 years, as well as interpretive exhibits explaining Cherokee history and culture. The museum also has a bookstore and shop featuring contemporary Cherokee crafts. On the grounds is a monument to those who died in the Removal as well as remains from burial sites flooded in the 1970s. The museum staff can direct you to monuments nearby that commemorate the flooded towns and ceremonial sites of their ancestors. The museum is open daily year-round. Fort Loudoun, a fort built by the British with Cherokee permission and originally intended as protection for the Cherokee, existed from 1756 to 1760. The convoluted history of relations between the Cherokee leaders, British soldiers, the settlers who were soon to become Americans, and the first United States Indian agents is clearly and sympathetically explained by Vicki Rozema in *Footsteps of the Cherokees: A Guide to the Eastern Homelands of the Cherokee Nation*, 1995; and also by Carroll Van West in the excellent *Tennessee's Historic Landscapes: A Traveler's Guide*, 1995. The remains of the Tellico blockhouse, built in 1794, can be seen. This is where the first Indian agents were stationed, sent not only for the protection of the Cherokee but also to negotiate any official business between the United States and the Cherokee. Tellico blockhouse also functioned as a trading post and served as an agricultural training center for the Cherokee. The reconstructed Fort Loudoun is open daily, year round.

Sixteen miles south is Englewood, founded in the late nineteenth century as a textile factory town. The **Englewood Textile Museum** (17 South Niota St., Englewood; 423/887-5455) has placed the emphasis of its interpretive exhibits upon the story of women in the labor force of the Appalachian region. The museum is housed in actual mill buildings donated by the grandson of an early mill owner. (The little-known story of Depression-era labor strikes among women textile workers in Tennessee and surrounding states has been captured in the 1995 documentary film *The Uprising of '34*, directed by George Stoney.) This free museum is closed on Sunday and Monday and during the winter months.

Athens, located about 10 miles west of Englewood, is the largest town in the region, with a population of around 15,000. The **McMinn County Living Heritage Museum** (522 W. Madison, Athens; 423/745-0329) has three floors of exhibits on local culture. Their annual quilt show will surprise visitors with the extent of both tradition and innovation to be seen in this historic art form. Kids will want to tour the **Mayfield Dairy** (423/745-2151 or 800/MAYFIELD), whose cheerful yellow trucks are seen all over the vicinity. Tours are free, and they have an ice-cream parlor where you can sample their wares every day but Sunday. Because it is accessible from I-75 and is about halfway between Knoxville and Chattanooga, Athens is a good place to spend the night for those who like to stay outside of the big city. If you want a special treat, try the **Woodlawn B&B** (110 Keith Ln., Athens; 423/745-8211 or 800/745-8213), an 1858 residence in downtown Athens located on five acres.

The town of **Etowah** ("muddy waters" to the Cherokee) was formed by the railroad, with the **L&N Railroad Depot** (727 Tennessee Ave., 423/263-7840)—a three-story Victorian built in 1906—as its first permanent structure. On the first floor is a museum housing a permanent installation created by Etowah residents entitled Growing Up with the L&N: Life and Times in a Railroad Town. Special events, including craft exhibits and train excursions, are held throughout the year. The museum is closed Mondays. Admission is free.

Further south on Highway 411 you'll reach Benton, where Cherokee leader Nancy Ward, who struggled to make peace between the white settlers and the Overhill Cherokee, is buried. Eight to ten miles further south you will reach the town of Ocoee. To the west is Cleveland, one of the last Cherokee gathering places in the Tennessee Overhill. The Tourist Bureau (2145 Keith Ave., 423/472-6587) offers a self-guided driving tour to Cherokee heritage land that includes a visit to **Red Clay State Historic Park** (423/478-0339). Turning east from Ocoee on Highway 64, a national forest scenic route winds 26 miles alongside the Ocoee River. The **Ocoee** ("Place of the River People") is a white-water river with Class IV rapids, and was the site of the 1996 Olympic trials and events. You'll be well within the **Cherokee National Forest**, a wonderland of outdoor recreational activity that offers wilderness activities, trout fishing, lake swimming, boating, camping, and horseback riding. Stop by the Ocoee Ranger Station on Highway 64 (423/338-5201) for information and directions to the **John Muir Trail**, an 18.8-mile path through diverse terrain.

    Ducktown and Copperhill, sites of major copper mines that operated for roughly 100 years beginning around 1850, offer startling evidence of environmental destruction, despite the fact that federal reforestation efforts in the area were begun as early as the 1930s. Mining operations at Ducktown's Burra Burra mine and others turned the **Great Copper Basin**—where the Cherokee had known of the rich deposits of copper ore long before they were "discovered" by those who moved in after the Cherokee Removal of 1838—into acres of denuded land covered with reddish residue from open-air copper smelting. Many Cherokee who remained behind became part of the region's labor force, working in mining, railroads, and other industries. The **Ducktown Basin Museum** (Burra Burra Hill, 423/496-5778) offers tours of the mine and exhibits explaining the "industrial archaeology" of the region as well as the Cherokee heritage. Two national register homes converted into bed-and-breakfasts—The **Company House** (125 Main St., 423/496-5634) and the **White House** (104 Main St., 423/496-4166)—will make your stay in Ducktown extra special. ◼

5

THE GREAT SMOKY MOUNTAINS

The highest peaks in the Appalachian chain rise up in Tennessee and North Carolina to become the Great Smoky Mountains, a land of legendary beauty, deep forests, and panoramic views. The Great Smoky Mountains National Park, opened in 1934, has become one of the most visited parks in the United States. On the west side of the park is the Qualla Boundary, 56,000 acres that was formerly the Eastern Cherokee reservation, which is still governed by the Cherokee Tribal Council. The Appalachian Trail crosses the park along the ridge, dividing Tennessee and North Carolina. At Newfound Gap, viewers can look off into either state and see rows and rows of mountains, often cloud-covered, receding slowly into the distance.

The Great Smoky Mountains National Park—home to impressive botanical specimens, many native and migrating birds, and some interesting wild creatures—is an International Biosphere Reserve. Unfortunately, the roads to the park are cluttered with motels, restaurants, souvenir stands, outlet malls, water slides, miniature golf courses, and various promotional shops and theaters of country music stars—the best known being "Dollywood." However, by timing your trip carefully and entering the park through alternative routes, you can still experience the majesty of untroubled nature. Hiking, biking, wildflower viewing, horseback riding, fly-fishing, listening for bird calls, and sleeping outside in the Great Smokies can be a uniquely restorative adventure. ◼

GREAT SMOKY MOUNTAINS NATIONAL PARK AREA

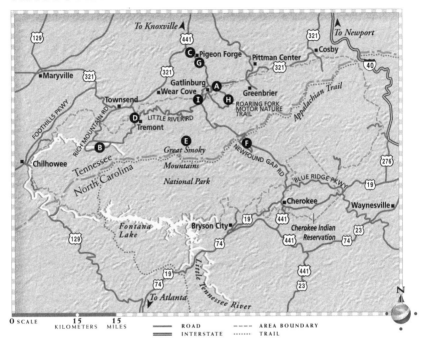

Sights

- **Ⓐ** Arrowmont School of Arts and Crafts
- **Ⓑ** Cades Cove Loop Road
- **Ⓒ** Dollywood
- **Ⓐ** Great Smoky Arts and Crafts Community
- **Ⓓ** Great Smoky Mountains Institute at Tremont
- **Ⓔ** Great Smoky Mountains National Park
- **Ⓕ** Newfound Gap/Appalachian Trail
- **Ⓐ** Ober Gatlinburg
- **Ⓖ** Old Mill
- **Ⓖ** Pigeon Forge Pottery
- **Ⓗ** Roaring Fork Motor Nature Trail
- **Ⓘ** Sugarlands Information Center

Note: Items with the same letter are located in the same town or area.

A PERFECT DAY IN THE GREAT SMOKY MOUNTAINS

Get up very early and take a thermos of coffee and some trail snacks into the park (or even better, camp there the night before) at Cades Cove. Try to be there as the mist rises on the huge open meadows of the valley. My husband likes to hike in about three miles up Abrams Creek toward Abrams Falls and fish back to where he started, wading in the rocky rushing water looking for brown or rainbow trout. You might wish to hike on to the falls; by mid-morning in summer it's usually hot enough for an exhilarating swim in the big pool of mountain-fresh water at its base. If it's off-season (early spring, late fall, or winter), it's always fun to stop in Gatlinburg and visit the gallery at Arrowmont, then lunch in town or enjoy a picnic along the Roaring Fork Motor Nature Trail. We often hike one of the many trails that afford a spectacular view as a reward for an afternoon of serious uphill walking, but more leisurely lowland trails can be just as gratifying for those interested in bird-watching or wildflower identification.

TRAVEL TIPS

This area has become so heavily visited on the Tennessee side that traffic is often backed up as far away as Pigeon Forge (five miles east) and even Sevierville (13 miles east).

Highway 441 between Sevierville—a charming small town with an unusual five-domed courthouse—and Pigeon Forge—once a sleepy community that contained little more than an old mill on the little Pigeon River—are now lined with motels and tourist attractions and can become a bottleneck for through traffic. There are several ways to approach the situation. One is to avoid it altogether by driving in from the north on Highway 321 through Newport or from the south on Highway 73 through Townsend. Another is to choose one of two alternate routes from Sevierville (Middle Creek Road or Pittman Center Road) and avoid as much of Pigeon Forge as possible.

SIGHTSEEING HIGHLIGHTS

✸✸✸ **Great Smoky Mountains National Park**—The main attraction, this park is one of Roosevelt's New Deal public works projects. Entering the park from Gatlinburg on Highway 441 will take visitors past the **Sugarlands Information Center**, where trail maps and seasonal information about road and hiking conditions are available, and then through Newfound Gap into North Carolina.

Stop at **Newfound Gap** (5,045 feet), where the **Appalachian Trail** crosses just a few hundred yards from the road, and read the historical markers concerning the park's founding. From there you can descend via the Indian Gap Trail to Alum Cave (a source of saltpeter, where mountain-dwelling Cherokee Indians once led impoverished Confederates hiding out in the mountains so that they could make gunpowder), or hike north along the high ridge to Mount LeConte, where the only overnight food and lodging accommodations in the park can be found at LeConte Lodge.

Walking or driving in the other direction will take you to Clingman's Dome, the second-highest peak in the park, at 6,642 feet. The road itself climbs to 6,311 feet, affording some pretty spectacular views as it heads over into North Carolina. **Roaring Fork Motor Nature Trail** enters the west side of the park from the heart of Gatlinburg and provides access to a number of hiking destinations including Rainbow Falls, Grotto Falls, and Trillium Gap.

You'll reach Cades Cove at the south end of the park by driving in through Townsend on Highway 73. An excellent auto-tour booklet can be obtained at the Cades Cove Visitors Center. On Saturday morning during late spring and summer, the **Cades Cove Loop Road** is open only for bicycling—would that it were always so! Many trails lead out of Cades Cove, including Abrams Falls Trail and the Rich Mountain Loop Trail. On the north side of the park there are entrances near Cosby and Greenbrier from Highway 321. This is one of the least-frequented areas of the park, and the hiking trails that lead in from here are short, steep, and afford spectacular views.

If you send in an annual membership fee of $15 to the Great Smoky Mountain Natural History Association, 115 Park Headquarters Road, Gatlinburg, Tennessee 37738, you will receive a quarterly newsletter highlighting changing attractions in the park and giving updated information on camping, fishing, horseback riding, nature programs, and volunteer opportunities for park ecosystem maintenance activities. The **Great Smoky Mountains Institute at Tremont** (423/448-6709), a nature center sponsored by the park and the Great Smoky Mountains Natural History Association, offers environmental education programs year-round on weekends and special youth summer camps. Participants stay overnight and have all meals at the institute; call for their current brochure. The Smoky Mountain Field

School, operated in conjunction with the community program at the University of Tennessee at Knoxville (423/974-0150), offers weekend adult workshops, hikes, and adventures led by experts on Smoky Mountain flora and fauna.

Details: Park information: 423/436-1200. (3 hours minimum)

✵ **Gatlinburg**—Once a charming mountain town, Gatlinburg is now not only a popular honeymoon spot but also a veritable tourist magnet for about half the year. Gatlinburg in the off-season can be quite pleasant, but watch out for overcrowding in summer and fall. Tennessee's only ski resort is located here, and many would like to boost the winter tourist season by promoting Gatlinburg as a ski town. **Ober Gatlinburg** has a peak elevation of 3,000 feet, much lower than the slopes to be found further north and across the state line in North Carolina at Boone, Banner Elk, and Wolf Laurel. Enough said. The main street of town (known as the Parkway) is crowded with restaurants, fudge and T-shirt shops, and lots of family entertainment attractions, the most credible of which is the Ripley's Believe It or Not Museum (423/436-5096).

In the very center of town is **Arrowmont School of Arts and Crafts** (566 Parkway, 423/436-5860) founded by Pi Beta Phi (the first sorority) in the early part of the century in an effort to promote and preserve mountain crafts. The sorority also built the Pi Beta Phi elementary school in 1912 for the children of mountain craftspeople and helped create a market for the traditional wares with their Arrowcraft Shop and mail-order catalogue. You can still visit the Arrowcraft Shop and purchase these traditional, handmade goods. Arrowmont, which has a complex of studios and dormitories in a secluded hollow right off the main road, is now an internationally known crafts school with resident artists and a year-round schedule of classes (write for a brochure: P.O. Box 567, Gatlinburg, TN 37738). The Arrowmont Gallery, library, and bookstore are open to the public.

The **Great Smoky Arts and Crafts Community**, located on Glades Road approximately three miles from downtown, houses more than 80 artist shops and studios that range from authentic furniture- and broom-makers to contemporary craft artists and watercolorists to cute craftsy items to downright schlock. The eight-mile loop takes in Buckhorn and Glades Roads and part of Highway 321 north. Many of the artist workshops are open year-round, all are free to the public, and there are a few eateries scattered along the way. The city trolley will take you out to Glades Road from the city center every half hour for $1. *Details: Department of Tourism: 800/267-7088. (1–3 hours)*

★ **Pigeon Forge**—Driving into Pigeon Forge can be a distressing experience as you wonder why anyone would want to visit the Smoky Mountain Police Museum, the Haunted Golf and Video Arcade, or Stars on Ice (impersonations of country-music stars in an ice-skating show); or spend their time at one of nine racetrack and go-cart arcades when real-life adventure is so near at hand up in the rugged mountain landscape that forms a backdrop for the town.

If you take Middle Creek Road from Sevierville, you will pass the entrance to **Dollywood** (800/DOLLYWOOD), Dolly Parton's amusement park, which has live music shows, upscale carnival rides, a dinner theater, and seasonal exhibits and events. Dolly is actually from this area and has been tremendously supportive of her hometown over the years, coming home for many years to perform annually at the high school to raise money for band uniforms. Perhaps her park reflects some of her genuine, down-home persona. Find out for yourself if you happen to be in the area between Memorial Day and Christmas.

As you start to come into Pigeon Forge you'll see both the **Old Mill** (2944 Middle Creek Rd.), an 1830s gristmill still in operation where you can buy stone-ground flour and meal; and **Pigeon Forge Pottery** (2919 Middle Creek Rd.), a charming spot where the same soft matte–finish gray-brown glazes have been created since its founding more than 50 years ago. Up until about 15 years ago, these were the only tourist sites in Pigeon Forge. Both are worth a look and, other than Arrowmont's Arrowcraft Shop, they are your best bet for purchasing gifts to take home. *Details: Pigeon Forge Department of Tourism: 800/251-9100. (30 minutes–3½ hours)*

FITNESS AND RECREATION

Great Smoky Mountains National Park (423/436-1200) offers boundless opportunities for hiking and walking. There are 149 official trails through the park. Pick up trail guides at the Sugarlands, Cades Cove, or Oconaluftee (in North Carolina) visitors centers. A comprehensive trail guide can be purchased for $16.95.

Horseback riding is also popular, and there are five authorized park concessions that can rent you a mount for $15 per hour: **Cades**

Cove (423/448-6286); **McCarter's** (423/436-5354), **Smoky Mountain** (423/436-5634) in Tennessee, and **Smokemont** (704/497-2373) in North Carolina. The **Wonderland Hotel** (see Lodging, below), located outside the park, also has stables.

Bicycles are recommended for use in the park only at Cades Cove, where the 11-mile loop trail is open in warm weather only to bicycles at least one morning a week. Generally the park roads are too heavily traveled to allow for bike traffic, and all park trails are off-limits to bikers.

Fishing is a major pursuit of both visitors and locals in the area. They make it easy here—you can obtain a license at the Gatlinburg Welcome Center or from some of the local merchants. Many actually begin fishing the Little Pigeon River as it passes through the city. A Tennessee or North Carolina fishing license is required for fishing in the park, but you don't need a trout stamp because park naturalists are eager to keep the nonnative rainbow trout population under control. By the same token, native brook trout are off-limits. **Old Smoky Outfitters** (511 Parkway, 423/430-1936) leads guided fishing trips. With the abundance of mountain streams feeding into the Pigeon and French Broad Rivers here, swimming, tubing, rafting, canoeing, and kayaking are also popular. The **Happy Hiker** (905 River Rd., 423/436-4303) can provide information about white-water rafting.

FOOD

Judging by the number of restaurants in town, you might conclude that visitors to Gatlinburg come primarily to eat and shop at discount malls. In the 10 or so years I have lived in the area, many of the charming old restaurants by the river and homey hotel dining rooms have disappeared, replaced by sure-to-be-crowded, buffet-style eateries or franchise restaurants. Of these, both **Ruby Tuesday** (Parkway, 423/436-9251), a fern bar–type restaurant that serves burgers and salads; and **Calhoun's** (1004 Parkway, 423/436-4100), which serves a full menu with a specialty of barbecued ribs, started in East Tennessee. The **Smoky Mountain Brewery** (behind Calhoun's at the same address, 423/436-4200) is a casual spot that has good pizza, microbrews, and live music on weekends. Contrary to what one might assume, there are few, if any, moderately priced, authentic country-cooking restaurants in the area, so consider finding lodgings in a cabin with a kitchenette and stocking up on groceries in order to save yourself time, money, and frustration.

When you do dine out, if you are willing to spend a little on a nice meal, here are some tried-and-true suggestions: **The Peddler** (820 River Rd., 423/436-0380), beside the river in a log cabin one street over from the Parkway in downtown Gatlinburg, offers good service and fine quality steaks cut-to-order at table-side. The **Park Grill** (1110 Parkway, 423/436-2300), an extravagantly designed log lodge located at the far end of town just before you enter the park, offers gourmet dining in a rustic atmosphere. Although they offer standard upscale fare, with a variety of meat and seafood entrées, their vegetarian entrées and desserts get special raves from some picky eaters that I know. **The Greenbrier** (370 Newman Rd., between Gatlinburg and Newport on Hwy. 321 North; 423/436-6318) is worth driving up a little mountain road to find because it's in a 1939 log cabin. The menu features prime rib and mountain trout.

In Pigeon Forge, turn off busy Highway 441 where it meets Highway 321 South. You'll find **Chef Jock's Tastebuds Café** (1198 Wear's Valley Rd., 423/428-9781), a small restaurant known for its wonderful French- and Italian-influenced cuisine. Bring your own wine and be prepared for a dining adventure—they serve ostrich tenderloin, as well as fresh trout, beef, chicken, and whatever strikes the chef's fancy. Chef Jock's is open Tuesday through Saturday for both lunch and dinner. A bit further out Wear's Valley Road, the **Wonderland Hotel** (3889 Lyon Springs Rd., 423/436-5490) serves real country food like steak and gravy, fried chicken, liver and onions, and fried mountain trout. It's open for breakfast and dinner, and prices are moderate.

LODGING

Between Pigeon Forge and Townsend on Highway 321 South, you'll find the **Wonderland Hotel**, the new version of a famous old hotel that used to be within the park's perimeter. The Wonderland (3889 Lyon Springs Rd., Sevierville; 423/436-5490) has lodge accommodations, a family-style dining room, and a stable for your horse. There are 30 rooms in the hotel, as well as three vacation cabins that are rented out when their owners are gone. Just up the road from the Wonderland, almost at the park boundary, is the **Little Greenbrier Lodge** (3685 Lyon Springs Rd., Sevierville; 423/429-2500 or 800/277-8100). Opened in 1939, Little Greenbrier Lodge has 10 rooms with both private and shared baths, a no-smoking policy, and includes a full breakfast with overnight accommodations.

GREAT SMOKY MOUNTAINS NATIONAL PARK AREA

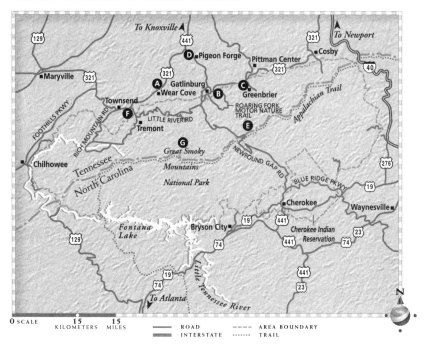

Food

- **A** Chef Jock's Tastebuds Café
- **B** Calhoun's
- **C** The Greenbrier
- **D** Park Grill
- **B** The Peddler
- **B** Ruby Tuesday
- **B** Smoky Mountain Brewery
- **A** Wonderland Hotel

Lodging

- **B** Buckhorn Inn
- **D** Highland Manor

Lodging (continued)

- **B** Hippensteal's Mountain View Inn
- **E** LeConte Lodge
- **C** Little Greenbrier Lodge
- **F** Richmont Inn
- **B** Roaring Fork Motel and Cottages
- **F** Talley Ho Inn
- **A** Wonderland Hotel

Camping

- **G** Great Smoky Mountains National Park
- **F** Tremont Hills Campground

Note: Items with the same letter are located in the same town or area.

If you take Highway 321 south into Townsend, you will have a choice of motels, cottages, and bed-and-breakfast inns on what the locals claim is the "peaceful side of the Smokies." If you prefer a plain, modern motel, the **Highland Manor** (7766 E. Lamar Alexander Pkwy., Hwy. 73, Townsend; 423/448-2211), on a hilltop with a swimming pool, has fairly reasonable rates and a few rooms with fireplaces. The **Talley Ho Inn** (8314 Hwy. 73, Townsend; 423/448-2465 or 800/448-2465), a 46-year-old motel which also has two cottages, also has fireplaces in some of its rooms. You may decide to pamper yourself at the five-year-old **Richmont Inn** (220 Winterberry Ln., Townsend; 423/448-6751)—built in the style of an Appalachian cantilevered barn—which offers deluxe rooms furnished with English and American antiques. A full breakfast is included with the stay. They are open year-round and may offer a discount during low season.

If you want to stay right in the city of Gatlinburg—although I would counsel against it—you might try one of the places along Roaring Fork Road, which ultimately leads to the park's Roaring Fork Motor Nature Trail. This area of town is not quite as heavily traveled as the main thoroughfare or the roads leading to the ski area. **Roaring Fork Motel and Cottages** (124 Roaring Fork Rd., 423/436-4385), which has a nice stone exterior, an outdoor pool, and moderate room rates, has been around as long as almost any place in town.

For an outdoor adventure, hike up to **LeConte Lodge** (423/436-4473). This rustic wooden complex, accessible only on foot and the only private lodging in the park, is still operated by the family of its builder, Jack Huff. To reach the top of LeConte—a 5,000-foot-plus peak often shrouded in clouds or covered with snow—one can choose a trail leading from the Roaring Fork Motor Nature Trail in Gatlinburg, from Cosby, or from Newfound Gap. Staying in the lodge or in a tiny two-person cabin is an exhilarating experience. Visitors should be prepared for cold nights and sudden rainstorms even in the midst of a hot, dry summer. The accommodations are often booked months in advance, and LeConte Lodge is only open from late-March to mid-November; you can write them in the off-season at P.O. Box 350, Gatlinburg, Tennessee 37738. Although the meals are good, you might wish to carry in your own bottle of wine and perhaps a few pieces of fruit or some fresh vegetables to add to the table, as all foodstuffs are still carried up the mountain only once weekly.

It's well worth a splurge to stay in a historic inn outside the city center, or in one of the many bed-and-breakfasts that have been built over the past 10 years. Outside of Gatlinburg on Highway 321 North is the charming old **Buckhorn Inn** (2140 Tudor Mountain Rd., 423/436-4668), established in 1938, which sits amid 35 acres of woodlands. There are six rooms at the inn—all with private baths—and six cottages. A full breakfast is included, and smoking is not permitted. A bed-and-breakfast recently opened by one of the area's most talented painters in an attempt to preserve the ambiance of long-ago Gatlinburg is **Hippensteal's Mountain View Inn** (Grassy Branch Rd., Gatlinburg; 800/527-8110 or 423/436-5761). Owner Vern Hippensteal has a gallery at 69 Buckhorn Road on the Arts and Crafts Loop. If all of these are booked, you might try the B&B Accommodations Service of the Smoky Mountains, 800/248-2923.

CAMPING

Great Smoky Mountains National Park has both established campgrounds and backcountry camping. Although all but one of the 10 established campgrounds can accommodate RVs, there are no hookups. The campgrounds have cold running water and flush toilets but no showers. Most sites cost $6 to $8 per night. While the campgrounds are generally open year-round, many have been forced to close during the winter months because of budget limitations. To book a campsite at Cades Cove, Elkmont, or Smokemont, call 800/365-CAMP.

There are more than 100 sites and shelters for backcountry camping in the park. Campers are required to have a permit (they are free and can be obtained from a ranger) in order to stay at one of the designated locations.   Reservations are required at 30 of the sites and can be made by calling 423/436-1231. You can pick up a backcountry map, listing all sites and shelters, for $1 at any park visitors center. Just before you enter the park, in Townsend, is the **Tremont Hills Campground** (Hwy. 73, Townsend; 423/448-6363), which has RV hookups, tent-camping sites, and some rustic cabins. Its location right on the river makes it the most appealing campground choice outside of the park.

6
NORTHEAST TENNESSEE

O nce the great stage road between Nashville and Washington, and then a major pre–Civil War railroad route between Knoxville and Wytheville, the over-mountain passage roughly paralleling Interstate 81 runs through mountain country. By the time one reaches Bristol, whose State Street forms the Tennessee-Virginia border, the great peaks of the Smokies are visible to the south while the Shenandoah range to the north has receded into the distance. This wide corridor through the mountains, which brought the Scots-Irish pioneer settlers into Tennessee and was one of the major entry points for railroad industrialization in the South, has—because of its isolated location and rugged terrain— remembered more of its pioneer heritage and retained more of the original character of the land the settlers first saw than any other part of the state.

The Appalachian Trail runs the length of this region, and several of the best preserved towns in Tennessee—Jonesborough, Greeneville, and Rogersville—can be seen very much as they were in the early days of Tennessee's battles for statehood. Later history is represented by the towns the railroad built: Newport, Johnson City, Erwin, and Elizabethton. These towns have no central square. Their linear arrangements not only mimicked the Shenandoah Valley towns on which they were modeled, but also allowed easy railroad access for loading raw materials and manufactured goods and for unloading supplies. ◼

NORTHEAST TENNESSEE

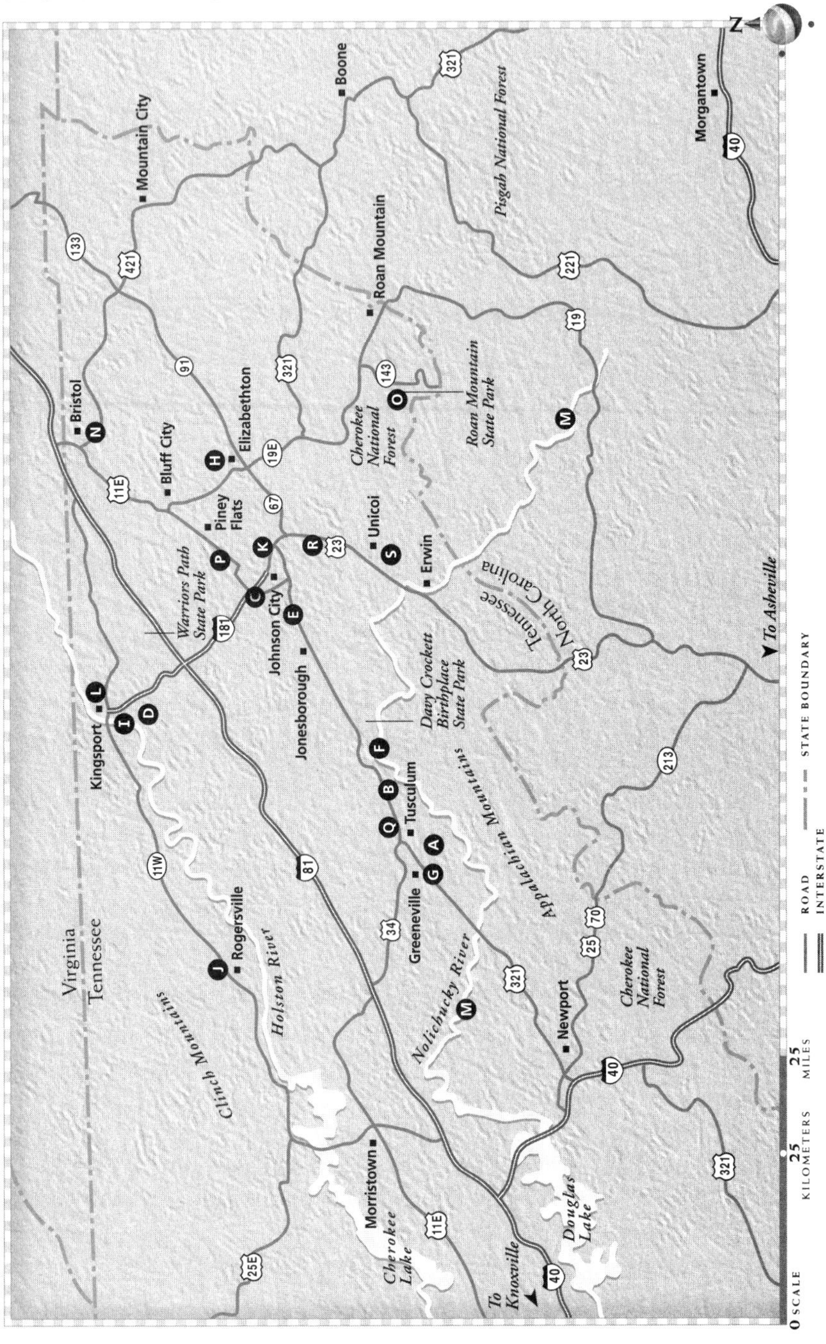

Morgantown

Boone

Mountain City

Roan Mountain

Pisgah National Forest

Bristol

Elizabethton

Bluff City

Roan Mountain State Park

N

H

Piney Flats

Unicoi

Cherokee National Forest

O

M

Warriors Path State Park

P

K

R

S

Erwin

C

E

Johnson City

Tennessee

North Carolina

To Asheville

Jonesborough

L

I

D

Davy Crockett Birthplace State Park

Appalachian Mountains

Kingsport

F

B

Tusculum

Q

A

G

Greeneville

Rogersville

Clinch Mountains

Holston River

Nolichucky River

J

M

Newport

Cherokee National Forest

Virginia
Tennessee

Morristown

Cherokee Lake

Douglas Lake

To Knoxville

O SCALE

25 KILOMETERS

25 MILES

ROAD
INTERSTATE
STATE BOUNDARY

Sights

- Ⓐ Andrew Johnson National Historic Site
- Ⓑ Andrew Johnson Museum and Library
- Ⓒ Archives of Appalachia
- Ⓓ Bays Mountain State Park
- Ⓒ Carroll Reece Museum
- Ⓔ Chester Inn
- Ⓕ Davy Crockett Birthplace State Park
- Ⓖ Dickson-Williams Mansion
- Ⓗ Doe River Covered Bridge
- Ⓘ Exchange Place
- Ⓙ Hale Springs Inn
- Ⓚ Hands On! Regional Museum
- Ⓓ Harry V. Steadman Mountain Heritage Farmstead Museum
- Ⓔ Jonesborough and Washington County History Museum and Historic District Headquarters
- Ⓛ Long Island of the Holston
- Ⓛ Netherland Inn
- Ⓜ Nolichucky River
- Ⓝ Paramount Theater
- Ⓞ Roan Mountain State Park
- Ⓟ Rocky Mount Historic Site
- Ⓙ Rogersville Depot Museum
- Ⓠ Samuel Doak House
- Ⓗ Sycamore Shoals State Historic Area
- Ⓡ Tipton-Haynes Historic Site
- Ⓢ Unicoi County Heritage Museum

Note: Items with the same letter are located in the same town or area.

A PERFECT DAY IN NORTHEAST TENNESSEE

After an overnight stay at one of the many charming B&Bs in Jonesborough, take a walk around the beautifully preserved historic district and visit the Washington County History Museum. Indulge in the Jonesborough Times and Tales Tour, an award-winning history brought to life in Jonesborough's historic homes and buildings, even if you don't generally do that sort of thing. After all, this is the headquarters of the National Storytelling Festival, and unless you are fortunate to have planned a visit during October, this may be your only taste of the ancient word-craft. Visit the craft artists shops and studios in historic downtown; then travel back into pioneer times, visiting Sycamore Shoals, the Carter Mansion, and Rocky Mount. Stop for lunch at the Ridgewood Restaurant in Bluff City, then move on to Kingsport to see the Long Island of the Holston River, from which Daniel Boone's Wilderness Road commenced. Stop for dinner in Johnson City and stay for outstanding acoustic music at the locally famous Down Home club.

JONESBOROUGH SIGHTSEEING HIGHLIGHTS

✮✮✮ **Chester Inn**—This frame structure dates from 1797 and is home to the National Storytelling Association (NSA). For the last 25 years or so, the NSA has been putting on a great big annual tale-telling meet here in early October. The association is planning an impressive new museum, which the festival's 10,000 annual attendees are making possible. At present the Chester Inn houses offices only.
  Details: 116 W. Main St., Jonesborough; 423/753-2171. (15 minutes)

✮✮✮ **Jonesborough and Washington County History Museum and Historic District Headquarters**—Learn about Tennessee's oldest town and its fascinating history. The Tennessee state seal was created by local jeweler/engravers; Andrew Jackson was admitted into law practice here; and the first antislavery newspaper, the *Manumission Intelligencer*, later *The Emancipator*, was published here. You can sign up at the museum for the highly recommended Jonesborough Times and Tales Tour (423/753-1010), available year-round by reservation only for $8 per person (since the tour includes special entry to private homes, children are not generally permitted).
  Details: 117 Boone St., Jonesborough; 423/753-1015. Mon–Fri 8–5, Sat–Sun 10–5. $2 adults, $1.50 seniors, $1 children. (30 minutes)

GREENEVILLE SIGHTSEEING HIGHLIGHTS

✮✮✮ **Andrew Johnson National Historic Site**—Dating from around 1830, this was the home and business establishment (tailor shop) of the 17th president of the United States, who also served as a member of congress, a senator and governor of Tennessee. He took office after President Lincoln's assassination.
  Details: College and Depot Sts., Greeneville; 423/638-3551. Daily 9–5. Admission is free. (1 hour)

✷✷ **Andrew Johnson Museum and Library**—Andrew Johnson was self-educated, and the 1,400 volumes housed here are a testament to his determination to rise above the profession of tailor. During his presidency, the United States purchased Alaska, and the Southern states were forced to atone to the North for the disruptions of the Civil War. Johnson faced impeachment charges relating to the reconciliation of North and South but was acquitted. Five years later he was elected to the Senate from Tennessee.

   Details: *Tusculum College, Hwy. 11E, Greeneville; 423/636-7348. Mon–Fri 9–5. Admission is free. (30 minutes)*

✷ **Davy Crockett Birthplace State Park**—The legendary Davy "born on a mountaintop in Tennessee" Crockett was actually born outside Greeneville in a log cabin near the Nolichucky River. This park features a reconstruction of his 1786 birthplace and a small museum. Crockett, one of Tennessee's early pioneers, was also a state senator and a hero of the Alamo. He died defending Texas there in 1836.

   Details: *1245 Davy Crockett Park Rd., Limestone (between Jonesborough and Greeneville); 423/257-2061. Daily 8–6. Admission is free. (30 minutes)*

✷ **Dickson-Williams Mansion**—This fine brick home was begun in 1815 and completed in 1821. The Marquis de Lafayette was once a guest here, as were many early Tennessee notables. During the Civil War, the house was taken over by both Northern and Southern troops at various times. Confederate leader John Hunt Morgan, a dashing figure who rallied Kentucky sympathizers toward the end of the war, was killed in the garden here in 1864.

   Details: *108 N. Irish St., Greeneville; 423/638-4111 (Chamber of Commerce). Open by appointment only. (1 hour)*

✷ **Samuel Doak House**—Now preserved as a museum by Tusculum College, Doak House was built in 1818 by Reverend Samuel Doak, a pioneer educator who founded the first school west of the Allegheny Mountains in 1780 (Washington College Academy) and Tusculum College in 1794.

   Details: *Tusculum College Campus, Highway 11E, Greeneville; 423/636-7348. Open Mon–Fri 9–5 by appointment only. Admission is free. (1 hour)*

KINGSPORT SIGHTSEEING HIGHLIGHTS

✪✪✪ **Long Island of the Holston**—This was the point of departure for Daniel Boone and the 30 men who set out to blaze a trail through the wilderness and establish boundaries for the claim of Richard Henderson's Transylvania Land Company in 1775. Nearby, the **Netherland Inn**, dating to 1818, was a key stage stop in close proximity to the important flatboat yard on the river. The three-story inn is authentically furnished and includes a children's museum. Visitors can walk the distance to imagine portage from one mode of transport to another in those days.

Details: Long Island of the Holston: Netherland Inn Rd., 423/229-9400. Open daily. Admission is free. Netherland Inn: 2144 Netherland Inn Rd., 423/246-6262. Sat–Mon 2–4:30. (1 hour)

✪ **Bays Mountain State Park**—This 3,000-acre nature preserve features the **Harry V. Steadman Mountain Heritage Farmstead Museum** and a planetarium, as well as hiking trails and a barge ride on a mountaintop lake. The museum collects artifacts of subsistence farming and mountaineer heritage. Displays illustrate the importance of resource conservation.

Details: 853 Bays Mountain Park Rd., Kingsport; 423/229-9447. Mon–Fri 8:30–5, Sat–Sun 1–8. Museum and planetarium open weekends only through most of the year, daily in summer. Admission to park $3/car, museum is free, planetarium shows $1.50/person. (1½ hours)

✪ **Exchange Place**—This early settlers' farm—originally granted in 1756 when the Virginia House of Burgesses had jurisdiction over the lands of Tennessee—has been restored to its 1850 form. Daniel Boone is said to have carved his name on a tree here in 1775. The name comes from a time when the house was also a stagecoach stop that exchanged state currency.

Details: 4812 Orebank Rd., Kingsport; 423/288-6071. Thu-Fri 10–2, Sat–Sun 2–4:30. Admission charged for special events only. (1 hour)

BRISTOL SIGHTSEEING HIGHLIGHTS

✪ **Paramount Theater Center for the Arts**—Dating from 1931, this newly restored theater is headquarters of the Birthplace of Country Music Alliance. The alliance is dedicated to the early history of country music as it evolved in and around this area, beginning with the 1927 Bristol Sessions, which produced the first professional country music recordings. The organization holds monthly Thursday evening concerts that emphasize the living tradition of southwest Virginia and northeast Tennessee music. To obtain a schedule of Alliance activities, write P.O. Box 216, Bristol, Tennessee/Virginia 37620.

Details: 518 State St., Bristol; 423/958-7456. Open for events only.

JOHNSON CITY SIGHTSEEING HIGHLIGHTS

✹✹ **Rocky Mount Historic Site**—While this house dates from 1770, its living history museum interprets the year 1791 when William Blount, who was visiting the Cobb Family, made this the first headquarters of the Southwest Territory.

Details: 200 Hyder Hill Rd. (Hwy. 11E), Piney Flats, TN; 423/538-7396 or 888/538-1791. Mon–Sat 10–5, Sun 2–6. $5 adults, $4.50 seniors, $3 students, ages 5 and under free. (1½ hours)

✹✹ **Tipton-Haynes Historic Site**—This building, the home of Colonel John Tipton, was built in 1783. The house and its grounds, which include 10 original and restored buildings, will give visitors insight into life before Tennessee was a state (the battle for the "Lost State of Franklin" took place here). While on the premises, visitors can see demonstrations and look inside a cave.

Details: 2620 South Roan St., Johnson City; 423/926-3631. Mon–Sat 10–5, Sun 2–5. $3 adults, $2.50 seniors, $1.50 ages 4–12. (1 hour)

✹ **Carroll Reece Museum**—A part of the Center for Appalachian Studies and Services (CASS), the museum is devoted not only to conserving the historical and artistic heritage of the region but also to bringing in historical and artistic influences from outside the region in its changing exhibits.

Details: East Tennessee State University campus, Johnson City; 423/929-4392. Mon–Sat 9–4, Sun 1–4. Admission is free. (1 hour)

✹ **Hands On! Regional Museum**—Twenty exhibits on topics that are interesting to kids are combined with activities designed to reinforce learning. Kids can pretend to work in a coal mine or even fly. Highly recommended by the mother of two inquisitive boys.

Details: 315 Main St., Johnson City; 423/434-HAND. Tue–Fri 9–5,

Sat 10–5, Sun 1–5, open Mon during summer. $5 adults, $4.50 seniors, $4 ages 3–18. (1½ hours)

Archives of Appalachia—This division of CASS houses more than 5 million manuscripts, a collection of photographs, and sound and image recordings on all aspects of Appalachian history and culture. The archives are open to the public.

Details: East Tennessee State University campus, Sherrod Library; 423/929-4338. Mon–Fri 8:30–4. Admission is free. (30 minutes)

ELIZABETHTON SIGHTSEEING HIGHLIGHTS

✯✯✯ **Roan Mountain State Park**—This scenic park includes Roan Mountain, which at 6,285 feet is the fifth-highest peak in the Appalachian chain (fourth highest in the Smokies). The park is justly famous for its massive stand of rhododendrons and its beautiful high-country scenery. Blueberries thrive here in late summer, and this is Tennessee's only park to offer cross-country skiing. Lodging is available either in cabins or tents.

Details: Hwy. 143, Roan Mountain; 423/772-3303. Open daily. Admission is free. (2 hours)

✯✯ **Sycamore Shoals State Historic Area**—Featuring the reconstructed Fort Watauga, this historic area was one of the first settlements outside the 13 colonies. The story of the Transylvania Purchase and the involvement of land speculator Richard Henderson and explorer Daniel Boone in opening up the Wilderness Road in 1775 is told. The Carter Mansion, built in 1780 on the banks of the Watauga River about three miles away and open only during the summer months, is run by the folks at Sycamore Shoals. Sycamore Shoals is also the site of *The Wataugans*, an outdoor drama held every July.

Details: Sycamore Shoals: 1651 W. Elk Ave., Elizabethton; 423/543-5808. Daily 9–5. Admission is free. Carter Mansion: 1013 E. Broad, Elizabethton; 423/543-5808. May–Aug daily 9–5. Admission is free. (2 hours)

✯ **Doe River Covered Bridge**—This is one of the four covered bridges still in use in Tennessee. It was built in 1882 out of oak planks, with hand-made nails forged over a blacksmith's fire. The bridge is on the National Register of Historic Sites.

Details: Hwy. 19E, Elizabethton; 423/547-3850. (15 minutes)

ERWIN SIGHTSEEING HIGHLIGHTS

✸✸ **Nolichucky River**—The 2,800-foot gorge of the Nolichucky River near Erwin affords spectacular views and churning white water and is a popular kayaking and rafting destination. *(30 minutes)*

✸ **Unicoi County Heritage Museum**—"Unaka" Indian displays and railroading memorabilia, along with other aspects of this mountain community's heritage, are exhibited here.
   Details: 1715 Old Johnson City Hwy. (Hwy. 107), Erwin; 423/743-9449. Daily 1-5. $1 adults, ages 12 and under free. (30 minutes)

ROGERSVILLE SIGHTSEEING HIGHLIGHTS

✸✸✸ **Hale Springs Inn**—The Hale Springs Inn, located on the central square of this historic town on the Wilderness Road, opened in 1824. It is the oldest continuously operated inn in Tennessee. A self-guided tour is available free of charge. The inn has 10 rooms with fireplaces for overnight stays, and their Colonial Dining Room is highly rated. Reservations are necessary.
   Details: 110 W. Main, Rogersville; 423/272-5171. Open daily. (30 minutes)

✸ **Rogersville Depot Museum**—This restored 1890s train station now houses a collection of historic Rogersville memorabilia. You can pick up a brochure describing a self-guided tour of Rogersville here or at the Hale Springs Inn.
   Details: 415 S. Depot St., Rogersville; 423/272-1961. Tue–Thu 10–4 or by appointment. $1 adults, 50¢ children under 12. (30 minutes)

FITNESS AND RECREATION

This rugged landscape offers the opportunity for a number of challenging outdoor activities, from hiking the Appalachian Trail to cross-country skiing to white-water rafting. Travelers might wish to plan a longer stay while in this part of the country to take advantage of the many unique recreational attributes of northeast Tennessee.

   The **Appalachian Trail** enters the area north of Bristol, touches Watauga Lake at Laurel Fork Gorge, and traverses Roan Mountain State Park, Cherokee National Forest, and Mount Pisgah

National Forest. It crosses the Nolichucky River near Erwin and straddles the Tennessee/Kentucky line all the way through Great Smoky Mountains National Park. Highways 421, 321, 19E, 23, 19W, 70, and 25/70 intersect the trail and provide access points for short hikes. For information contact the Appalachian Trail Conference at 304/535-6331. Just across the North Carolina line where Highway 25/70 parallels the French Broad River is the tiny town of **Hot Springs**, which still has at least one operative bathhouse.

Roan Mountain State Park, on Highway 143 near the North Carolina line, is best known for Catawba rhododendron plantings covering 600 acres. The flowers bloom in June. This spectacular park has cabins, camping, hiking, and cross-country skiing. For information call 423/772-3303.

Bays Mountain Park and Planetarium (423/229-9447), outside of Kingsport, is a mecca for those with kids. In addition to the ever-popular planetarium, Bays Mountain has hiking trails, a barge ride, and an outstanding nature interpretive center, which includes the Mountain Heritage Farmstead Museum and illustrates pioneer methods of resource conservation.

Steele Creek Park (423/989-4850) in Bristol is a 2,000-acre municipal park which includes a golf course, nature center, 25 miles of hiking trails, a children's train ride, and a mountain lake.

In Johnson City, **Buffalo Mountain Park** (423/283-5815) is a rewarding place to stretch the legs after a day of historic homes and museums. Its hiking trails have scenic overlooks.

Both the **Davy Crockett Birthplace State Park**, outside of Greeneville; and **Warriors Path State Park**, in Kingsport, have swimming pools. Warriors Path also offers resort amenities such as horseback riding, boating, fishing, and golf. Call 423/239-8531 for reservations and information.

If you want to arrange a white-water rafting expedition, you might check out the following list of rafting companies with an outdoor outfitter such as **Mahoney's in Johnson City** (702 Sunset Dr., 423/282-5413): **B-Cliff White-water Rafting** (Watauga River, Elizabethton; 800/592-2262), **Cherokee Adventures White-water Rafting** (Nolichucky River, Erwin; 423/743-7733 or 800/445-7238), **Nantahala Outdoor Center** (includes the Nolichucky and handles four other rivers as well; Bryson City, NC; 800/232-RAFT), **USA Raft** (Nolichucky and French Broad Rivers, Erwin; 800/USA-RAFT). There are lots of golf courses in the area besides those mentioned in conjunction with public and state parks. The **Roan Valley Golf Course** (423/727-7931) on Highway 421 near Mountain City is a public course noted for its spectacular views.

Cavers will be interested in **Bristol Caverns**, the largest cave in the eastern Smoky Mountains (Hwy. 421 S., 423/878-2011); and **Appalachian Caverns** (near Bluff City, 423/323-2337), which has one area that opens up to a height of more than 100 feet. Bristol Caverns was reportedly discovered in 1863, but it is likely that various nomadic Indian groups had used it for several centuries as they had Appalachian Caverns and Mammoth Cave.

FOOD

Good choices for lunch in downtown Jonesborough include **Cornbread's** (107 E. Main, 423/753-7766), good for a basic plate lunch; the **Dillworth Diner** (105 E. Main, 423/753-9009), perfect for an upscale diner meal; and the **Main Street Cafe** (117 W. Main, 423/753-2460), which makes healthy sandwiches and picnic lunches to go. For an elegant dining experience, try the **Parson's Table** (102 Woodrow, 423/753-8002)—an 1870s church converted into a restaurant. Although it seems odd at first, the romantic setting works and the chef-owner does a nice job. It's worth a splurge. Another unusual conversion is that of plank-front, rural grocery store to fine restaurant, as at **Harmony Grocery** (Harmony, 423/348-6183), located just outside of Jonesborough. Specialties include Creole cuisine.

In Johnson City, **Galloway's Restaurant** (806 N. Roane, 423/926-1166), open for both lunch and dinner, is a popular spot. Located in a cozy bungalow, Galloway's specialty is pasta, but evenings feature Italian-inspired veal and other dishes. **The Peerless** (2531 N. Roane, 423/282-2351) is a 60-year-old steakhouse that is well liked by the locals. **The Firehouse** (627 W. Walnut, 423/929-7377) is a 1900s firehouse with a 1925 fire engine on display and both barbecue and steaks on the menu.

In Kingsport, **Skoby's** (1001 Konnarock Rd., 423/245-2761), with its two theme rooms—a diner and a butcher shop—is a popular spot for upscale dining. The "Pantry" is the only part of the restaurant open for lunch. An Italian restaurant that offers good food at a good price is **Giuseppe's** (2530 E. Stone Dr., 423/288-2761).

Bristol Bagel & Bakery Co. (501 State St., 706/466-6222) makes their bagels on the premises and serves espresso and cappuccino

NORTHEAST TENNESSEE

Z

Morgantown ■

Boone ■

321

40

Pisgah National Forest

221

Mountain City ■

133

421

91

Roan Mountain ■

19

Bristol ■
A

321

143
K

Bluff City ■
F

Elizabethton ■

19E

Cherokee
National
Forest

Roan Mountain
State Park

11E

Piney
Flats ■

67

Unicoi ■
J

23

Erwin ■

Warriors Path
State Park

D

Tennessee
North Carolina

Johnson City ■
C

187

To Asheville ▼

23

Davy Crockett
Birthplace
State Park

Jonesborough ■

Kingsport ■
E

I

Tusculum ■

213

81

Appalachian Mountains

34

Greeneville ■
G

25 70

Cherokee
National
Forest
H

11W

Rogersville ■
B

321

25

Clinch Mountains

Holston River

Nolichucky River

Newport ■

40

Virginia
Tennessee

Morristown ■

11E

321

25E

Cherokee
Lake

To
Knoxville ▼

40

Douglas
Lake

ROAD
INTERSTATE

STATE BOUNDARY

0 SCALE   25
KILOMETERS

25
MILES

Food

- Ⓐ Bristol Bagel & Bakery Co.
- Ⓑ Colonial Dining Room
- Ⓒ Cornbread's
- Ⓒ Dillworth Diner
- Ⓓ The Firehouse
- Ⓓ Galloway's Restaurant
- Ⓔ Giuseppe's
- Ⓒ Harmony Grocery
- Ⓒ Main Street Cafe
- Ⓒ Parson's Table
- Ⓓ The Peerless
- Ⓕ Ridgewood Restaurant
- Ⓔ Skoby's
- Ⓐ Troutdale Dining Room
- Ⓖ West Main Restaurant

Lodging

- Ⓖ Aiken-Brow House
- Ⓖ Franklin House

Lodging (continued)

- Ⓓ Garden Plaza Hotel
- Ⓖ General Morgan Inn
- Ⓑ Hale Springs Inn
- Ⓒ Hawley House
- Ⓖ May Ledbetter House
- Ⓖ Jonesborough Bed-and-Breakfast
- Ⓖ Old Yellow Vic
- Ⓖ Snapp Inn B&B

Camping

- Ⓗ Cherokee National Forest
- Ⓘ Davy Crockett Birthplace State Park
- Ⓙ North Indian Creek Campground
- Ⓚ Roan Mountain State Resort Park
- Ⓔ Warriors Path State Park
- Ⓙ Woodsmoke Campground

Note: Items with the same letter are located in the same town or area.

in a historic downtown neighborhood. They also have locations in Kingsport and Johnson City. For a special treat in Bristol splurge at the **Troutdale Dining Room** (412 Sixth St., 423/968-9099). It's in a Victorian house and is open for dinner only. They have been given excellent reviews for their fine American cuisine. Everything is made with fresh ingredients and on the premises, and entrées include local mountain trout.

The **Ridgewood Restaurant** in Bluff City (900 Elizabethton Hwy., 423/538-7543) has been serving its famous barbecue for many years. For good, plain country cooking, Greenville residents rely on

West Main Restaurant (915 West Main, 423/638-8818). **Brumley's** (General Morgan Inn, 111 N. Main; 423/787-1000) serves both lunch and dinner. In Erwin stop in at the **Blue Ridge** (202 S. Elm, 423/743-6181) for breakfast, lunch, dinner, and some fine home cooking. A candlelight dinner at the **Colonial Dining Room** in Rogersville (Hale Springs Inn, 110 W. Main; 423/272-5171) is a memorable experience both for the regional cuisine and the historic ambiance.

LODGING

Jonesborough has a multitude of bed-and-breakfast accommodations, many of which are in historic homes. Among those in the historic district are: the 1850s **Aiken-Brow House** (104 Third Ave. S., 423/753-9440), which includes two bedrooms with private baths; the **Franklin House** (116 Franklin Ave., 423/753-3819), which dates from 1840; the **Hawley House** (114 E. Woodrow, 423/753-8869), which dates from the late 1700s and whose owners claim it's the oldest building in town; the **Jonesborough Bed-and-Breakfast** (100 Woodrow, 423/753-9223), which dates from the 1830s; **May-Ledbetter House** (130 W. Main, 423/753-7568), a Victorian with the Windows on Main restaurant downstairs and three bedrooms upstairs; and the **Old Yellow Vic** (411 W. Main, 423/753-9558), an 1887 Victorian with an ornate porch.

In Rogersville the **Hale Springs Inn** (110 W. Main, 423/272-5171), a restored stage stop on the Wilderness Road, has been in continuous operation since 1824. Ten rooms with fireplaces and private baths at moderate prices await. A continental breakfast and a fine dining room should be all the enticement anyone needs to make it to this out-of-the-way destination.

The **General Morgan Inn** in Greensville (111 North Main, 423/787-1001), originally four interconnecting 1890s railroad hotels, has been turned into a historic luxury hotel. A continental breakfast is served in the hotel dining room. Just out of town, near Davy Crockett's birthplace, you'll find the **Snapp Inn B&B** (1990 Davy Crockett Park Rd., Limestone; 423/257-2482) in an 1815 Federal-style home that features two bedrooms with private baths, a view of the mountains, and a full breakfast.

Garden Plaza Hotel (211 Mockingbird Ln., 423/929-2000) is a fine modern facility near the Medical Center and a shopping plaza in Johnson City.

CAMPING

Tennessee state parks in the vicinity include the **Davy Crockett Birthplace State Park** (Limestone, 423/257-2167), which has a both a tent-only campground and hookups; **Roan Mountain State Resort Park** (Hwy. 143, Roan Mountain; 423/772-3303), which has cabins as well as tent camping; and **Warriors Path State Park** (Hwy. 36, Kingsport; 423/239-8531), which has campsites and hookups. There are lots of commercial RV parks and campgrounds in the area. Two that are especially nice for RV travelers are the **North Indian Creek Campground** (Hwy. 107, Unicoi; 423/743-4502) near the Nolichucky River Gorge, which has 27 sites with hookups; and the **Woodsmoke Campground** (Hwy. 181, Unicoi; 423/743-2116), which is located in the woods with a small stream and has 16 sites with hookups and four tent sites. The **Cherokee National Forest** (423/476-9700) borders this entire area.

NIGHTLIFE

East Tennessee State University (ETSU) provides a variety of cultural activities for Johnson City. Listen to its campus public radio station WETS, 89.5, for happenings in and around the Johnson City area. ETSU's strong music department features no fewer than five student bluegrass bands and a classical music program. The university is also home to CASS, the Center for Appalachian Studies and Services, which is dedicated to research and public outreach in the Appalachian region.

The **Down Home** (423/929-9822) is a well-loved acoustic music club in Johnson City. Their recorded announcement lists shows for up to a month in advance, so you can make your plans around their schedule should you so desire. If you are in the mood for traditional country music, check with Bristol's **Paramount Theater** (423/968-7456) to see what they have scheduled. Kids will enjoy the novelty of seeing the outdoor summer theater performance of *The Wataugans*, a dramatic reenactment of the events that took place at Sycamore Shoals when Richard Henderson negotiated the Transylvania Purchase with the Cherokee Indians in 1775. For details, contact the Sycamore Shoals State Historic Area in Elizabethton (423/543-5808).

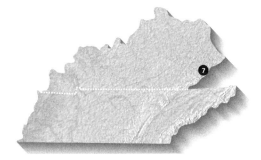

7
EASTERN KENTUCKY

Driving through the mountainous heart of Eastern Kentucky on well-paved four-lane highways, you'll almost forget you're in Appalachia. Not too many years ago, the name was synonymous with abject poverty and lack of education. Now the region has reclaimed its proud heritage.

Those who live in this wildly beautiful country are self-reliant and resilient. A wry wit, fervent religious faith, reverence for nature, and belief in hard work and luck have enabled the "mountain people," as locals call themselves, to triumph through years of economic depression.

While strip-mining is no longer widely practiced, coal is still Kentucky's largest export, and more coal is now mined here than at any time over the past twenty years. Operations are now underground and mostly mechanized. Because techniques involve fewer laborers in the mines, there are fewer mining jobs, and residents have been forced to seek other kinds of employment. Often, this means moving away from the region.

But new grass-roots organizations have sprung up to reshape the community. Health cooperatives, vegetable growers associations, and church missions are here in force. You'll also find traditional craft associations, folk festivals, and performance venues. The kindness, humor, and generosity you'll encounter here is unparalleled, and the deep quiet of the woods and sweeping canyon vistas will linger long after you have returned home. ◣

EASTERN KENTUCKY

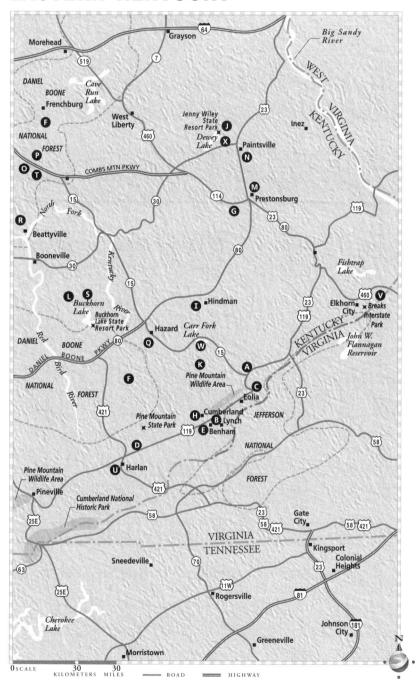

Morehead

Grayson

64

Big Sandy River

WEST VIRGINIA

519

7

DANIEL
BOONE
Frenchburg

Cave Run Lake

West Liberty

Jenny Wiley State Resort Park

Dewey Lake

Inez

KENTUCKY

F

NATIONAL

460

J

X

Paintsville

P

FOREST

N

O T

COMBS MTN PKWY

15

30

114

M

Prestonsburg

119

North Fork

G

23

80

R

Beattyville

Booneville

30

Kentucky River

15

80

Fishtrap Lake

L S

Buckhorn Lake

Buckhorn Lake State Resort Park

I

Hindman

23

119

Elkhorn City

460

V

Breaks Interstate Park

DANIEL

Red River

BOONE

Hazard

Carr Fork Lake

KENTUCKY

VIRGINIA

John W. Flannagan Reservoir

Q

W

Bird River

PKWY

80

15

NATIONAL

FOREST

F

K

A

Pine Mountain Wildlife Area

C

Eolia

JEFFERSON

421

H

Cumberland

B

Lynch

23

Pine Mountain State Park

119

E

Benham

NATIONAL

58

D

FOREST

U

Harlan

Pine Mountain Wildlife Area

421

Pineville

Cumberland National Historic Park

58

23

Gate City

58

421

25E

58

421

63

VIRGINIA
TENNESSEE

Kingsport

Colonial Heights

Sneedeville

70

23

25E

11W

Rogersville

81

Cherokee Lake

Johnson City

181

Greeneville

Morristown

N

0 SCALE   30   30
KILOMETERS   MILES   ——— ROAD   === HIGHWAY

Sights

- **Ⓐ** Appalshop
- **Ⓑ** Apple Tree Orchard
- **Ⓒ** Bad Branch Falls
- **Ⓓ** Blanton Forest
- **Ⓔ** Coal Miners Memorial Park
- **Ⓕ** Daniel Boone National Forest
- **Ⓖ** David Appalachian Crafts
- **Ⓗ** Downtown Cumberland Historical Walking Tour
- **Ⓘ** Hindman Settlement School
- **Ⓙ** Jenny Wiley Outdoor Theatre
- **Ⓚ** Kentucky Coal Mining Museum
- **Ⓚ** Lilley Cornett Woods
- **Ⓛ** Morris Fork Crafts
- **Ⓜ** Mountain Arts Center
- **Ⓝ** Mountain Home Place
- **Ⓞ** Natural Bridge State Park and Red River Gorge
- **Ⓗ** Poor Fork Arts and Crafts Store
- **Ⓑ** Portal 31 Walking Tour
- **Ⓝ** Van Lear General Store

Food

- **Ⓔ** Apple Room
- **Ⓐ** Courthouse Cafe
- **Ⓟ** Hemlock Lodge
- **Ⓗ** Hoagie Shop

Food *(continued)*

- **Ⓟ** Miguel's Pizza
- **Ⓠ** North Fork Grille
- **Ⓡ** Purple Cow

Lodging

- **Ⓢ** Buckhorn Lake State Resort Park
- **Ⓣ** Cliffview Resort
- **Ⓙ** Jenny Wiley State Resort Park
- **Ⓞ** Natural Bridge State Resort Park
- **Ⓔ** Old Schoolhouse Inn
- **Ⓣ** Quiltmaker's Inn
- **Ⓤ** River's Edge Country Inn
- **Ⓐ** Salyers House

Camping

- **Ⓥ** Breaks Interstate Park
- **Ⓦ** Carr Creek State Park
- **Ⓟ** Cliffview Resort
- **Ⓧ** German Ridge Campground
- **Ⓙ** Jenny Wiley State Resort Park
- **Ⓗ** Kingdom Come State Park
- **Ⓟ** Koomer Ridge
- **Ⓞ** Natural Bridge State Park
- **Ⓢ** Tailwater
- **Ⓢ** Trace Branch

Note: Items with the same letter are located in the same town or area.

A PERFECT DAY IN EASTERN KENTUCKY

After entering Kentucky through the impressively engineered Cumberland Gap tunnel, drive the beautiful Kingdom Come Parkway (Highway 119) into the heart of coal-mining country, along the eastern slope of Pine Mountain, with the Cumberland River at your side. This route will put you on the Mountain Craft Trail, a whimsical backroads tour of destinations such as J. D. Maggard's Country Store in Eolia and the Oven Fork Mercantile.

Cross Pine Mountain at Whitesburg, stopping for lunch and to catch your breath after winding down the mountain. A leisurely afternoon's drive will get you into Prestonsburg in time to swim at Jenny Wiley State Resort Park before showtime at either Jenny Wiley's outdoor theater or the sparkling new Mountain Arts Center.

SIGHTSEEING HIGHLIGHTS

✩✩✩ **Appalshop**—This nonprofit organization was founded 25 years ago to document and preserve mountain culture. The group produces documentary films and sound recordings and maintains radio station WMMT (88.7) and a resident theater company. Appalshop filmmakers are much admired for their "soft" documentary approach, allowing mountain people to tell their own stories and have a voice in their own future. The radio station also lives by this credo. It is programmed almost entirely by around 50 volunteers. Shows vary from *Good Morning Gospel* to *Deep in Tradition: Old-time Bluegrass with Buck Maggard* to the issue-oriented *Mountain Talk* call-in program. My favorite offering is the hilarious *Little Debbie's Hillbilly Throwdown*, which features "real gone hillbilly, rockabilly and y'alternative." Appalshop should be a first stop for anyone interested in Appalachia, past or present. The group also organizes the annual Seedtime on the Cumberland performing arts festival in May.

Details: 306 Madison, Whitesburg; 606/633-0108. Mon–Fri 9–5. *(30 minutes)*

✩✩✩ **Daniel Boone National Forest**—This massive natural area encompasses 21 counties in Eastern Kentucky. Visitors come for hiking, horseback riding, canoeing, rock climbing, cross-country skiing, hunting, and fishing. Rangers are charged with maintaining the watershed, protecting the environment, and preserving the culture of the area. There are no lodgings within the forest, although camping is permitted at designated sites. Bordering the forest are several state parks with lodging. *Details: Forest Supervisor, 1700 Bypass Rd., Winchester; 606/745-3100. Topographic maps available from the University of Kentucky, Room 104, Mining and Mineral Resources Building, Lexington, KY 40506, 606/257-3896. (3 hours–2 days)*

✪✪✪ **Jenny Wiley Outdoor Theatre**—Located in Jenny Wiley State Resort Park, this outdoor amphitheater hosts shows from June to August. In addition to *The Legend of Jenny Wiley*, the dramatic story of a young pioneer woman who was kidnapped by Shawnee and Cherokee Indians and managed to escape after more than a year in captivity, the theater produces musicals based on both regional favorites and timeless classics. *Details: Jenny Wiley State Resort Park, Prestonburg; 606/886-9274; www.JWtheatre.com. Mid-June–Aug, performances at 8:15. Tickets $8–$15.*

✪✪✪ **Kentucky Coal Mining Museum**—Once the company store in Benham, the town that Wisconsin Steel (later International Harvester) built in 1926, this three-story museum, which opened in 1994, displays coal-mining artifacts and exhibits. A video history of early days in the mines and displays of fossil and geological specimens make this simple museum a good source of information. The upper floor is soon to house a tribute to East Kentucky native Loretta Lynn. *Details: Main Street (Hwy. 160), Benham; 606/848-1530. Mon–Sat 10–5, Sun 1–4. $3 adults, $2 seniors, $1 children. (30 minutes)*

✪✪✪ **Mountain Arts Center**—This state-of-the-art music venue has a 24-track recording studio, rehearsal rooms, and an art gallery in the lobby. All 1,050 seats offer unobstructed views of the stage. The acoustics, which allow reproduction-quality live recording, have been winning praise since the center opened in October 1996. Programming ranges from the Kentucky Opry, an updated version of the Nashville stage show, to local gospel groups, big bands, ballet, and pop and Broadway shows. *Details: 50 Hal Rogers Dr. (Hwy 114), Prestonsburg, 606/889-9125 or 888/622-2787. Tickets for the Kentucky Opry, which performs once or twice per month, begin at $10. Five-person family ticket $30.*

✪✪✪ **Natural Bridge State Park and Red River Gorge**—These two areas stand side by side just outside of Slade, bordering the Daniel

Boone National Forest's Clifty Wilderness area. The Natural Bridge is a 75-foot sandstone slab over which visitors may walk. Natural Bridge State Park is one of Kentucky's original state parks, founded in 1926.

The Mountain Parkway is the most direct route into Red River Gorge, which offers a 30-mile driving loop for viewing as many as 100 natural stone arches. Visitors can also enjoy hiking trails and some of the country's best rock climbing. The gorge was formed by the Red River, a National Wild and Scenic River with designated put-ins for canoeists. The Sheltowee Trace, which runs the length of the Daniel Boone National Forest, also runs through the gorge and is marked by a turtle symbol.

Details: *Natural Bridge State Park, 2135 Natural Bridge Road, Slade; 606/663-2214. Red River Gorge, exit 33 at Slade from Bert T. Combs Mountain Parkway. (2–3 hours)*

★★★ **Portal 31 Walking Tour**—Two miles down the road from Benham, U.S. Steel purchased the township of Lynch and 40,000 acres in 1917. Today visitors can walk the site of Mine No. 31, erected in 1920 and operated into the 1960s. The sight includes a coal tipple, once the largest in the world.

Details: *Hwy 160, Lynch; 606/848-3204. Daily 8–5. Free. (1 hour)*

★★ **Coal Miners Memorial Park**—The park, next door to the Kentucky Coal Mining Museum in Benham, was created on the site of L&N railroad tracks laid in 1911. A long wall contains memorial bricks engraved with birth and death dates of local miners, and bricks are still being added. The park hosts free Friday night music fests, where visitors and locals can hear bluegrass and gospel singing.

Details: *Main Street (Hwy. 60), Benham. (30 minuites)*

★★ **Downtown Cumberland Historical Walking Tour**—Once known as Poor Fork, Cumberland is the largest town in Harlan County, with a population of just over 3,500 and a strong coal-mining legacy. This neatly kept little town looks much like it did in 1930. Stop in at the Hoagie Shop for breakfast or lunch, then pick up a brochure for the Mountain Crafts Trail at Poor Fork Arts and Crafts Store.

Details: *Cumberland Tourism Commission, 104 Freeman St., Cumberland; 606/589-5812. (1 hour)*

✶✶ Hindman Settlement School—This beautiful small campus, modeled on the concept of Chicago's Hull House, was built in 1902 as an educational outpost for mountain children. The first of many such schools in the South, Hindman was not only a boarding school but also a center for community service and local pride. Well-educated young ladies from northeastern colleges came to Kentucky to teach, and the Hindman School library was one of the first and finest in the state. Today the school library is the Knott County Public Library, and the school itself focuses on dyslexia in children and adult literacy. Summer programs include the Appalachian Writer's Workshop and an Appalachian Family Folk Week, held in early June.

Details: Hwy. 160 and Hwy. 80, Hindman, 606/785-5475. (1 hour)

✶✶ Morris Fork Crafts—About 30 miles west of Hazard, near Buckhorn Lake, you'll find a community craft cooperative tucked back in a long valley. Morris Fork Crafts sits next to the old stone Morris Fork Presbyterian Church, which started the shop in 1978. It's now independently run by members of the local community, and more than 100 artisans contribute to the large inventory. Morris Fork participates in crafts fairs around the country and sells works from a catalog. You will find well-made goods at fair (but not cheap) prices. Small quilts are priced from $100. Rag rugs start at $20, and a hand-carved Noah's ark sells for $65. The cooperative holds an annual fair on the fourth Saturday in September.

Details: Hwy. 28 to 930 Morris Fork Rd., Booneville; 606/398-2194. Mon–Fri 9–3; weekends by appointment. (30 minutes)

✶✶ Mountain Home Place—Here you'll learn about rural life in mid-nineteenth-century Kentucky. You'll see costumed guides who work fields using teams of oxen, make butter, and do farm chores as you walk around on your own.

Details: Paintsville Lake, Paintsville, 606/297-1850. Apr–Oct Wed–Sat 9–5, Sun 1–4. $5. (2 hours)

✶✶ Poor Fork Arts and Crafts Store—Ten years ago, local folks formed the Poor Fork Arts and Craft Guild and organized their "really off the beaten path" Mountain Crafts Trail. The trail, shown on a hand-drawn brochure and map, includes tiny establishments on and around Highway 119. One of the largest stops on the trail, the Poor Fork Arts and Crafts Store includes 4,500 square feet of display space on both sides of Main Street in Cumberland. Stop in to examine a wide range of hand-made items, including beautifully crafted mountain dulcimers and quilts and a menagerie of highly expressive and humorous gourd-art figures. *Details: 218 W. Main St., Cumberland; 606/589-5812. Mon–Sat 10–5. (½ hour)*

★ **Apple Tree Orchard**—Just outside of Benham, Cumberland, and Lynch, is an apple orchard that is well worth a stop, especially in early fall. Try the Scarlet Gala Apple, on which Apple Tree has a patent. It's a crisp, light-red apple that combines the best qualities of Golden Delicious and Macintosh. You may find yourself ordering a bushel. *Details: Hwy. 119, two miles north of Cumberland, 606/589-5735. Mon–Sat 9–5. (15 minutes)*

★ **Bad Branch Falls**—The largest Nature Conservancy preserve in Kentucky, this 1,640-acre gorge in the Cumberland Mountains is made of sandstone. Almost always in shadow, the habitat nurtures many plants usually found only at higher elevations. A waterfall drops over 60 feet on the mountain's south face. *Details: Hwy. 932 and Hwy. 119, approximately seven miles south of Whitesburg. (1 hour)*

★ **Blanton Forest**—The site of a Boy Scout camp for many years and still called Camp Blanton, this virgin timber forest is currently being developed into a public site. *Details: Hwy. 119 just north of Harlan, 606/573-9871. (1 hour)*

★ **David Appalachian Crafts**—Tucked in an out-of-the-way spot just outside Prestonsburg is a highly successful craft cooperative that sells white oak baskets, quilts, and handwoven goods. The David School, an impressive new log structure built in the style of a mountain lodge, has ties to the cooperative and is located next door. You'll drive past some operating coal mines to get to the site. *Details: Hwy. 404, six miles from Prestonsburg; 606/886-2377. Mon–Fri 9–4. Free. (30 minutes)*

★ **Lilley Cornett Woods**—As many as 90 species of trees—some of them here when the Pilgrims landed—are found at this site. The woods are accessible only by guided tour. Be warned: You'll climb 900 feet up a steep slope on the tour.

Details: Hwy. 1103, 28 miles north of Whitesburg; 606/633-5828. *Visitor's center open May–Aug daily 9–5, Apr, Sept, and Oct weekends only. Free. (2 hours)*

✯ **Van Lear General Store**—Once a coal company store, the place is now owned by the brother of country singers Loretta Lynn and Crystal Gayle.
Details: Inquire at the Paintsville Visitor's Center, 304 Main St. Paintsville, 800/542-5790. (30 minutes)

FITNESS AND RECREATION

There's lots of hiking to be had in this mountainous region. For 38 miles along the ridge of Pine Mountain (2,800 feet), runs the **Little Shepherd Trail**, accessible to both hikers and horseback riders. It can be accessed through **Kingdom Come State Park**, 606/589-2479, on Pine Mountain near Cumberland. Kingdom Come also has 14 hiking trails and year-round fishing in a mountain lake. Two old growth forests, **Blanton Forest** near Harlan, 606/573-9871, and **Lilley Cornett Woods**, Highway 1103 north of Pine Mountain and west of Whitesburg, 606/633-5828, can only be visited in the company of designated tour guides. Just off Highway 119 at Highway 932 near Eolia is **Bad Branch State Nature Preserve**, managed by the Kentucky State Nature Preserves Commission, 502/573-2886, and the Nature Conservancy, 606/259-9655. Here, a spectacular short hike into a deep gorge features a 60-foot waterfall. For more of the same, continue northeast on 119 to **Breaks Interstate Park**, 703/865-4413 or 800/982-5122, operated by the states of Kentucky and Virginia. The park, which features plunging ravines carved by the Russell Fork River, offers white-water recreation, horseback riding, a seasonal lodge, a restaurant, year-round cabin accommodations, and camping.

The U.S. Army Corps of Engineers operates several lakes in this part of Kentucky. They are popular for boating and fishing. These lakes include **Martins Fork Lake** near Harlan, 606/573-1468, and **Carr Fork Lake** near Hazard, 606/642-3308. Kentucky state parks designated as resort parks feature golf courses and swimming pools, in addition to lakes, lodges, restaurants, cabins, and camping facilities. **Jenny Wiley, Buckhorn Lake**, and **Paintsville Lake** are all resort parks.

FOOD

Restaurants other than the fast-food chains are few and far between in these parts, so it's wise to stock up when you find something that looks promising. However, there are a few restaurants in the area worth noting. The **Purple Cow** on Main Street in Beattyville, 606/464-9222, is a classic soda fountain/diner. The hand-painted sign and the police cruisers parked curbside tipped me off to this place. One whole wall is a skillfully painted mural featuring the restaurant's namesake—more blue than purple—seated in a wooded landscape. Inside you'll find folks at formica counters eating and chatting. Sit down to the plate lunch special and get an earful, or take a cheeseburger and indulgently creamy chocolate milkshake and go on your merry way. Open weekdays for breakfast, lunch and dinner; weekends for breakfast and lunch.

The **Hoagie Shop**, Third and Main, Cumberland; 606/589-2218, may sound like an unlikely breakfast spot, but locals swear by it for all three meals. Italian sausage and pepper sandwiches and other meaty, cheesy specials make up the bulk of the fare here, but breakfast includes freshly baked biscuits and fried apples, grits, and eggs. Just down the road, at the Old Schoolhouse Inn, 100 Central Avenue, Benham; 606/848-3000, the **Apple Room** serves fine spaghetti with meat sauce and a slice of cheese bread to go with it. Open only for dinner, seven nights.

The **North Fork Grille**, 470 Main Street, Hazard, 606/436-0769, occupies two 1913 storefronts downtown. In one section, a full bar with pool tables and a live music stage off to the side greets visitors. The other storefront is filled with nicely set tables. A menu promising steaks, pasta, and fresh fish lives up to the recommendations of friends in a nearby city. The Grille, which also has a nice wine list, draws customers from around the region for moderately priced, relaxed, quality dining—and good music on weekends to boot.

In Slade, the Natural Bridge State Park's **Hemlock Lodge** (606/663-2214) offers all three meals at reasonable prices. The view is great, and the place does breakfast with a vengeance—from perfectly cooked ham, eggs, and biscuits to healthy bran muffins and fresh fruit. **Miguel's Pizza**, just outside the park (Hwy. 11, Slade), is the unofficial headquarters of the Red River Gorge Climber's Coalition. Serving dinner only, Miguel makes whole grain crust pizzas that have earned him rave reviews.

Whitesburg's **Courthouse Cafe** (104 N. Webb Ave.); 606/633-5859) is open for both lunch and dinner, with a nice array of sandwiches, salads, and two dinner specials nightly. The Tanglewood pie, banana with cream cheese in a crust, is original.

LODGING

On Highway 119 (Kingdom Come Parkway) just before you reach Harlan is **River's Edge Country Inn**, 85 Bradford Loop, Wallins, 606/664-2612 or 606/664/3748. The house, which overlooks the Cumberland River, was built at the turn of the century. It has been restored and now has six guestrooms and two shared baths. A full breakfast is included in the room rate. Note that small children, pets, and smokers are verboten here.

The **Old Schoolhouse Inn** (100 Central Avenue, Benham; 606/ 848-3000 or 800/231-0627), built in 1926 by the Wisconsin Steel Corporation, has 40 guest rooms. Until 1992 the building was the town's elementary school. A major remodeling venture outfitted every room (quite large and with lots of tall windows) with a private a bath and luxurious furnishings. Dinner is the only meal served in the inn's Apple Room restaurant, so visitors are on their own for lunch and breakfast.

Just twenty miles or so outside of Hazard is **Buckhorn Lake State Resort Park** (Hwy. 1833, Buckhorn; 606/398-7510 or 800/325-0058). The park has a standard motel-type lodge overlooking a beautiful mountain lake as well as modern cabins with two bedrooms and two baths. The **Quiltmaker's Inn** (Main St., Hindman; 606/785-5622) is a dormitory-style hotel built in 1937 over a storefront. Rooms share baths between them, and every bed is covered by a handmade quilt. Clean and simple, air-conditioned, and with a television in every room, this friendly hotel is owned by proprietors of the clothing store below. Breakfast is a simple, continental-style affair in a communal dining room—and the price is right.

Prestonsburg's **Jenny Wiley State Resort Park** (off Hwy. 23 on Hwy. 3, 606/886-2711) is on beautiful Dewey Lake. The modern lodge has 49 rooms, and there are simple one- and two-bedroom cottages here as well. This park has an active naturalist program that would make a two-night stay desirable for those with children, and there is a nine-hole golf course for parents to enjoy. An interpretive center has a great taxidermy display, and well-planned programs focus on native plant and animal life and local history.

Near Slade is **Natural Bridge State Resort Park** (2135 Natural Bridge Road, 606/663-2214), which features some old Civilian

Conservation Corps structures. The lodge and cabins are of more recent vintage, but they are nice nonetheless, nestled in quiet locations, and offer a comfortable, reasonably priced overnight stay. This park books up early, especially in summer and fall, so call ahead. About eight miles down the road is the **Cliffview Resort** (Hwy. 715 and Hwy. 11, Rogers, 606/668-6550), a new development on 1,500 wooded acres that features horseback riding, fishing, canoeing, and hiking. A variety of furnished cabins are offered, and there is a log inn as well. Meals are provided only on weekends, but there is a camp commissary for picnic and basic food needs.

Whitesburg has a lone bed-and-breakfast in the **Salyers House** (126 Hays Street, 606/633-2532), a 1932 cottage furnished in Victorian style. There are four spacious guest rooms, each with a private bath, and there is handsome antique furniture throughout. Breakfast, continental-style, is provided, and the innkeeper offers a discount for corporate travelers.

CAMPING

Kingdom Come State Park in Cumberland allows primitive camping for $8.50 a night for two; campers must register with the ranger, 606/589-2479. In Elkorn City, **Breaks Interstate Park** has 122 sites with hookups. Call 703/865-4413 or 800/982-5122 for information. Rates are $12 a night for two.

Carr Creek State Park, south of Hazard on Highways 80 and 158, 606/642-4050, has 39 sites with hookups. The U.S. Army Corps of Engineers has two campgrounds at Buckhorn Lake: **Tailwater** (606/398-7220) off Highway 28, which has 30 sites with hookups, and **Trace Branch** (606/398-7251) on Highway 257, which has 30 primitive campsites.

In Prestonsburg, **Jenny Wiley State Resort Park**, 606/886-2711, has a 117-site campground with full hookups. It is open April through October. **German Ridge Campground** (606/886-6709) on Dewey Lake is run by the U.S. Army Corps of Engineers.

Cliffview Resort, 606/668-6550, about eight miles out of Slade, has both primitive campsites with shower access and primitive cabins for around $10 per person. **Koomer Ridge**, 606/663-2852, in the Daniel Boone National Forest at Red River Gorge, has 54 primitive sites. **Natural Bridge State Park** has two campgrounds with showers and hookups and some primitive campsights as well. Remember, reservations are not taken at Kentucky state parks. Call 606/663-2214 for park information.

SPECIAL EVENTS

Once you are within earshot, listen to Appalshop's Mountain Community Radio (88.7 FM) for announcements about happenings in eastern Kentucky, southwestern Virginia, and northeastern Tennessee. Notable annual events include Appalshop's own **Seedtime on the Cumberland**, held in late May, which includes not only traditional mountain music but also contemporary plays. The **Festival of the Mountain Masters** (Hwy. 421 S., Village Center Mall, Harlan, 606/573-2900), held the Friday and Saturday after Thanksgiving, is a great place to learn about harvest activities, from sheep shearing, spinning, and weaving to molasses making.

ROAD TRIPS: COUNTRY MUSIC HIGHWAY AND THE KINGDOM COME PARKWAY

Highway 23—Country Music Highway—is 150 miles of two- and sometimes four-lane road, stretching from the Virginia border through northeastern Kentucky to the borders of Ohio and West Virginia. Locals will be proud to tell you that country stars Loretta Lynn, Ricky Skaggs, Dwight Yoakam, Patty Loveless, and the late Keith Whitley all hail from these parts. At the north end of the road, in Ashland, you'll find the **Paramount Performing Arts Center**, a 1930s art deco palace—one of the major country-music venues in the United States. About midway between the Virginia and Ohio borders, in Prestonsburg, sits the **Mountain Arts Center,** a spectacular new complex (see Sightseeing Highlights). Nearby Paintsville features both **Loretta Lynn's girlhood home** and the **Mountain Homeplace**, a restoration of a working mountain farm. At the southern end of the highway, as it winds through the mountains into Virginia at Elkhorn City, is **Breaks Interstate Park** (see Fitness and Recreation).

Highway 119—the Kingdom Come Parkway—stretches nearly the height of the state, from Pineville to Pikeville. This well-maintained two-lane road "stays mostly on the plain," traversing the long valley just to the east of Pine Mountain, accompanied part of the way by the Cumberland River. The drive will take you past jutting rocks, steep embankments, and two stands of old growth forest that eluded loggers during the early decades of settlement.

8

CUMBERLAND GAP AND BEREA

In 1775 Daniel Boone and a party of 30 men blazed a trail through the Cumberland Gap. Boone was following in the footsteps of those who came before—Thomas Walker in 1750, who had given it a name; the scouts, hunting parties, and war parties of Indian tribes, who regarded the area as common ground belonging to none; and, as always, the animals which had first found the passage through the high hilly country.

Today visitors driving through the Cumberland Gap on the four-lane Highway 25 will notice the destruction that coal mining and road building have forced upon the landscape, and see a number of small Appalachian cities and towns tucked into pockets of poor soil or wedged up against unforgiving rock and rushing rivers. A stop in the town of Berea will help fill in the history of Appalachian Kentucky. The history of Berea College shows how the preservation of the craft tradition has worked in the service of higher education for mountain youth. Berea is also a living example of the first experiment in interracial living in the pre–Civil War South. Just north of Berea is White Hall, home of abolitionist politician Cassius Marcellus Clay, one of the founders of Berea College and a friend of Abraham Lincoln's. The destinies of the earliest citizens of Kentucky and the strong-willed and proud mountain peoples who have stayed in this sparsely populated Appalachian region despite severe economic disadvantages, remain inextricably linked. ◼

CUMBERLAND GAP

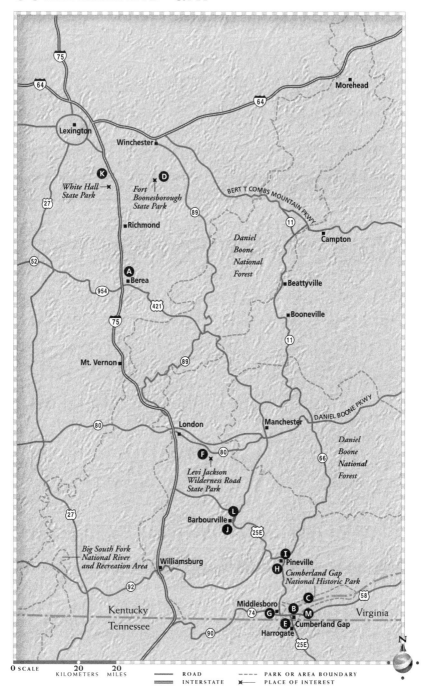

75

64

Morehead

64

Lexington

Winchester

K

White Hall
State Park

D

Fort
Boonesborough
State Park

89

BERT T COMBS MOUNTAIN PKWY

11

Campton

27

Richmond

Daniel
Boone
National
Forest

52

A
Berea

Beattyville

954

75

421

Booneville

11

Mt. Vernon

89

DANIEL BOONE PKWY

80

London

Manchester

Daniel
Boone
National
Forest

F

80

66

Levi Jackson
Wilderness Road
State Park

27

L

Barbourville

J

25E

Big South Fork
National River
and Recreation Area

Williamsburg

I

Pineville

H

Cumberland Gap
National Historic Park

C

92

58

Kentucky

Middlesboro

B

M

Virginia

Tennessee

74

G

E

Cumberland Gap

90

Harrogate

25E

N

0 SCALE   20   20
      KILOMETERS   MILES

—————— ROAD   - - - - - PARK OR AREA BOUNDARY
══════ INTERSTATE   ×——— PLACE OF INTEREST

Sights

- **Ⓐ** Berea
- **Ⓑ** Cumberland Gap
- **Ⓒ** Cumberland Gap National Historic Park
- **Ⓓ** Fort Boonesborough
- **Ⓔ** Harrogate/Lincoln Museum
- **Ⓒ** Hensley Settlement
- **Ⓕ** Levi Jackson Wilderness Road State Park
- **Ⓖ** Middlesboro
- **Ⓗ** Pine Mountain Lake State Resort Park
- **Ⓘ** Pineville
- **Ⓖ** Ridgerunner B&B
- **Ⓙ** Thomas Walker State Historic Site
- **Ⓚ** White Hall/Clermont
- **Ⓑ** Ye Olde Tea and Coffee Shoppe

Food

- **Ⓓ** Old Drugstore
- **Ⓛ** Vintage House
- **Ⓓ** Webb's Kitchen
- **Ⓑ** Ye Olde Tea and Coffee Shop

Lodging

- **Ⓑ** Cumberland Gap Inn
- **Ⓖ** Holiday Inn
- **Ⓗ** Pine Mountain Lake State Resort Park
- **Ⓖ** Ridgerunner B&B

Camping

- **Ⓒ** Cumberland Gap National Park
- **Ⓓ** Fort Boonesborough State Park
- **Ⓕ** Levi Jackson Wilderness Road State Park
- **Ⓜ** Wilderness Road Campground

Note: Items with the same letter are located in the same town or area.

A PERFECT DAY IN CUMBERLAND GAP AND BEREA

For the best glimpse of the deep woods and rugged terrain encountered by settlers moving through the area in the early 1800s, spend a night in the Cumberland Gap National Historic Park. Be sure to reach the Pinnacle, from which point you can see three states. In the town of Cumberland Gap, on the eastern side of the mountain, enjoy an excellent lunch of chicken and dumplings or a Dijon tenderloin sandwich in a historic setting at the upscale Ye Olde Coffee and Tea Shoppe. Drive north along Highway 25 to Berea, stopping for Wilderness Road sights at your leisure. Spend the late afternoon touring the campus, browsing the college bookstore for books by Appalachian authors, and visiting the many craft shops of Berea College; then dine on regional specialties in Berea's famous Boone Tavern Dining Room before turning in upstairs for a sleep that will take you back in time.

DANIEL BOONE AND THE WILDERNESS ROAD

Daniel Boone actually explored the Cumberland Gap area around 1769, but it was the signing of the Treaty of Sycamore Shoals six years later between the Cherokee and the Transylvania Land Company that gave white settlers Cherokee permission to inhabit the entire watershed of the Cumberland River as well as the southern watershed of the Kentucky River. Under the auspices of Transylvania Land Company owner Richard Henderson, Boone established Fort Boonesborough on the Kentucky River near what is now Richmond, and ultimately moved his family there.

In the decades that followed, many settlers from the areas that are now Virginia, Tennessee, and North Carolina walked and rode along Boone's route. Some wanted to make their way toward the more populated Fort Harrod, which in 1774 had been established as the first permanent English settlement west of the Alleghenies. The designated Wilderness Road began to diverge from Boone's Trace, near where London, Kentucky, is today. It can still be followed along what is now Highway 150 from Mount Vernon to Harrodsburg, where visitors can see the reconstructed Fort Harrod and watch the outdoor drama *The Legend of Daniel Boone* during the summer months. Call 800/852-6663 for more information.

SIGHTSEEING HIGHLIGHTS

✯✯✯ **Berea**—This small city, located on Highway 25 or just off I-75 at exits 76 and 77, is 37 miles north of London and 35 miles south of Lexington. Berea has become known as the "folk arts and crafts capital of Kentucky" and is home to the small, private liberal arts college of the same name. The college square in the center of town is ringed with crafts shops, as is Old Town Berea, located near the old train depot on North Broadway. There are also a number of antique shops along Highway 25 South.

Berea College offers tours of its campus, as well as its **Appalachian Museum** and its **Log House Craft Shop** and student workshops. Berea was not only the first integrated school in the South, but also the first to offer work-study, tuition-free education to the best and brightest Appalachian youth. Students at Berea learn to produce the Berea-style woodcraft, ironware, weaving, and pottery that is sold to support the school. A spirit of enlightened enterprise pervades this serene mountain town; just walking onto the campus is inspiring. Be sure to seek out the Fine Art Department's **Doris Ullman Galleries**, located in the Rogers-Traylor Art Building, for outstanding exhibits of contemporary regional art. The Boone Tavern Hotel, on the college square and founded in 1909, offers comfortable rooms furnished with Berea-made furniture. The wait staff, comprised of Berea students, serves breakfast, lunch, and dinner in the Boone Tavern Dining Room.

Details: Berea Campus: Main St., 606/986-9341, ext. 5018. Campus tours Mon–Fri 9–10 a.m. and 1 p.m., Sat 9 a.m. and 2 p.m. Free. Berea College Museum: 103 Jackson, 606/986-9341. Mon–Sat 9–6, Sun 1–6, closed Jan. $1.50. (2 hours)

★★★ **Cumberland Gap**—Cumberland Gap, Harrogate, and Middlesboro were founded in the late 1800s by Alexander Arthur and the American Association, British venture capitalists in the railroad, coal, and steel industries who were financed by the Bank of England. The story of their bold plans and ultimate failure adds a fascinating second chapter to the history of the region. A free printed walking tour of Cumberland Gap is available by stopping in at the town hall. In Cumberland, visit the **Newlee Iron Furnace**. Dating from the 1820s, this primitive furnace—a limestone rock chimney for melting iron ore mined from the mountain above, served by a waterwheel and bellows arrangement—inspired the speculative development of the American Association in the late 1880s. Nearby is the hand-laid limestone railroad tunnel (built in 1880) through the gap that signaled the beginning of industrialization for the region.

Details: Colwyn St., Cumberland Gap; 423/869-3860 or 800/332-8164. (1 hour)

★★★ **Cumberland Gap National Historic Park**—The Pinnacle Overlook onto the gap itself can be reached by a short walk up a paved path behind the visitors center. Cumberland Gap has a fascinating Civil War history—it changed hands four times during the war, as it was a major conduit for supplies and soldiers moving in both directions. This fact is delineated in historic markers and the artifacts that remain. The 20,000-acre Cumberland Gap Historic National Park, which spans Virginia, Kentucky, and Tennessee, offers a variety of ranger-led activities as well as hiking trails and campgrounds where you are unlikely to encounter many other visitors, even in the busiest of summer seasons. There is a nice visitors center with interpretive historical exhibits on the Kentucky side of the gap. The **Hensley Settlement**—a preserved mountain community of three farmsteads originally built around 1905—can be reached by hiking into the park about 11 miles. Two Park Service–employed farmer-demonstrators maintain the buildings and fields using old farming methods.

Details: Visitors center, Hwy. 25; 606/248-2817. Daily 8–5, summers 8–6. Admission is free. (2 hours)

★★ **Fort Boonesborough**—Now a state park, this is the site of Fort Boone. It was established by Daniel Boone on April 1, 1775, as several log huts near a salt lick by the Kentucky River. After the arrival of Richard Henderson and his Transylvania Colony, the fort was moved and built into four blockhouses and 26 log cabins. The fort has been reconstructed, and an excellent walking trail guide prepared by the Kentucky Historical Society assists visitors in retracing the paths of major events in the history of this key pioneer outpost. A "forage trail" brochure calls attention to the ways in which the first white settlers made use of nature's bounty for their survival.

Details: Hwy. 627, six miles northeast of White Hall; 606/527-3131. Summer daily 9–5; Nov–Mar Wed–Sun 9–5. $4.50 adults, $2.25 children. (1½ hours)

★★ **White Hall State Historic Site**—White Hall is just off I-75 at exit 95. This imposing 3½-story brick house sits alone on vast acreage. It was the home of Cassius Marcellus Clay, a staunch abolitionist, friend of Abraham Lincoln's, and ambassador to Russia through most of the 1860s. Clay's father, Green Clay, was one of the wealthiest men in Kentucky when he built the elegant **Clermont** in 1797. An early surveyor of the Kentucky territory for the State of Virginia, Green Clay bought a large tract of land and founded a distillery nearby. White Hall (circa 1860), adjoining Clermont, had the first indoor plumbing in the state. All of the bricks for both homes were manufactured on the property. Furnished with some original pieces and period furnishings throughout, White Hall has a fascinating museum on the top floor.

Details: Hwys. 25 and 421, Richmond; 606/623-9178. Apr–Oct Tue–Sun 9–4:30. $4.50 adults, $2.50 children. (1 hour)

✸✸ **Wilderness Road Tours**—Former coal mine operator Tom Shattuck, a resident of Middlesboro and an amateur historian of Daniel Boone and the Wilderness Road, leads tours of the area. His comfortable van runs twice daily from Middlesboro and Pineville and covers Cumberland Gap, the Wilderness Road, Daniel Boone's Trace, Civil War Breastworks, and the history of Cumberland Gap and the original Middlesboro.

Details: 224 Greenwood Rd., Middlesboro; 606/248-2626. Tours start at $14 per person and can be customized. (2 hours minimum)

✸ **Ye Olde Tea and Coffee Shoppe**—This restaurant was created in 1991 by combining three buildings that originally housed the bank, the post office and general merchandise store, and the hardware store, all dating from 1889.

Details: 528 Colwyn St., Cumberland Gap; 800/899-4844. Daily for lunch and dinner. (30 minutes)

Harrogate—This town once housed the American Association's 700-room Four Seasons Resort hotel. It is now home to Lincoln Memorial University, whose **Lincoln Museum** has a fine collection of memorabilia relating to the one-time president. The university was founded by Lincoln's friend General O. O. Howard.

Details: Cumberland Gap Pkwy., Harrogate; 423/869-6235. Mon–Fri 9–4, Sat 11–4, Sun 1–4. $2 adults, $1.50 seniors, $1 ages 6–12. (1 hour)

Levi Jackson Wilderness Road State Park—Located just south of London, this park commemorates a site where both the Wilderness Road and Boone's Trace are known to have passed. Inside the park are a working gristmill, a pioneer cemetery, and the Mountain Life Museum.

Details: Hwy. 25S, London; 606/878-8000. Museum open Apr–Oct daily 9–4:30. $1.25 adults. (1 hour)

Middlesboro—The American Association had its greatest influence on Middlesboro, a town planned to hold 100,000, with grand Cumberland Avenue laid out 100 feet wide. Founder Alexander Arthur dreamed of creating the Pittsburgh of the South and built beautiful downtown

Victorian gothic and Romanesque buildings and lovely homes in a hilly neighborhood now called Arthur Heights. The Ridgerunner B&B (see Lodging) is in one of these original homes. The nearby 1889 Middlesboro Golf Club (see Fitness and Recreation), which has nine holes, is of British design and is one of the oldest continuously played courses in the country. Unfortunately, its original clubhouse is no longer standing. The club is private, but visitors are allowed. The Middlesboro County Airport has a free museum exhibit featuring Glacier Girl, a WWII B-52 that was buried under the ice for many years.

Details: Bell County Chamber of Commerce: 800/988-1075 (30 minutes –2 hours)

Pineville—Located 13 miles north of Middlesboro, Pineville is situated at the second gap—a steep water-pass through the mountains—back from Cumberland. The sight of a massive flood wall at the entrance to the town is a reminder of the fragility of our environment. **Pine Mountain Lake State Resort Park** (606/337-3066), founded in 1924 and located on a mountaintop two miles outside the city, is Kentucky's first state park and is thought to be its most beautiful because of its well-groomed wood and stone buildings.

Details: Bell County Chamber of Commerce: 800/988-1075 (30 minutes)

Thomas Walker State Historic Site—Barbourville is home to this historic site, which consists of little more than a picnic area and is located approximately 11 miles south of the city in a protected valley. Walker, who found the Gap in 1750 on a surveying trip, named it after the duke of Cumberland. A physician, he was the personal doctor and trusted friend of Peter Jefferson, the father of Thomas Jefferson, in Charlottesville, Virginia. Upon Peter's death, 12-year-old Thomas became Walker's godson, and the young Jefferson is thought to have been much influenced by Walker's mentorship. The Vintage House restaurant is on the town square in Barbourville's oldest building.

Details: 25 E. to Hwy. 459, Barbourville; 606/546-4400. Open daily. Admission is free. (30 minutes)

FITNESS AND RECREATION

Cumberland Gap National Historic Park (606/248-2817) offers a variety of ranger-led activities as well as hiking trails and campgrounds.

Horses are permitted on many park trails and in three of the overnight campgrounds. There is a private livery stable near Ewing, Virginia, outside of the park on Highway 58. Bikes can be ridden on all paved roads and on some off-road trails as well.

Pine Mountain Lake State Resort Park (606/337-3066), which sponsors the 10K "At the Top" run along the crest of Pine Mountain every April, also has a swimming pool and a nine-hole golf course. **Levi Jackson Wilderness Road State Park** (606/878-8000) offers hiking trails and a swimming pool. **Fort Boonesborough State Park** (606/527-3131) has designated hiking trails, a swimming pool, and a miniature golf course. The **Middlesboro Country Club** (606/248-3831) has an historic nine-hole course.

FOOD

Ye Olde Tea and Coffee Shop (511 Colwyn Ave., Cumberland Gap; 800/899-4844), which features an extensive menu and gets rave reviews from many quarters, is open for dinner; and yes, they also serve good coffee. Across the street in a small storefront building is **Webb's Kitchen** (423 Colwyn, Cumberland Gap; 423/869-5877) which serves fine down-home meals. The **Old Drugstore** (515 Colwyn, Cumberland Gap; 423/869-0455) serves good milkshakes and sandwiches.

The **Vintage House** (101 N. Main, Barbourville; 606/546-5414) offers good sandwiches and specials for lunch Wednesday through Friday. It also serves dinner Thursday through Saturday (menu changes weekly); reservations are recommended.

In Berea the **Boone Tavern Dining Room** (Main St., 800/366-9358) serves breakfast, lunch, and dinner. No alcohol is served, but regional specialties like spoon bread and homemade yeast rolls, fried green tomatoes, black-eyed pea dip, corn pudding, and pecan-crusted catfish make this a requisite stop on any itinerary. It's best to make reservations for meals. Try the **Cardinal Deli**, just a few doors down, for breakfast or lunch with the locals; or **Papaleno's** or the **Berea Coffee and Tea Company**, next door, for a morning or afternoon pick-me-up.

LODGING

There is a **Holiday Inn** (423/869-3631 or 800/HOLIDAY) right off Highway 25 at Cumberland Gap. It mars the incredible view but provides a convenient place to overnight. The same folks that own Ye

BEREA

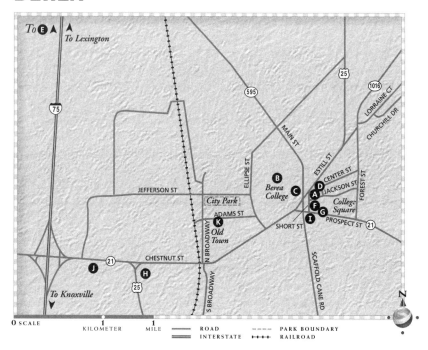

Sights

A Appalachian Museum

B Berea College

C Doris Ullman Galleries

D Log House Craft Shop

E Fort Boonesborough

Food

F Berea Coffee and Tea Company

G Boone Tavern Dining Room

F Cardinal Deli

F Papaleno's

Lodging

H Berea's Shady Lane

I Boone Tavern

J Holiday Motel

K Morning Glory

Note: Items with the same letter are located in the same area.

Olde Tea and Coffee Shop have opened the very nice **Cumberland Gap Inn** (511 Colwyn Ave., Cumberland Gap; 423/869-9172). In Middlesboro, the **Ridgerunner B&B** (208 Arthur Heights, 606/248-4299) is highly recommended; as is **Pine Mountain Lake State Resort Park** (Pineville, 800/325-1712), which offers rustic cottages and a 30-room lodge.

The **Boone Tavern** (Main St., 800/366-9358) in Berea has 59 small but clean and quiet rooms at reasonable rates. All rooms are furnished with early versions of the cottage-industry craft furniture for which Berea is known. If you happen to reach Berea when the tavern is full, try one of the B&Bs in town: **Berea's Shady Lane** (123 Mount Vernon Rd., Berea; 606/986-9851), which has two guest rooms with baths; or **Morning Glory** (140 N. Broadway, 606/986-8661), which is located upstairs in a former pharmacy in Old Town Berea. Downstairs is Weaver's Bottom, a craft studio belonging to the B&B owners. The **Holiday Motel** (Berea exit off I-75, 606/986-3771) is a clean, locally owned option. There are several national chain motels located just off I-75.

CAMPING

Fort Boonesborough State Park (606/527-3131) has a large camping area with hookups and primitive camping sites near the Kentucky River. Sites may not be reserved in advance.

Cumberland Gap National Park has several campgrounds (no hookups) and comfort stations with hot showers. One of the campgrounds has a simple cabin with six bunks and a fireplace. The **Wilderness Road Campground** (606/248-2817)—on Virginia Highway 58, two miles from the gap—is open year-round for tents and trailers. Except for group camping, reservations are not accepted. **Levi Jackson Wilderness Road State Park** (606/878-8000) offers year-round camping with hookups.

SPECIAL EVENTS

One of the best ways to get to know this region is to participate in the celebration of Appalachian traditional culture. Any one of these events would be worth planning a trip around. **Middlesboro's Cumberland Mountain Fall Festival**, in October, features the **Official State Banjo Contest** (606/248-1075). Barbourville has an annual **Daniel Boone Festival** (606/546-6062), also in October, that has been ongoing for more than 45 years. Pine Mountain State Resort Park (606/337-3066) sponsors a **Great American Dulcimer Convention** in September and the **Mountain Laurel Festival** in May. Levi Jackson Wilderness Road State Park has a **Mountain Folk Festival** (606/986-9341) weekend in September that features contra dancing. London sponsors the **Camp Wildcat** reenactment of the first Union victory of the Civil War in 1861. The visitors center (800/348-0095) has more information.

Berea hosts the **Kentucky Guild of Artists and Craftsmen's Spring and Fall Fairs** (606/986-3192) in May and October; the **Big Hill Mountain Bluegrass Festival** (606/986-2540) in August; and the **Celebration of Traditional Music** (606/986-9341) in October.

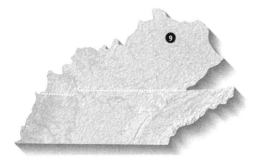

9
LEXINGTON

The Kentucky bluegrass region, centered around Lexington, nourishes the world's champion thoroughbreds. The famous lush grass is fed by underground water that runs through the limestone beneath the softly rolling terrain. The beneficial effects of this same water are also reaped by the Kentucky bourbon distillers nearby. A drive along Paris Pike or Iron Works Road passes some of the loveliest horse farms in the country. Driving onto the well-manicured grounds of Keeneland Race Course will make anyone feel like a member of the privileged elite.

Lexington, Kentucky's second largest city, was founded in 1775. In its beautiful old neighborhoods one finds small British-style parks—like Gratz Park—that function as green spaces for enormous Federal-period brick houses. In the midst of the historic district sits Transylvania University, dating from 1780, the first institution of higher learning in the western United States. Stroll the labyrinth of streets around Gratz Park and Transylvania that bear names like Upper, Limestone, Cheapside, Mill, and Market, and you will absorb some of Lexington's early history. The girlhood home of Mary Todd Lincoln is here, as are the law offices of one of Abraham Lincoln's mentors, the "Great Compromiser" Henry Clay.

Activities at the University of Kentucky are an important part of Lexington life. The Singletary Art Center provides outstanding cultural offerings and an excellent art museum. Rupp Arena, the well-known home court for UK's powerful Wildcat basketball team, is part of Lexington's convention center in the heart of downtown. ◣

GREATER LEXINGTON

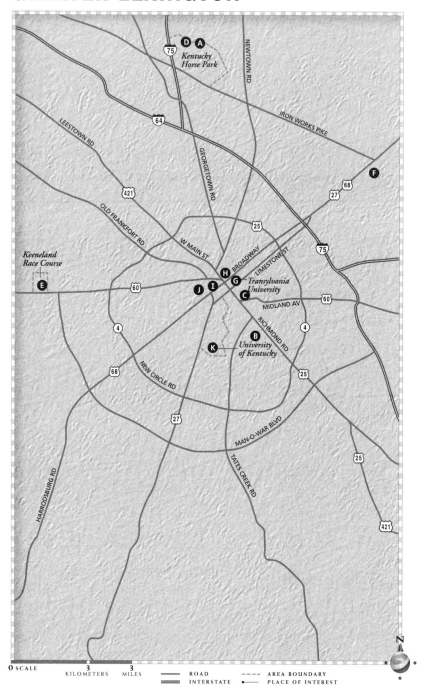

D A
75 Kentucky
Horse Park

NEWTOWN RD

IRON WORKS PIKE

LEESTOWN RD

64

GEORGETOWN RD

F
68
27

421

OLD FRANKFORT RD

25

W MAIN ST

75

Keeneland
Race Course

BROADWAY

LIMESTONE ST

H
G Transylvania
University

60

J I

60

C

E

MIDLAND AV

4

RICHMOND RD

4

B
University
of Kentucky

K

68

NEW CIRCLE RD

25

25

27

MAN-O-WAR BLVD

25

HARRODSBURG RD

TATES CREEK RD

421

N

0 SCALE   3   3
   KILOMETERS MILES   ———— ROAD   ---- AREA BOUNDARY
                       ═══ INTERSTATE   •—— PLACE OF INTEREST

Sights

Ⓐ American Saddlebred
Museum

Ⓑ Ashland, the Henry Clay Estate

Ⓒ Hopemont, the Hunt-Morgan
House

Ⓓ International Museum of the
Horse

Ⓔ Keeneland

Ⓕ Kentucky Center for the Horse

Ⓖ Kentucky Gallery of Fine Crafts
and Art

Ⓓ Kentucky Horse Park

Ⓗ Lexington Children's Museum

Ⓘ Mary Todd Lincoln House

Ⓖ Morlan Gallery

Ⓙ Red Mile Harness Racetrack

Ⓖ Transylvania University

Ⓚ University of Kentucky Art
Museum

Ⓚ University of Kentucky

Note: Items with the same letter are located in the same area.

A PERFECT DAY IN LEXINGTON

An early-morning drive west out Versailles Road to Keeneland for a glimpse of the morning workouts and breakfast at the Track Kitchen are the closest most of us will come to feeling like a bluegrass horse owner. Later drive along Rice Road to Old Frankfort Pike and Yarnalltown Road. Stop at the Kentucky Horse Park on Iron Works Pike and spend a couple of hours in the museums and open stables. To see how thoroughbreds are trained to race, continue on Iron Works Pike to the Kentucky Center for the Horse, where tours are available. Head back into Lexington's historic Gratz Park neighborhood for lunch and a walking tour that includes visits to historic homes or a stop at the lively, interactive Lexington Children's Museum. In the late afternoon wind down with a quiet hour at UK's art museum. A carriage ride around downtown Lexington makes a nice end to the day. Afterward, dine on regional specialties at the highly esteemed Merrick Inn, and attend an evening performance at UK's Singletary Center for the Arts, the restored 1890s Lexington Opera House, or the 1920s Kentucky Theater in downtown Lexington.

KENTUCKY HORSE CULTURE

Horse-racing events are surprisingly accessible to visitors. Keeneland's hedge-lined racecourse and beautiful limestone grandstands are available during the 15-day race seasons in spring and fall to anyone with the price of a basic ticket (under $10), and parking is free. Race-goers can bring their own picnics, purchase barbecue and burgoo at the track, or make reservations to dine on higher-priced fare at one of the several enclosed dining rooms at Keeneland. There is no charge to watch the daily morning workouts held there year round, and visitors are welcome at the Track Kitchen cafeteria for a reasonably priced breakfast with Keeneland employees and visiting trainers.

The Red Mile harness racetrack provides equally low-cost seats and a variety of dining options for its series of races for two months in late spring and two weeks in fall. No two courses run simultaneous events and Kentucky's system of intertrack wagering and simulcast racing at many of its major racecourses ensures a statewide audience for every event.

SIGHTSEEING HIGHLIGHTS

★★★ **Driving Tour**—The Lexington Convention and Visitors Bureau, located at Rose and Vine, distributes a terrific bluegrass driving-tour map that shows the location of more than 100 horse farms in and around Lexington. I highly recommend driving this circuit as a general orientation to the area. Turn the map over and you have a walking tour of Lexington's center. Entering the city via one of the old roads, such as Old Frankfort Pike and Versailles Road from the west, or Richmond Road from the south, will also whet your appetite for Kentucky horse culture.

Details: Lexington Convention and Visitors Bureau: 301 E. Vine, 800/845-3959. Mon–Fri 8:30–5, Sat 10–5, Sun noon–5; extended hours in summer. (2 hours)

★★★ **Keeneland**—This racecourse, opened in 1936, is Kentucky's most beautiful. The motto of Keeneland's founders is "racing as it was meant to be," and that means there is no public address system, so the twice-yearly race meetings (15 days in April and in October) are conducted without the roar of announcers. An unreserved grandstand seat goes for as little as $2.50, reserved seats for under $10.

Details: *4201 Versailles Rd., 800/456-3412. Daily for training work-outs 6 a.m. to 10 a.m. Admission is free. (2 hours)*

✮✮✮ **Kentucky Center for the Horse**—This is a real training facility for thoroughbreds who are being taught the rigors of the race. There are 1,100 stalls here for visiting "students," and tours are given twice daily.

Details: *3380 Paris Pike (intersection of Iron Works Pike and Paris Pike), 606/293-1853. Tours Mon–Sat 9 and 10:30 a.m.; additional tour at 1 p.m. in summer. $10 (by reservation only). (1½ hours)*

✮✮✮ **Kentucky Horse Park**—The park is run by the state of Kentucky. The **International Museum of the Horse** is located on the grounds, as are stables and exhibits that demonstrate many aspects of horse breeding and training. The grounds are extensive and beautiful. Kids of all ages will feel privileged to have been able to see the real thing at such close range.

Details: *4089 Iron Works Pike, 606/233-4303 or 800/678-8813. Apr–Oct and Nov–Mar Wed–Sun 9–5. $9.95 adults, $4.95 ages 7–12; parking is free. (2 hours)*

✮✮ **American Saddlebred Museum**—The museum is also part of the Kentucky Horse Park complex, although it is maintained by its own nonprofit organization. The museum displays chronicle the history and development of the American horse, which was created from the lineage of the earliest horses in this country, from English thoroughbreds to Indian ponies. This museum will be of tremendous interest to anyone who owns a horse. It is possible to buy a combined ticket at a discount for both the Kentucky Horse Park and the Saddlebred Museum.

Details: *4089 Iron Works Pike, 606/259-2746. Wed–Sun 9–5, Apr–October daily; extended hours in summer. $3 adults, $2 ages 7–12. (1 hour)*

✮✮ **Red Mile Harness Racetrack**—This track features the kind of racing that used to be common all over the South, with a single horse hitched to a streamlined sulky from which a lightly perched jockey leans back gracefully. The Red Mile holds racing meets in May, June, and late September through early October, and a seat in the grandstand is only $2.

Details: South Broadway; 606/255-0752. Open daily for morning workouts. Admission is free. (1 hour)

HISTORIC LEXINGTON SIGHTSEEING HIGHLIGHTS

✴✴ **Hopemont, the Hunt-Morgan House**—Hopemont was built in 1814 by Kentucky's first millionaire, John Wesley Hunt. His grandson, General John Hunt Morgan, who had attended Transylvania University and, as a Confederate general, terrorized Union generals with his erratic attacks, stayed here often during the Civil War. Another distinguished relative who also inhabited the house was Thomas Hunt Morgan, who won the Nobel Prize for his research in science and genetics in 1933. The house is a beautiful example of early Kentucky architecture.

Details: 201 N. Mill, 606/233-3290. March–Dec Tue–Sat 10–4, Sun 2–5. $5 adults, $2.50 ages 7–12. (1 hour)

✴✴ **Mary Todd Lincoln House**—This 22-room home is where Mary Todd grew to adulthood after her family moved to Lexington in 1832. Abraham Lincoln visited her here three times. He particularly cherished Mary's father's library. Both Todd and Lincoln artifacts are on display.

Details: 578 W. Main, 606/233-9999. Mid-March–Nov Tue–Sat 10–4; last tour at 3:15. $5 adults, $2.50 ages 7–12. (1 hour)

✴✴ **University of Kentucky**—The 23,000-seat Rupp Arena is home to the legendary powerhouse Kentucky Wildcats. The arena is located on the university campus downtown on West Vine next to the Lexington Convention Center, and open free on weekdays from 8:30 to 5:30 for anyone who'd like to peek inside. Singletary Center for the Arts, also on the UK campus, serves as a performing arts center for the whole city. Located within the center is the **University of Kentucky Art Museum**, an impressive museum with both permanent collections and three large galleries for changing exhibits.

Details: Rose St. and Euclid Ave.; Singletary Center for the Arts schedule and ticket information: 606/257-4929. Art Museum: 606/257-5716. Tue–Sun noon–5. Admission is free. (1 hour)

✴ **Ashland, the Henry Clay Estate**—Ashland is a bit of an architectural hybrid since it was remodeled by Clay's son after his death.

Nonetheless, the home and memorabilia that belonged to Kentucky's great statesman is interesting.

Details: 120 Sycamore Rd. (not far from the University of Kentucky), 606/266-8581. Feb–Dec Tue–Sat 10–4:30, Sun 1–4:30. $6 adults, $3 ages 7–12. (1 hour)

✯ **Lexington Children's Museum**—This hands-on museum, with exhibits designed primarily for children from 12 months to 12 years, is always filled with lively young visitors. The museum has grown from community interest and has both semipermanent and permanent exhibits (a multicultural series changes once a year; the current one is on China).

Details: Victorian Square complex, Main and Broadway; 606/258-3256. Mon–Fri 10–6, Sat 10–5, Sun 1–5; closed Mon during school year. $3 adults, $2 ages 7–12. (1½ hours)

✯ **Transylvania University**—This first college of higher learning west of the Alleghenies was founded in 1780. The **Morlan Gallery** in the Mitchell Fine Arts Center features changing exhibits. Campus tours are available by appointment.

Details: 300 N. Broadway, 606/233-8210. Gallery open Mon–Fri noon–5. Admission is free. (1 hour)

Kentucky Gallery of Fine Crafts and Art—The Kentucky Guild of Artists and Craftsmen juries members only into the shows here. You'll see traditional techniques and materials as well as some inspired twists on old themes in this show/sale gallery space.

Details: 139 W. Short, 606/281-1166. Mon–Sat 10–6. Admission is free. (30 minutes)

FITNESS AND RECREATION

Besides taking a walking tour of historic neighborhoods, the next most natural form of exercise around Lexington—unless you have access to a horse—would be biking or running along the beautiful horse-country roads. The **Raven Run Nature Sanctuary** (Richmond Rd., 606/272-6105), located southeast of Lexington along the palisades of the Kentucky River, offers extensive hiking and biking opportunities along with wildlife-watching.

Golf is widely popular in the area, and there are a number of courses available for public use. One of the best known is **Kearney Links** (606/253-1981), a British-style course that has been used for national golf events. On Richmond Road right in town is the **Lakeside Golf Course** (606/263-5315). **Connemara** (Nicholasville, just south of Lexington on Hwy. 27; 606/885-4331), which was once a horse farm, is highly touted for its beauty.

If visiting horse country makes your kids want to try riding for themselves, the **Kentucky Horse Park** offers a 50-minute trail ride for $10. A 45-minute drive from Lexington will reach several stables that can provide a more extensive horseback-riding outing. Try **Big Red Stables** in Harrodsburg (606/734-3118), where a trail ride on their extensive property is $20/hour.

FOOD

In downtown Lexington breakfasts come highly recommended at **Linda's Sandwich Shop** (214 S. Limestone, 606/252-6264), where you can get eggs, country ham, and all the trimmings (including grits). For fresh-baked goodies and strong coffee, try **Magee's Bakery** (726 E. Main, 606/255-9481). For lunch, **DeSha's** (109 N. Broadway, 606/259-3771)—located downtown in Victorian Square—is a Lexington favorite for Kentucky specialties and after-work socializing and is open seven days a week. Other downtown lunch choices include the plain-looking but authentic **Tonio's Super Burritos** (102 S. Vine St., 606/254-3722). For supper you might try the original **Columbia Steakhouse** (201 N. Limestone, 606/253-3135), a 50-year-old moderately priced eatery that spawned several other Columbia steak houses in Kentucky. A hipper crowd frequents the **Atomic Café** (265 N. Limestone, 606/254-1969). It serves Caribbean specialties with a few American favorites, and has outdoor seating and live music.

Some of Lexington's most highly touted food and service can be found at the charming and romantic **A la Lucie** (159 N. Limestone, 606/252-5277), which has daily fresh seafood and pasta specials as well as classic beef and lamb preparations. Totally different but equally loved is the **Merrick Inn** (3380 Tate's Creek Rd., just east of downtown; 606/269-5417), where the cooking is Southern, the ambiance is gracious, and there is an extensive wine list. Merrick Inn even opens for supper on Sundays during Keeneland's spring and fall race meetings so that Lexingtonians have a place to dine after the competitions.

In the university area, if you need a respite from the excesses of country ham and Kentucky Hot Brown sandwiches, stop by **Everybody's Natural Foods & Deli** (503 Euclid, 606/255-4162) at the edge of the UK campus. The **Kentucky Inn** (525 Waller Pike, 606/254-1177) is well known for its country-cooking buffet, open for lunch and dinner. **Rogers Restaurant** (808 S. Broadway, 606/254-1077), whose menu changes daily, is Lexington's oldest restaurant (dating from 1923) and is marked by a classic neon sign out front and a neighborhood bar in the back. They serve plain, homemade food for lunch and dinner.

LODGING

The **Camberley Club Hotel at Gratz** (120 W. Second, 606/231-1777 or 800/555-8000) is a quiet, elegant hotel that is nearly hidden in a historic neighborhood. Rooms start at $130, but ask about AAA, AARP, and other discounts when the hotel isn't heavily booked. This is the only hotel in the historic district; it's within walking distance of almost everything, including downtown. Continental breakfast is served to guests only. The Dining Room and the Tap Room Lounge offer public dining evenings.

Lexington has two nice large downtown convention hotels, the **Hyatt Regency** and the **Radisson**, both of which are near Rupp Arena. Near UK is the older **Kentucky Inn** (525 Waller Pike, 606/254-1177), which is a basic family-owned motel with 100 rooms and a pool.

CAMPING

The **Kentucky Horse Park** (4089 Iron Works Pike, 606/233-4303, ext. 257) offers year-round camping for less than $20 a night.

NIGHTLIFE

The limestone-filtered water that's good for making bourbon whiskey is also a fine beginning for brewing beer. Two new breweries have opened recently in Lexington, each with their own local brews. **Lexington City Brewery** (1050 S. Broadway, 606/259-BREW) has a fine Burley Red as well as a lager named after a legendary Lexington dog, Smiley Pete, whose story can be read on a historic marker

DOWNTOWN LEXINGTON

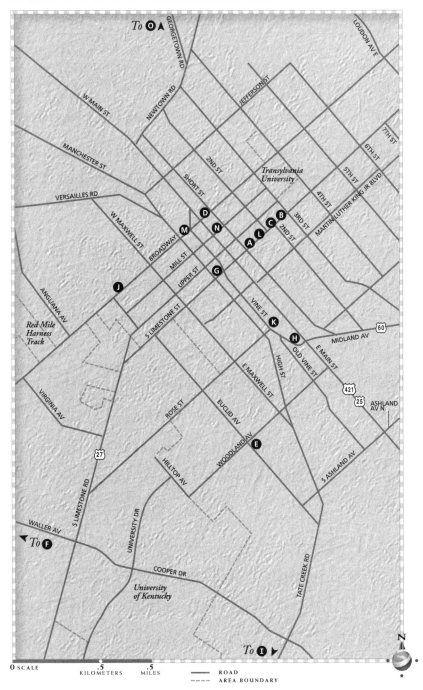

To O ▲

GEORGETOWN RD

LOUDON AV E

W MAIN ST

NEWTOWN RD

JEFFERSON ST

7TH ST

6TH ST

MANCHESTER ST

2ND ST

Transylvania University

5TH ST

MARTIN LUTHER KING JR BLVD

4TH ST

SHORT ST

VERSAILLES RD

3RD ST

W MAXWELL ST

D

N

C **B**

2ND ST

BROADWAY

M

A **L**

MILL ST

UPPER ST

G

ANGLIANA AV

J

S LIMESTONE ST

VINE ST

K

Red Mile Harness Track

H

OLD VINE ST

MIDLAND AV

60

E MAIN ST

VIRGINIA AV

E MAXWELL ST

HIGH ST

421

27

ROSE ST

EUCLID AV

25

ASHLAND AV N

WOODLAND AV

E

S ASHLAND AV

HILLTOP AV

UNIVERSITY DR

WALLER AV

To **F** ◀

TATE CREEK RD

COOPER DR

University of Kentucky

S LIMESTONE RD

To **I** ▼

N

0 SCALE
.5 KILOMETERS   .5 MILES
——— ROAD
- - - - AREA BOUNDARY

Food

- **A** A la Lucie
- **B** Atomic Café
- **C** Columbia Steakhouse
- **D** DeSha's
- **E** Everybody's Natural Foods & Deli
- **F** Kentucky Inn
- **G** Linda's Sandwich Shop
- **H** Magee's Bakery
- **I** Merrick Inn
- **J** Rogers Restaurant
- **K** Tonio's Super Burritos

Lodging

- **L** Camberley Club Hotel at Graz
- **M** Hyatt Regency
- **F** Kentucky Inn
- **N** Radisson

Camping

- **O** Kentucky Horse Park

Note: Items with the same letter are located in the same place.

downtown. The restaurant offers an extensive menu and makes a great place to watch UK basketball, especially since tickets to Rupp Arena are scarce. **Lexington Brewing Company** (401 Cross, 606/252-6004) makes Limestone Ale and Kentucky Hemp Beer (hemp used to be one of Kentucky's major crops years ago), and offers brewery tours by appointment. **Cheapside Bar & Grill** (131 Cheapside, 606/254-0046), a downtown Lexington favorite, has music almost every night and is also a good place for lunch.

For concert events check out both the **Kentucky Theatre** (214 E. Main, 606/231-6997), a 1920s movie theater that also shows foreign and classic films; and the **Lexington Opera House**, dating from the 1880s and also home to the **Lexington Ballet**. Lexington's primary source of cultural programming is the **Singletary Center for the Art**s (606/257-4929). Located on the UK campus, it features major performing arts, music, and theater events throughout the year.

Scenic Route: Highway 60 from Lexington to Louisville

Highway 60 parallels I-64 and passes through the historic Kentucky countryside and leads into the capital city of Frankfort, once Frank's Ford across the Kentucky River.

First follow Old Frankfort Pike out of Lexington, and you'll see one of the densest groupings of horse farms in the area. The road then intersects with Highway 60 and I-64. Take Highway 62 (exit 65 from I-64) into **Midway**, a railroad town founded in 1832. Midway has antique shops running down both sides of the railroad track. Try the **Depot Restaurant** (128 Main St., 606/846-4745) and be sure to taste the Trackside Pie (a version of Kentucky Derby Pie). Or call for dinner reservations at the historic **Holly Hill Inn** (N. Winter St., 606/846-4732)

Named the state capital in 1792, **Frankfort**, a beautiful small city on the river, has preserved a number of distinguished Federal-style homes and public buildings dating from the early 1800s. Remnants of Frankfort's historical past can be found all over the city.

HIGHWAY 60

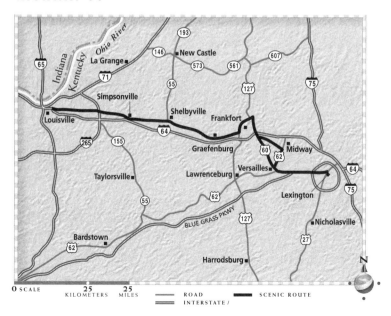

Daniel and Rebecca Boone are buried here. The exquisite 1831 state capitol building, designed by Gideon Schyrock, now houses the **Kentucky Historical Society Library** (502/564-3016), whose special collections date to 1750. Bibb lettuce is named after an early citizen-horticulturist. The only Frank Lloyd Wright house in Kentucky is here, and you may tour of the old-fashioned kitchens of **Rebecca-Ruth Candy** (112 E. Second St.), where the "bourbon ball" was invented. Stop by the visitors center at Gooch House on Capital Avenue to pick up a walking tour map. The center will also give you a local restaurant guide that features no less than six diners—the one I wish I'd tried was **Sweet Nectar** (205 Steele St.).

Continuing on I-64, at exit 28 is **Simpsonville**. Here you can have a meal or late afternoon tea at an 1817 stagecoach inn, the tiny **Old Stone Inn** (502/722-8882), one of the first stone houses in Kentucky. About seven miles down Highway 60 is **Shelbyville**, whose late Victorian-era downtown is listed on the National Register of Historic Places. Antique stores abound in this small town, and the historic **Science Hill Inn** (502/633-2825), a highly-acclaimed dining room, is also located here. ◼

10

LOUISVILLE

L ouisville, Kentucky's largest city, is located at the historically unnavigable Falls of the Ohio. Long before white settlers arrived, rocky outcroppings in the river formed a natural barrier that snagged plant life and provided a crossroads for the ancient people and animals of the last ice age.

The city of Louisville was founded in 1788 by Revolutionary War general George Rogers Clark as a settlement on the portage site of Corn Island, a strategic position which controlled British troop movement on the river and served as a base of operations for the exploration of the Northwest Territory. In 1804, Clark's brother William departed with Meriwether Lewis to explore the lands that had been acquired in Thomas Jefferson's Louisiana Purchase of 1803. In 1808, John James Audubon began his career as a shop owner in Louisville, doing some of his earliest studies of nature at the Falls of the Ohio before he settled downriver at Henderson, Kentucky, in 1810. Always a center of river trade and a transportation hub, by the late nineteenth century Louisville had reached the height of prosperity. The three-story brick townhouses of Old Louisville's Belgravia and St. James Court neighborhoods and the four- and five-story warehouse buildings of Main and Market Streets testify to that financial prominence.

Today the still-thriving hotels, restored theaters, active Kentucky Center for the Arts, and postmodern Humana and Providian Center skyscrapers attest to downtown Louisville's continued cultural and financial health. ◪

LOUISVILLE

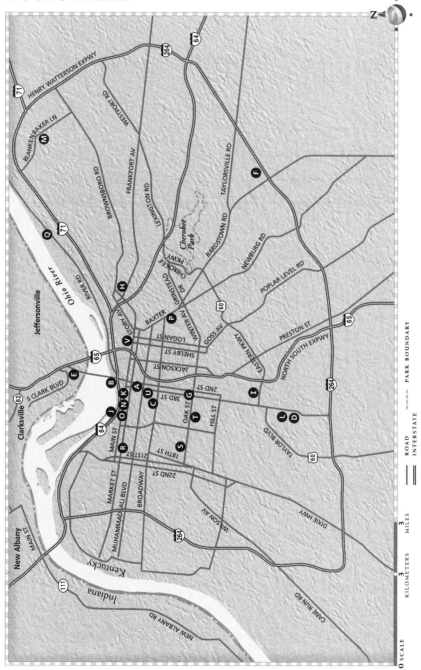

Sights

A Actor's Theater

B Belle of Louisville

C Brennan House

D Churchill Downs

E Falls of the Ohio Interpretive Center

F Farmington

G Filson Club

H Hadley Pottery

I J. B. Speed Art Museum

J Kentucky Art and Craft Foundation

K Kentucky Center for the Arts

L Kentucky Derby Museum

M Locust Grove

N Louisville Science Center

O Louisville Slugger Museum

P Louisville Stoneware

Q Louisville Visual Art Association

R Main Street

S Old Louisville

T Old Louisville Information Center

U Palace Theatre

V Thomas Edison House

A PERFECT DAY IN LOUISVILLE

Arrive at Lynn's Paradise Café early (to avoid the line at this popular spot) for a hearty and healthful breakfast amidst eclectic folk-art decor. You might be inspired to wander Bardstown Road for some antique and junk browsing afterward—ask for some good leads at Lynn's. Drive across the river to the Falls of the Ohio Interpretive Center where you can "see" Louisville long before it was a city and understand its relationship to the Ohio River that formed its northern boundary and, for more than 150 years, has been its lifeline to the rest of the world.

Stroll down Main Street looking at the architectural details on these hundred-year-old buildings. There are several galleries in the neighborhood; pick up a Louisville Gallery Guide at the elegant Kentucky Art and Craft Foundation Gallery for addresses. Try Check's in Germantown for lunch. Afterward drive out to the Watertower Gallery, a former water plant whose pump rooms now serve as exhibit spaces. Don't miss the Kentucky Derby Museum (and Churchill Downs in season). Have an early dinner at one of Louisville's renowned new American-cuisine restaurants then move on to Actor's Theatre. End your evening with a top-shelf bourbon in the Old Seelbach Bar.

SIGHTSEEING HIGHLIGHTS

✪✪✪ **Belle of Louisville**—For a closer look at river life, take an afternoon cruise on this sternwheeler, first chartered as the packet boat *Idlewild* in 1914 and now the oldest operating steamboat on the Ohio. In 1998 the *Belle* missed its annual Derby Festival race due to maintenance, but now it's being restored to its former glory, and a regular schedule is anticipated by late 1998. Another boat, the *Spirit of Jefferson*, offers a popular Sunday brunch cruise.
Details: 401 W. River Rd.; 502/574-2355 or, through Ticketmaster, 502/361-3100. (4 hours)

✪✪✪ **Churchill Downs**—Churchill Downs has hosted the Kentucky Derby every first Saturday in May since 1875. Seating in the club-house, built in 1895, can be enjoyed for a $3.50 ticket during the racing season, late April to July 1 and late October through November. Grandstand seats go for $2.50. With the exception of the Derby, tickets can usually be purchased on the day of the race. The annual Derby Week Festival (800/928-FEST) brings as many as 1 million people to town for a variety of activities leading up to the big day.

Next door, the **Kentucky Derby Museum** includes tours of Churchill Downs in the admission ticket. In addition to one of the most powerful slide presentations you will ever see and interactive stations that provide Derby history, there are also semipermanent changing exhibits. On current view is an exposition of the important early role of African Americans in thoroughbred racing.
Details: Churchill Downs: 700 Central, 502/636-4400. Kentucky Derby Museum: 704 Central, 502/637-1111. Daily 9–5. $5 adults, $2 children under 12. (1½ hours)

✪✪✪ **Falls of the Ohio Interpretive Center**—Located a stone's throw from downtown Louisville, the center provides a thorough introduction to the amazing geologic history of the area and kindles the observing spirit of any nature lover. More than 265 species of birds and 125 species of fish have been recorded in this 1,400-acre wildlife preserve. The superb orientation film begins with a fine explanation of the Devonian period, 400 million years ago, when the southern part of the North American continent was covered by warm seas. Due to a series of geologic events, not the least of which was the scraping effect of the glaciers that created the Ohio River Valley, fossils of marine life from the Devonian period can still be found outside on the shoals of the river. The center also contains a fine historical museum.

Details: 2nd Ave., Clarksville, IN; 812/280-9970. Mon–Sat 9–5, Sun 1–5. $2 adults, $1 children under 12. (1 hour)

✹✹✹ **J. B. Speed Art Museum**—The museum was founded in 1927 by Hattie Bishop Speed in memory of her husband, James. The museum's strengths are its collections of old master and medieval paintings, but it has been steadily acquiring important works by contemporary American artists over the past 20 years or so. Newly reopened after a major overhaul, the Speed Museum now includes an Interactive Learning Center for children.

Details: 2035 S. Third, 502/634-2700. Tue–Fri 10:30–4, Thu nights until 8, Sat 10:30–5, Sun noon–5. Museum admission is free; Learning Center $3.50. (1 hour)

✹✹✹ **Louisville Visual Art Association**—This multifaceted organization reflects the enthusiastic spirit of Louisville's ecumenical arts community. It is located in the oldest (dating from 1858), tallest, and most ornamented water tower in the country. The association is responsible for the Pegasus Gallery at the Louisville International Airport and for exciting child and adult art programming, including the "Boat Race Party" on Kentucky Derby weekend and the Waterside Music and Arts Festival in July. Changing exhibits of contemporary local and regional art are displayed.

Details: 3005 Upper River Rd., 502/896-2146. Mon–Fri 9–5, Sat 9–3, Sun noon–4. Admission is free; donations requested. (1 hour)

✹✹✹ **Main Street**—This historic downtown business district contains the second largest number of cast iron building facades in the country. Among the newer buildings you'll notice the **Kentucky Center for the Arts**, at Sixth and Main, and the postmodern Humana Headquarters Building across the street designed by Michael Graves. The **Louisville Science Center** (727 W. Main, 502/561-6100. Mon–Thu 10–5, Fri–Sat 10–9, Sun noon–5. $7 adults, $6 children) was one of the first interactive science exploratory museums in the country. The **Kentucky Art and Craft Foundation** (609 W. Main, 502/589-0102. Mon–Sat 10–4. Admission is free) features changing exhibits of outstanding Kentucky artists and a sales room. **Actor's Theatre** (316 W. Main, 502/584-1208) is in an 1830s bank building designed by Gideon Schyrock, an important early Kentucky architect who also designed the original state capitol building in Frankfort (now the Kentucky Historical Society).

The **Louisville Slugger Museum** (8th and Main, 502/588-7228. Mon–Sat 9–5, tours hourly 9:30–4:30. $5 per person), built by Hillerich and Bradsby Company, makers of Louisville Slugger bats, has just moved onto Main Street (you can't miss the 120-foot bat on the sidewalk).

Details: Walking tours available from the Main Street Association (101 N. 7th, 502/561-3493). (2 hours)

✯✯ **Brennan House**—Occupied by a single family since its construction in 1868, this historic home contains original Victorian furnishings.
Details: 631 S. Fifth St., 502/540-5145. Mar–Dec Tue–Sat 10:30–3:30. $3 adults, $1.50 ages 6–12. (30 minutes)

✯✯ **Farmington**—This fine Federal-style 14-room home was built in 1810 from a design by Thomas Jefferson and has been restored to its original interior color scheme.
Details: 3033 Bardstown Rd.; 502/452-9920. Mon–Sat 10–4:30, Sun 1:30–4:30. $4 adults, $2 students ages 6–17, children under 6 free. (1 hour)

✯✯ **Filson Club**—A historical and genealogical society founded in 1884, the Filson Club has its museum and library in a 1901 Beaux Arts building in Old Louisville that is open to the public. While it's worth checking out for the architecture, it's even more interesting if you have something pertinent to look up.
Details: 1310 S. Third St., 502/535-5083. Library open Mon–Fri 9–5, Sat 9–noon. $3 per person. Museum open Mon–Fri 9–5. Admission is free. (30 minutes)

✯✯ **Locust Grove**—The home of Louisville's founder, George Rogers Clark, Locust Grove was built in 1790 on 55 acres located east of the city. Imagine where you would put your home if you could settle anywhere in town!

Details: 561 Blankenbaker Ln., 502/897-9845. Mon–Sat 10–4:30, Sun 1:30–4:30. $4 adults, $2 students ages 6–17, children free. (1 hour)

✩✩ **Old Louisville**—This well-preserved historic district includes the Brennan House and Filson Club, as well as lots of B&Bs in old houses and many magnificent residences. The St. James Court Art Show (502/635-1842) takes place on St. James Place every October and the Kentucky Shakespeare Festival (502/583-8738) is held here every summer for free in Central Park. Old Louisville can be explored with the aid of a walking-tour map distributed by the **Old Louisville Information Center**.

Details: Old Louisville Information Center, 4th and Magnolia; 502/635-5244. Mon–Fri. (1½ hours)

✩✩ **Thomas Edison House**—Edison lived in this Butchertown row house from 1866 to 1867 while he worked for Western Union Telegraph. A guided tour takes visitors through the house. There is also a small museum dedicated to this amazing American inventor.

Details: 729–31 E. Washington, 502/585-5247. Tue–Sat 10–2. $4 adults, $2 students ages 6–17, children under 6 free. (1 hour)

Old Louisville

Kentucky Dept. of Travel Development

☆ **Palace Theatre**—Newly restored to its 1928 glory, the Palace serves as a concert venue for popular acts. Designed by John Ebersole for vaudeville productions and silent films, the Palace still has its original private box seats and is nothing short of wonderfully gaudy. Walking in this part of Louisville can recall the splendor of yesteryear. Call to see if someone you'd like to hear is playing while you're in town.
Details: 625 Fourth St., near the Brown Hotel; 502/583-4335. Tours Tue and Thu 10–2. $2 per person. (45 minutes)

Louisville Stoneware and Hadley Pottery—These establishments feature different versions of folk-style blue-figured stoneware. Unique souvenir dog dishes and baby gifts with a Louisville look are available. Both stores are open for tours Monday through Friday, with show-rooms open Saturday morning.
Details: Louisville Stoneware: 731 Brent St., 502/582-1900. Hadley Pottery: 1570 Story Ave., 502/584-2171 or 800/626-1800. (30 minutes)

FITNESS AND RECREATION

The paved **Riverwalk** along the Ohio River from 4th to 18th Streets makes a good short jogging trail close to downtown. Speaking of the river that started it all, **Canoe Kentucky** (800/K-CANOE), headquartered in Frankfort, offers access to 12 of the state's best paddling streams.

The **Louisville Wheelmen**, founded in 1897, sponsors bicycling events and can give information about good bike rides in the area. Contacted them via the Internet at www.thepoint.net/~kycycle/.

Louisville is a town that loves festivals. The **Kentucky Derby Festival**, complete with a boat race between the *Belle of Louisville* and the *Delta Queen*, begins in mid-April and lasts until the Derby in early May. The **Humana Festival of New American Plays** has gained a reputation for artistic excellence. It takes place from late February through March, and some of the downtown hotels offer special festival packages to encourage visitors. Call Actors Theatre (502/584-1208) for information. The 20-year-old **Corn Island Storytelling Festival** is held in several city park locations and focuses on the passing down of history through storytelling. The **Kentucky Shakespeare Festival** is held during June and July in Old

Louisville. Call the Louisville Convention and Visitors Bureau (800/792-5595) for schedules.

FOOD

Downtown for breakfast? Grab a cup and a breakfast pastry at **John Conti Gourmet Coffee** (500 S. 4th, 502/583-1216) next to the Seelbach Hotel downtown. This Louisville coffee company has a roasting plant (502/499-8602) out on Bardstown Road. For lunch in the downtown area go to **J. Graham's** (a casual dining spot) at the Camberley Brown Hotel (335 W. Broadway, 502/583-1234). Try their original Kentucky Hot brown, an open-faced turkey sandwich topped with Mornay sauce, cheese, tomato, and bacon. Wash it down with an Oldenburg Ale, brewed in northern Kentucky.

For an inexpensive and unusual dinner downtown, try **Café Kilimanjaro** (649 S. Fourth St., 502/583-4332), where you can often find Jamaican jerk chicken or Ethiopian Doro Wat cooking outside in a metal barrel, along with world music on Friday and Saturday nights. The Seelbach Hotel's **Oakroom** (500 S. Fourth Ave., 502/585-3200) offers a fine $19.98 prix fixe meal before 6:30 every evening. Another excellent downtown restaurant is **Vicenzo's** (150 S. Fifth, 502/580-1350), a pricey Italian establishment that offers risottos, pastas, and a large number of veal entrées.

In the midtown area, which includes Bardstown Road, try **Lynn's Paradise Café** (984 Barret Rd., 502/583-EGGS). You'll recognize it by the large metal coffee pot out front and the gaily decorated exterior. Lynn's serves only the freshest produce (she works with the Kentucky Organic Growers Association and the Farm Growers of America) and whips up famous scones, pancakes, and French toast chock full of fruits and nuts. Lynn's is also open for lunch and dinner. Local favorites for lunch include the **Bristol Bar and Grille** (1321 Bardstown Rd., 502/456-1702), which also has a restaurant in the Kentucky Center for the Arts (502/583-3342); **Check's Cafe** (1101 E. Burnet, in Germantown; 502/637-9515), which makes fried chicken, burgers, beer, bratwursts, and what they claim is the best chili in town; and **Cunningham's** (900 S. Fifth, 502/587-0526), near Old Louisville, where they serve fish sandwiches, steaks, and burgers.

For a fine evening of dining, sample the artistry of Louisville's trend-setting chefs at **Shariat's** (2901 Brownsboro Rd., 502/899-7878), where you can sample regional specialties like poached pears

LOUISVILLE

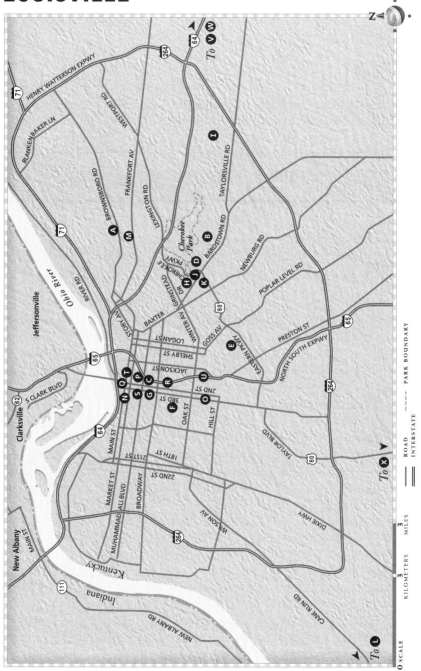

Food

- Ⓐ Azalea
- Ⓑ Bristol Bar and Grille
- Ⓒ Café Kilimanjaro
- Ⓓ Café Metro
- Ⓔ Check's Cafe
- Ⓕ Cunningham's
- Ⓖ J. Graham's
- Ⓗ Jack Fry's
- Ⓘ John Conti Gourmet Coffee
- Ⓘ Le Relais
- Ⓙ Lilly's
- Ⓚ Lynn's Paradise Café
- Ⓛ Mike Linnig's
- Ⓖ Oakroom
- Ⓜ Shariat's
- Ⓝ Vicenzo's

Lodging

- Ⓖ Camberley Brown Hotel
- Ⓞ Columbine
- Ⓟ Doubletree Downtown
- Ⓠ Galt House
- Ⓡ Holiday Inn
- Ⓢ Hyatt Regency
- Ⓣ Inn at Jewish Hospital
- Ⓞ Inn at the Park
- Ⓞ Old Louisville Inn
- Ⓞ Rose Blossom
- Ⓖ The Seelbach
- Ⓞ Towne House
- Ⓤ Towne House Annex
- Ⓥ Travelodge Convention Center

Camping

- Ⓦ Guist Creek Campground
- Ⓧ Otter Creek Park

Note: Items with the same letter are located in the same area.

and Kentucky ham, Kentucky Bibb lettuce with Bourbon vinaigrette, and sumptuous vegetarian offerings. Also try **Lilly's** (1147 Bardstown Rd., 502/451-0447), which might offer wild mushrooms over grits as an appetizer, free-range chicken potpie, or Kentucky lamb chops with mint pesto. **Jack Fry's** (1007 Bardstown Rd., 502/452-9244), which always has fresh fish entrées; and **Azalea** (3612 Brownsboro Rd., 502/895-5493), whose menu consistently has an imaginative flair, are slightly less expensive. **Café Metro** (1700 Bardstown Rd.,

502/458-4830) features grilled fish and daily special soups and pastas and a menu that changes every several months. Any one of these will be worth the splurge for an adventure in cutting-edge regional haute cuisine.

One of Louisville's most established dining spots is **Le Relais** (Taylorsville Rd., 502/451-9020), at the old Bowman Field Airport. Its dishes rely on authentic French preparation but its English-language menu displays a self-confident, inventive flair. You might wish to sample the smoked salmon profiterole with crème fraîche and a caper relish, or a New York strip with a cognac and green peppercorn sauce. For great seafood try **Mike Linnig's** (9308 Cane Run Rd., off Waterson Expressway about 20 minutes west along the river; 502/937-1235). Seafood, mostly fried, and lots of it, is the order of the day at this friendly and casual place.

LODGING

Louisville has two elegant old hotels downtown: **The Seelbach** (500 S. Fourth, 800/333-3399) and the **Camberley Brown** (335 W. Broadway, 502/583-1234). While both charge upwards of $120 for standard, beautifully appointed rooms, they do give AAA and AARP discounts when rooms are available and offer special theater packages and regular weekend packages. The **Galt House** (Fourth St. and River Rd., 502/589-5200 or 800/626-1814), another fine hotel of more recent vintage, faces the Ohio River. The **Hyatt Regency Louisville** (320 W. Jefferson, 502/587-3434), **Holiday Inn Downtown** (120 W. Broadway, 502/582-2241), **Doubletree Downtown** (101 E. Jefferson, 502/491-4830), and **Travelodge Convention Center** (401 S. Second St., 502/583-2841) are reliable national chain hotels located in the heart of downtown. Marriott runs the very nice **Inn at Jewish Hospital** (Jefferson and First, 502/582-2481).

In Old Louisville, just south of downtown, there are lots of great B&B accommodations. The **Old Louisville Inn** (1359 S. Third, 502/635-1574) is a 1901 house with 11 guest rooms built by an early railroad magnate. Other delightful historic homes offering bed-and-breakfast accommodations in Old Louisville are the **Rose Blossom** (1353 S. Fourth, 502/636-0295), an 1884 three-story Victorian; **Inn at the Park** (1332 S. Fourth, facing Central Park; 502/637-6930), an 1886 Richardsonian Romanesque mansion with six rooms with private baths; **Towne House** (1460 St. James Court, 502/636-5673), which has four guest rooms and is located on a tree-lined English-style ellipse; the **Towne House Annex** (105 W. Ormsby, 502/636-1705), a turn-of-the-century house and antique shop with two suites, one of which occupies the entire third floor; and the **Columbine** (1707 S. Third, 800/635-5010), which has five guest rooms with private baths.

CAMPING

On the way to Frankfort, east of Louisville near Shelbyville, at I-64 exit 35, is beautiful Guist Creek Lake and **Guist Creek Campground** (502/633-1934). Open April through October, the campground has 15 primitive camping sites and 28 full hookups. Thirty-five minutes south of Louisville, on the way to Fort Knox (Hwy. 31W), you'll find **Otter Creek Park** (502/583-3577), a city park with a view of the Ohio River. There are more than 200 tent and full-hookup campsites here, all of which are available on a first-come, first-served basis. The park also has a lodge and cabins.

NIGHTLIFE

The **Palace Theater**, a newly renovated downtown venue (625 Fourth Ave., 502/583-4555) books popular music acts; call for a schedule. In the O'Malley's Corner complex downtown is **Coyotes** (Second and Liberty, 502/589-FUNN), which offers big-name country music acts, comedy, and local bands in a club setting. At **Bearno's by the Bridge** (131 W. Main St., 502/584-7720) you can hear live alternative local music, have your palm read, and enjoy live comedy. They also serve an extensive pasta-based Italian menu.

Actor's Theater, which presents an exciting yearly schedule in two downtown theaters, hosts the **Humana Festival of New American Plays** in late February and March. They are located in a historic building at 316 West Main. Stop by the box office or call 502/584-1205 or 800/4ATL-TIX for tickets, which run from $16 to $36. The **MacCauley Theater** (Fourth and Broadway) is scheduled in conjunction with the **Kentucky Center for the Arts** (502/562-0100 or 800/775-7777) and offers plays, musicals, dance, and classical and popular music events. On the three stages of the Kentucky Center for the Arts, you'll find the **Louisville Orchestra**, the **Louisville Ballet**, the **Kentucky Opera**, and much more.

Two of Louisville's favorite bars featuring live music are the

Butchertown Pub (1335 Story, 502/583-2242), where you can hear rock 'n' roll and blues bands; and the **Phoenix Hill Tavern** (644 Baxter, 502/589-4957), which features New Age rock and reggae.

11

BARDSTOWN AND HISTORIC CENTRAL KENTUCKY

The counties surrounding Bardstown form the historic center of Kentucky. Bardstown, home of Federal Hill—the mansion that inspired Stephen Foster's "My Old Kentucky Home"—is a charming town that merits a several-day visit. Located southwest of Lexington in the heart of Kentucky's distillery country, this is the place to learn about the state's traditional Southern hospitality. The surrounding small towns and historic sites will easily take two days to explore. This area contains the first settlements west of the Allegheny Mountains. Fort Harrod, now reconstructed in a park on its original location, was built in 1774 as a shelter for pioneer families.

Bardstown was founded from a Virginia land grant in 1780. The Kentucky state constitution was written in nearby Danville in the years before Kentucky was granted statehood in 1792. The Shaker Village at Pleasant Hill, active from 1805 to 1910, was the third largest Shaker community in the United States, with as many as 500 residents at its height. Visitors to Perryville and its surrounding landmarks of the War Between the States will experience the divided loyalties of Kentucky and Tennessee firsthand. South of Bardstown is Abraham Lincoln's 1809 birthplace at Hodgenville and his boyhood home at Knob Creek. ◾

BARDSTOWN

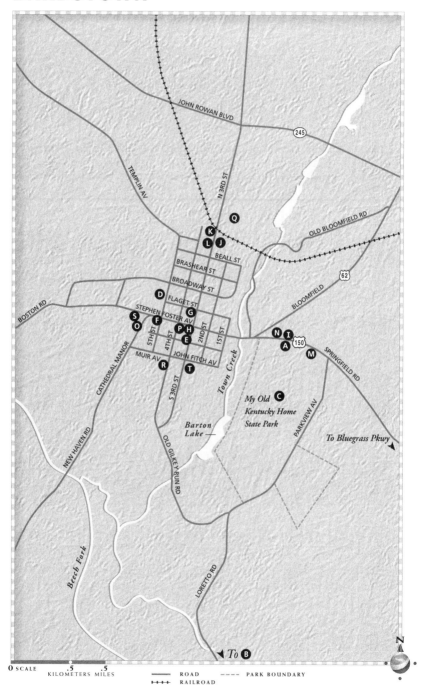

JOHN ROWAN BLVD

245

TEMPLIN AV

N 3RD ST

OLD BLOOMFIELD RD

Q

K
L J

BEALL ST

BRASHEAR ST

BROADWAY ST

62

D

FLAGET ST

BLOOMFIELD

STEPHEN FOSTER AV

G

BOSTON RD

S
O

F

P H

N I

A

150

5TH ST

4TH ST

2ND ST

1ST ST

E

M

SPRINGFIELD RD

MUIR AV

JOHN FITCH AV

R

T

CATHEDRAL MANOR

S 3RD ST

PARKVIEW AV

My Old
Kentucky Home
State Park

C

NEW HAVEN RD

Barton
Lake —

To Bluegrass Pkwy

OLD GILKEY RUN RD

Beech Fork

Town Creek

LORETTO RD

N

◄ To B

O SCALE
KILOMETERS MILES
.5   .5

——— ROAD   - - - - PARK BOUNDARY
┝┿┿┿┥ RAILROAD

Sights

Ⓐ Federal Hill

Ⓑ Maker's Mark Distillery Tour

Ⓒ My Old Kentucky Home State Park

Ⓓ Oscar Getz Museum of Whiskey History/Bardstown Historical Museum

Ⓔ Old Talbott Tavern

Ⓕ St. Joseph Proto-Cathedral

Food

Ⓖ Beall's Row Coffee and Ale House

Ⓗ Hurst Drug Store's Old-Fashioned Soda Fountain

Ⓘ Kurtz Restaurant

Food (continued)

Ⓙ McKinney House

Ⓚ My Old Kentucky Dinner Train

Ⓛ Tom Pig's

Lodging

Ⓜ Bardstown Inn

Ⓝ Bardstown Parkview Motel

Ⓞ Best Western General Nelson Motel

Ⓟ Jailer's Inn

Ⓠ The Mansion

Ⓡ McLean House

Ⓢ Old Kentucky Home

Ⓣ Victorian Lights

Ⓚ Wilson Motel

Note: Items with the same letter are located in the same place.

A PERFECT DAY IN AND AROUND BARDSTOWN

Walk the old streets of central Bardstown, stopping at Beall's Row Coffee and Ale House for coffee and a muffin and dawdling in some of the antique shops. The walk to the Bardstown Historical Society Museum takes you past beautiful, early-1800s houses that are still private residences. Enjoy the Oscar Getz Museum of Whiskey History, which will whet your appetite for a taste of the real thing. Have a family-style lunch at Kurtz Restaurant and then walk across the street to My Old Kentucky Home for a guided tour. A leisurely drive out into the rolling countryside will take you through Perryville and Harrodsburg on the way to Pleasant Hill. Spend the afternoon musing over Shaker exhibits and demonstrations before a quiet supper in the Trustee's Office Dining Room.

MORE BARDSTOWN HISTORY

Bardstown was founded in 1780 when William Bard came to claim his brother David's Virginia land grant. A courthouse of hand-hewn logs was built in 1785, and the town was incorporated in 1788 as part of Virginia's "Kentucky district." Kentucky's distillery industry, whose records date it as far back as 1776 in this vicinity, arose here because of the high percentage of limestone in the water.

BARDSTOWN SIGHTSEEING HIGHLIGHTS

✰✰✰ **Federal Hill**—Better known as My Old Kentucky Home, Federal Hill was built in 1818 by Judge John Rowan Sr. It was after a visit here in 1853 that Stephen Foster penned his famous song. Tours are led by guides dressed in period costume. **My Old Kentucky Home State Park** surrounds the historic site. From June until Labor Day, *Stephen Foster—The Musical* is performed in the amphitheater here. The 40-year-old production now includes orchestration by the Louisville Symphony and is getting rave reviews.

Details: Stephen Foster Ave. (Hwy. 62), Bardstown; 502/348-3502 or 800/323-7803. Daily 9–5, summer 8:30–6. $4 adults, $2 children. Stephen Foster—The Musical *performances: 800/626-1563, fax 502/349-0574, internet www.stephenfoster.org. Tue–Sun at 8 p.m., Sat at 2. $14 adults, $7 ages 7–12, under 7 free. Order tickets in advance. (1 hour)*

✰✰✰ **Old Talbott Tavern**—Opened in the late 1770s, this tavern began as a stagecoach stop. There are plenty of interesting tales to be told of its many early visitors. George Rogers Clark and John James Audubon stayed here, and an upstairs room contains a late-eighteenth-century mural painted by one of Louis Philippe's entourage. Talbott Tavern provided wonderful food and lodging until a fire partially destroyed the upper level in 1998. At present the murals are undergoing restoration and the building is being renovated.

Details: 107 West Stephen Foster, 502/348-3494. (30 minutes)

✰✰ **Maker's Mark Distillery Tour**—This tour is highly recommended by those who have toured them all. Also located in and around Bardstown are the Heaven Hill (Evan Williams, Elijah Craig), Barton Brands, and Jim Beam distilleries. These three distilleries also offer free tours; it might be fun to see them all.

Details: Hwy. 52, Loretto; 502/865-2099. Tours Mon–Sat 10:30–3:30, Sun 1:30–3:30. Admission is free. (1½ hours)

★★ **Oscar Getz Museum of Whiskey History and Bardstown Historical Museum**—Housed in beautiful old Spalding Hall behind the cathedral, these museums contain many fascinating artifacts of local culture and history. Downstairs, Thomas Merton Books (310 Xavier Dr.; 502/348-6488) carries a large selection of publications by and about the famous Trappist monk/philosopher who lived just south of Bardstown at the Abbey of Gethsemani.

Details: 114 N. Fifth, 502/348-2999. Tue–Sat 10–4, Sun 1–4; summer Tue–Sat 9–5, Sun 1–5. Admission is free. (1 hour)

★★ **St. Joseph Proto-Cathedral**—This church, built between 1816 and 1819, was the first Catholic church west of the Alleghenies. The Cathedral has a fine collection of European paintings.

Details: 310 W. Stephen Foster; 502/348-3126. Mon–Fri 9–5, Sat 9–3, Sun 1-5. Admission is free. (30 minutes)

★ **Abbey of Gethsemani**—Twelve miles south of Bardstown, the Abbey, founded in 1848, is home to the largest order of Cistercian (Trappist) monks in the country. Scholar and religious mystic Thomas Merton lived and wrote here for many years. It is possible to arrange for a retreat stay at the monastery. The monastic vow of silence is observed, and contributions for room and board are voluntary. Reservations may be made by writing to: Abbey of Gethsemani, Trappist, Kentucky, 40051

Details: Hwy. 31E to 247, Bardstown; 502/549-3177. Open to the public daily for vespers at 5:30 p.m. Admission is free. (30 minutes)

★ **Art and Antiques**—While in Bardstown be sure to stroll up and down North Third Street while peeking in shops filled with antique furniture and cool old stuff. Down a side street is Sutherland Gallery (97 W. Flaget, 502/349-0139), where all of the art on display is by contemporary Kentucky artists. The owner can recommend artists' studios that are worth visiting. *(1 hour)*

★ **Hodgenville**—This town—home to the **Lincoln Birthplace National Historic Site**, **Lincoln Boyhood Home**, and **Lincoln Museum**—is the center of "Lincolniana." At the birthplace, the cabin in which the ex-president was born on February 12, 1809 has been enclosed inside a granite monument. Six miles north as you come in from Bardstown is **Knob Creek**, where a period reconstruction of the cabin in which young Lincoln lived until he was around eight years old has been set at the documented site—in a valley next to the water. The Lincoln Museum in downtown Hodgenville on the town square contains works of art illustrating scenes from Lincoln's life as well as memorabilia.

Details: Hwy. 31E (30 miles southwest of Bardstown). Abraham Lincoln Birthplace National Historic Site: 502/358-3137. Daily 8–4:45, summer daily 8–6:45. Admission is free. Lincoln's Boyhood Home: 502/549-3741. Apr–Oct 10–5, summer 10–6. $1 adults, 50¢ ages 6–12. Lincoln Museum: 502/358-3163. Mon–Sat 8:30–5, Sun 12:30–5. $3 adults, $1.50 ages 6-12. (3 hours)

New Haven—Just south of Bardstown on Highway 31 is the departure point for the **Kentucky Railway Museum's** 22-mile ride behind a 1905 steam locomotive. There are vintage railcars and railroad artifacts at the depot museum. Handicapped accessible.

Details: Hwy. 31E; 800/272-0152. Museum: Mon–Sat 9–5, Sun 1–5. $3 adults, $1 ages 1–12. Train: Apr–Dec Mon–Sat at 2 p.m.; additional rides in summer. $12.50 adults, $8 ages 1–12. (2 hours)

Springfield—Another site on the Abraham Lincoln trail is the 1816 **Washington County Courthouse**, which contains the marriage bond of Lincoln's parents. The oldest continuously used courthouse in the state, this one has documents dating to 1792. The **Lincoln Homestead State Park** houses a replica of Thomas Lincoln's boyhood cabin as well as the actual **Berry House**, in which Nancy Hanks grew up. The two families lived in the area after arriving here in the 1780s and 1790s over the Wilderness Road. Don't miss the antique store downtown in the grand turn-of-the-century Springfield Opera House.

Details: Washington County Courthouse: Hwy. 150 and 55, Springfield; 606/336-5425. Mon–Fri 9–4:30, Sat 9–noon. Admission is free. Lincoln Homestead State Park: 5079 Lincoln Park Rd., off Hwy. 528, Springfield; 606/336-7461. Daily 8–6. Berry House admission May–Sept is $1. (1 hour)

HARRODSBURG SIGHTSEEING HIGHLIGHTS

✪✪✪ **Old Fort Harrod State Park**—Harrodsburg was founded by Captain James Harrod and 32 other men who traveled from

Pennsylvania to stake out land. They arrived at the site in July 1774 and built a blockhouse fort, the first permanent English settlement west of the Allegheny Mountains. Inside this reproduction of Harrod's fort is a living history interpretation with working craftspeople and animals. The site is authentic, as confirmed by the presence of the pioneer cemetery nearby dating back to the earliest days of the settlement. Visit the **Mansion Museum**, which dates from the 1830s, to see a wide range of historical artifacts. *The Legend of Daniel Boone*, an outdoor drama, is performed during the summer in the park amphitheater. Call 800/85-BOONE for times and prices.

Details: Hwys. 68 and 127, Harrodsburg; 606/734-3314. Nov–mid-Mar daily 8–4:30, 8:30–5 the rest of the year. $3.50 adults. (1 hour)

☆☆☆ **Shaker Village at Pleasant Hill**—Located just outside of Harrodsburg on 2,700 acres of rolling land, the Shaker Village weaves an almost magical spell over visitors. Excellent explanatory tours are offered, along with demonstrations of daily activities and a ride on a river steamer that shows how the community of Shakers—who at their peak in the 1830s were about 500 persons strong—loaded and transported their wares to export markets down river. The central buildings are located on a high, bare hill and their yellowish cut-limestone facades form an austere contrast to the rolling bluegrass fields surrounding the village. Visitors can sample the simple but excellent Shaker recipes in a summertime tearoom, or take meals in the Trustee's House Dining Room. There is also a fine gift and book shop here, and lodging is available.

Details: Hwy. 68, 606/734-5411. Daily 9–6; during winter hours are slightly shorter and several buildings are closed, with ticket prices reduced accordingly. $9 adults, $4.50 ages 12–17, $2.50 ages 6–11. $6 per person for Dixie Belle *riverboat excursion. (2 hours)*

☆☆ **Perryville**—This town, named after Oliver Hazard Perry, was founded in 1817. It has become well known because of the Battle of Perryville, fought here in 1862. With troops on both sides arriving from the south through Tennessee, this battle was considered the "Battle for Kentucky." More than 7,500 men died, and although the battle was not a clear victory or loss for either side, the Confederates retreated. A reenactment of the battle is held in early October, on the Sunday closest to the anniversary date of October eighth. Before the war Perryville was a prosperous town with a number of homes and historic businesses built on what was known as Merchants Row along the Chaplin River during the 1840s and 1850s. Many of these are still standing, offering visitors a look at an intact city street from the period. The River House Café (Merchants Row, Perryville; 606/332-8101), a neighborhood restaurant that will give you a walking-tour map of the town, is in a building that had been used as a casket-making shop, a post office, and a general store. Across the river on the residential side of town the Elmwood Inn (205 E. Fourth St., Perryville; 606/332-2400)— formerly Elmwood Academy, which was used as a hospital after the famous battle—now serves afternoon tea (by reservation only).

Details: Perryville Battlefield State Historic Site: Hwys. 68 and 150, Perryville; 606/332-8631. Apr–Oct daily 9–5. $2 adults, $1 children. (1 hour)

Danville—Danville was critical to Kentucky's formation because the first constitution was drafted here between 1788 and 1792. Stop in at the visitors center for walking-tour directions, as there is lots of history here. **Constitution Square State Historic Site** includes the early post office, jail, and courthouse. **Centre College**, founded in 1819, is also here, and its oldest building can be toured. Centre's Norton Center for the Arts (606/236-4692), which presents music, theater, and visual arts, is the cultural hub of the community.

Details: Visitors Center: McClure-Barbee House, 304 S. Fourth; 800/755-0076. Mon–Fri 9–4. Constitution Square State Historic Site: 134 S. Second, 606/236-5089. Daily 9–dark. Admission is free. Centre College: Main St., 606/238-5343. Old Centre open Mon–Fri 10–4; Norton Center for the Arts, (606/236-4692) open Mon–Fri 10–4. (2 hours)

FITNESS AND RECREATION

Daily walking tours of downtown Bardstown, old Harrodsburg, or Shaker Village at Pleasant Hill will keep you both mentally stimulated and well-exercised during your stay in the area. The *Dixie Belle* river-boat makes hour-long trips from Shaker Landing (enter through Shaker Village), April through October. The prices are reasonable ($6 adults, $4 children), and the boat is a real sternwheeler (handicapped accessible). **My Old Kentucky Home State Park** (502/349-6542) offers an 18-hole golf course, as does the **Lincoln Homestead State Park** (606/336-7461) in Springfield.

Running through these historic towns would be fun, as they are fairly flat and there is a lot to see. Horseback riding at **Big Red**

Stables (Harrodsburg, 606/734-3118; open daily at 9 a.m., $20 per hour) makes a great day out, especially for families. The stables are located on more than 2,000 acres and offer guided rides for those who prefer to ride with a group. Biking on country roads is even possible as a means of transportation because the distances between towns are not great. There is an annual two-day ride between Louisville and Bardstown called **My Old Kentucky Home Tour,** held in mid-September. It's sponsored by the Louisville Wheelmen (502/893-4232), a biking club founded in 1897.

FOOD

In the heart of downtown Bardstown, **Beall's Row Coffee and Ale House** (114 N. Third St., 502/348-9594) offers informal dining in a charming storefront for breakfast, lunch, and dinner. Breakfast and lunch are inexpensive; dinner prices are moderate. Six blocks away is a tiny place named **Tom Pig's** (732 N. Third St., 502/348-9404). They serve a good plate lunch, and the place is always packed with local folks. Across from My Old Kentucky Home you'll find **Kurtz Restaurant** (418 E. Stephen Foster Ave., 502/348-8964) a charming establishment made of cut stone. Kurtz serves great food with a regional emphasis at moderate prices. The atmosphere is informal and the staff is knowledgeable and friendly.

For a quick lunch, stop in at **Hurst Discount Drug Store's Old-Fashioned Soda Fountain** (Court Square, 502/348-9261). You can sit at the counter as they make you a brown cow (root beer float). Up the street is Hurst's (119 N. Third St., 502/348-8929), a popular steak house that also serves great breakfasts.

For nice atmosphere, try **McKinney House** (formerly the Bardstonian, 521 N. Third St., 502/348-1958), located in a restored antebellum home. Open for lunch and dinner and serving sandwiches, salads, pastas, prime rib, and steak, McKinney House has a cozy bar area on the upper level. You could spend your evening out riding on **My Old Kentucky Dinner Train** (602 N.Third St., 502/348-7300). The cost of the meal—highly touted by locals—and the two-hour train ride in restored 1940s dining cars is $37 for lunch and $60 for dinner. Children must be age five or older, and the train is handicapped acces-sible. In New Haven, just south of Bardstown, the **Sherwood Inn** (138 S. Main St., New Haven; 502/529-3386), an old railroad hotel right by the tracks, gets good reviews for food and drink, and provides a nice

BARDSTOWN AREA

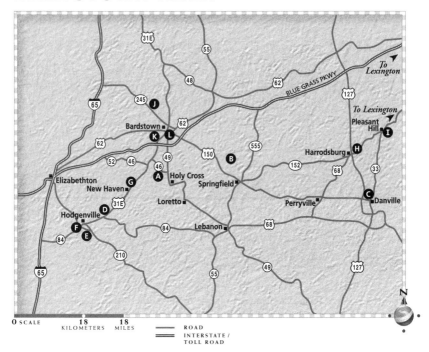

Sights

- **A** Abbey of Gethsemani
- **B** Berry House
- **C** Centre College
- **C** Constitution Square State Historic Site
- **D** Knob Creek
- **E** Lincoln Birthplace National Historic Site
- **B** Lincoln Homestead State Park
- **F** Lincoln Museum
- **G** Kentucky Railway Museum
- **H** Old Fort Harrod State Park
- **I** Shaker Village at Pleasant Hill

Food

- **H** Beaumont Inn
- **G** Sherwood Inn

Food *(continued)*

- **I** Trustee's Office at Shaker Village

Lodging

- **H** Beaumont Inn
- **C** Randolph House
- **G** Sherwood Inn
- **I** Trustee's House at Pleasant Hill
- **C** Twin Hollies Retreat

Camping

- **J** Holt's Campground
- **K** My Old Kentucky Home State Park
- **L** White Acres Campground

Note: Items with the same letter are located in the same town or area.

evening out for Bardstonians. They also have rooms available (see Lodging).

In Harrodsburg, the **Beaumont Inn** (Hwy. 127, Harrodsburg; 606/734-3381) serves outstanding meals in the dining rooms of a three-story brick structure that was constructed as a girls' school in 1845. Regional specialties include fried chicken, country ham, and corn-batter cakes. Reservations are a must for non-guests (see Lodging). **Trustee's Office at Shaker Village** (3501 Lexington Rd., Harrodsburg; 606/734-5411) serves a simple menu of country ham, roast turkey, catfish, or other seasonal entrées with assorted fresh vegetables and their famous lemon pie. Prices, all inclusive, can reach up to $20 for a wonderful meal. Breakfast, lunch, and dinner are served, but liquor is not. Reservations are often necessary for non-guests (see Lodging).

LODGING

The list of bed-and-breakfasts in and around Bardstown is extensive. **The Mansion** (1003 N. Third Ave., 502/348-2586) is a gorgeous antebellum home. Its only drawback is that it's a long walk away from downtown. The rooms all have private baths and are furnished with antiques. Even if they're full, they do offer public tours by reservation (800/399-2586).

Victorian Lights (112 S. Third St., 502/348-8087) is downtown, as is the three-room **Jailer's Inn** (111 W. Stephen, 502/348-5551), which really was the old jail until about 10 years ago. The front portion of the building, made of stone, dates from 1819. The Old Talbott Tavern is currently closed for repairs, but **McLean House** (107 W. Stephen Foster, 502/348-3494), next door, is open. It has five guest rooms and is operated by the same management.

If you just want a simple motel, try the clean and quiet **Wilson Motel** (530 N. Third, 502/348-3364). It's locally owned and includes 15 units and a pool. The **Bardstown Parkview Motel** (418 E. Stephen Foster, 502/348-5983 or 800/732-2384), next to Kurtz Restaurant and across the street from My Old Kentucky Home, is a fine choice; as is the **Bardstown Inn** (510 E. Stephen Foster, 800/894-1601), which is locally run and only about five years old. **Old Kentucky Home** (414 W. Stephen Foster, 800/772-1174) has 36 rooms and a pool. Across the street is the **Best Western General Nelson Motel** (411 W. Stephen Foster, 800/225-3977), a large establishment with a pool. On the outskirts of town are the Holiday, Ramada, Hampton, Comfort, and Red Carpet Inns.

In Harrodsburg, the **Beaumont Inn** (Hwy. 127, 800/352-3992) has been operated by four generations of the Dedman family since it opened in 1919. Guests can choose rooms in the original brick building, with its high ceilings and antique furniture, or they can stay in a new, tastefully furnished eight-room building across the street. The inn has an outdoor pool open in season, and the neighborhood surrounding the inn is nice for a short stroll. The Beaumont is an institution unto itself, and has little museum vignettes on display in various corners of its gracious sitting rooms. A splurge here is highly recommended, but guests expecting to sample Kentucky bourbon need to bring their own, as no liquor is served. The **Trustee's House at Pleasant Hill** (3501 Lexington Rd., 800/734-5611) offers lodging in sparsely furnished but comfortable historic quarters. Staying here guarantees a peaceful night's rest. There are 81 rooms in the main building and four cottages.

Danville, just nine miles south of Harrodsburg, is a bed-and-breakfast mecca. **Twin Hollies Retreat** (406 Maple, 606/236-8954) and **Randolph House** (463 W. Lexington, 606/236-9594) are two bed-and-breakfasts in antebellum homes. Call the Kentucky Bed-and-Breakfast Association (800/292-2632) for recommendations if these are booked.

CAMPING

My Old Kentucky Home State Park (Hwy. 150, Bardstown; 502/348-3502) has 39 sites with hookups and 15 sites for tent camping. The Visitors Bureau recommends two commercial campgrounds outside of Bardstown: **White Acres** (Hwy. 62W, 502/348-9677), which has 100 sites with hookups; and **Holt's** (Hwy. 1430 at Hwy. 245, 502/348-6717), which has both hookups and tent camping.

NIGHTLIFE

During the Christmas season many Bardstown attractions—including My Old Kentucky Home and some of the distilleries—offer candlelight tours on weekends. This is not only very festive, but also true to history, as many of the homes in Bardstown once had only candlelight illumination. The pre-Christmas season is a nice time to be in Bardstown, as the small shops are filled with gift ideas, the brick sidewalks might have a dusting of snow, and the old-time pace might be just what you need to get you into a truly joyful Christmas spirit. In summer, *Stephen Foster—The Musical* is presented nightly at eight at My Old Kentucky Home State Park's outdoor theater (800/626-1563). Mondays are dark, and Saturday matinees are held at two o'clock in the indoor facility, which also serves as a rain venue.

You'll find music here, too, in the form of bluegrass and Irish-influenced acoustic performers. They're at **Beall's Row** every Friday and Saturday during the summer. Or just go find a bar with friendly atmosphere and ask what they know about whiskey. You might get a chance to taste some hard-to-find top-shelf local bourbons and talk about their merits with some true connoisseurs. Booker Noe, grandson of Jim Beam, is much revered in these parts for his single-batch whiskey, Booker's, which is indeed a smooth-sipping whiskey. If you time it right you might catch the **Kentucky Bourbon Festival** (800/638-4877) the third week of September.

12
BOWLING GREEN AND MAMMOTH CAVE

This area of south-central Kentucky is approximately one hour north of Nashville, just off I-65 headed north to Louisville. Its most spectacular natural feature is Mammoth Cave. Once a tourist destination second only to Niagara Falls in popularity, Mammoth Cave is now an international biosphere reserve and national park interpretive and recreation site. This is cave country; nearby towns are named Horse Cave and Cave City.

Bowling Green, home to Western Kentucky University, offers the visitor a central point from which to explore a wide range of activities—from the quiet ingenuity of the early-nineteenth-century Shaker settlement at South Union to the style and innovation of the Corvette, America's best-known sports car, at its assembly plant and new museum. Bowling Green has a surprisingly cosmopolitan air for a city its size. One finds serious theater at the Capitol Arts Center, located in a historic building downtown along with a public art gallery. An 82-mile scenic driving tour of the region touts both its natural and historic attributes. WKU houses an impressive museum of state and local history, and an archeological collection related to the exploration of Mammoth Cave.

East of Bowling Green, the countryside is flat, rich farmland—once prime tobacco-raising ground. Smoking barns still dot the landscape, and small towns like Franklin, Auburn, and Smith's Grove are filled with Victorian architecture and antique shops. ◾

BOWLING GREEN AND
MAMMOTH CAVE

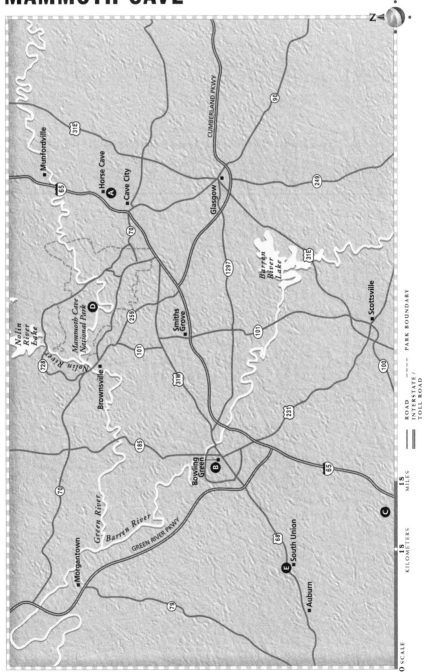

Z

Munfordville

31E

65

Horse Cave

Cave City

A

CUMBERLAND PKWY

90

Glasgow

249

70

1297

31E

Barren
River
Lake

Nolin
River
Lake

Mammoth Cave
National Park

D

259

Smiths
Grove

101

Scottsville

728

Nolin River

101

100

31W

Brownsville

231

185

Bowling
Green

B

65

70

Green River

Barren River

GREEN RIVER PKWY

South Union

68

Morgantown

E

Auburn

C

79

O SCALE

18
KILOMETERS

18
MILES

ROAD

INTERSTATE /
TOLL ROAD

PARK BOUNDARY

Sights

- **A** American Cave Museum and Hidden River Cave
- **B** Bowling Green Walking Tours
- **B** Capitol Arts Center
- **D** Civil War Heritage Trail
- **A** Horse Cave Theatre
- **C** Kentucky Downs
- **B** Kentucky Museum and Library
- **D** Mammoth Cave
- **B** National Corvette Museum and GM Corvette Assembly Plant
- **B** Riverview
- **E** Shaker Museum at South Union
- **E** Shaker Tavern

Note: Items with the same letter are located in the same town or area.

A PERFECT DAY IN BOWLING GREEN

After an overnight stay at one of the Mammoth Cave Hotel cabins, strike out early on one of the ranger-guided tours of the cave (tours begin as early as 8 a.m., and crowds can be a problem). Pack a picnic and explore the wonders of Mammoth Cave National Park, perhaps taking a boat ride on the Green River. Or head into Bowling Green for a tour of the Corvette Factory and the one-of-a-kind museum across the street. Lunch in historic downtown at the Parakeet Café. The Kentucky Museum at WKU has a wonderful exhibit about Victorian childhood that kids will love. Drive out to South Union and wander leisurely through the Shaker Museum and grounds. Dine on regional specialties and spend the night at the 1869 Shaker Tavern. If you are up for some nightlife, check to see if the Phoenix Theatre or the Capitol Arts Center has anything in production.

BOWLING GREEN SIGHTSEEING HIGHLIGHTS

✸✸✸ **Shaker Museum at South Union**—The settlement at South Union, located about 10 miles southwest of Bowling Green, was started in 1807 by a band of 30 Shakers who traveled west to Kentucky under the leadership of Brother Benjamin Seth Youngs and Sister Molly Goodrich. At its height in 1827, South Union numbered 350 converts from the surrounding communities, and its furniture-making industry was at peak production. Six thousand acres of land and 250 buildings made up the original community, which lasted until 1922. The Centre House (1824) is beautifully interpreted and historically intact, with a museum store containing a fine selection of books by and about the Shakers. Informative tours are available and programs, including workshops in making Shaker-style furnishings, are held throughout the year.

Near the railroad tracks just to the south stands the 1869 **Shaker Tavern** (Hwy. 73, South Union; 502/542-6801), constructed as a business venture in hopes of attracting visitors from the outside world who would continue to patronize Shaker industries. The Tavern is now operated as a bed-and-breakfast only.

Details: *Hwy. 68/80, between Russellville and Bowling Green; 502/542-4167. Mar–Mid-Dec Mon–Sat 9–5, Sun 1–5. $3 adults, $1 children under 12. (2 hours)*

✯ **Capitol Arts Center**—Located in a restored 1939 art deco theater building on the main square, the center features an art gallery and a full schedule of music and dance performances, film, theater, and other activities sponsored by the Capitol Arts Alliance.

Details: *416 E. Main, 502/782-2787. Center box office and gallery open Mon–Fri 9–4. Admission to gallery is free. (30 minutes)*

✯ **Kentucky Downs**—This track offers thoroughbred racing in September, year-round simulcast, and off-track betting at other times. If you want to sit inside, you can do so at the Turf Club Restaurant and Bar. Franklin is a small, pretty town filled with antique shops, so make sure to leave some time to explore.

Details: *Hwy. 31, exit 2 on I-65; 502/586-7778. Call ahead for post times. General admission is $2 per person. (1 hour)*

✯ **Kentucky Museum and Library**—This museum of regional and state history was founded in 1931 with the creation of an archive for significant materials relating to Kentucky history. The library holds important collections of Kentucky books, manuscripts, and information on folk life. The museum facility presents an impressive yearly schedule of changing exhibits as well as semipermanent interpretive exhibits, such as *Growing Up Victorian* and *Main Street: Mirror of Change*, designed to bring local and regional history to life. The Nelson Collection of artifacts from Mammoth Cave National Park is housed at the museum, and cooperative research projects between the two entities are ongoing. Many exhibits place a special emphasis on children as the audience and a number of interactive interpretive activities are used.

Details: Kentucky St., Western Kentucky University; 502/745-2592. Tue–Sat 9:30–4, Sun 1–4. $2 adults, $1 children under 12. (1½ hours)

✸ **National Corvette Museum and GM Corvette Assembly Plant**— No big surprises here, just lots of classic vettes, including experimental models never driven, and lovingly restored oldies. It's sort of the MTV of museums—lots of hype and glamour but a pretty narrow story line. The Corvette Assembly Plant (502/745-8228) offers free tours at 9 a.m. and 1 p.m. Monday through Friday. At times when a new design is underway, the plant closes all touring activity until the car is released.

Details: Exit 28 on I-65, the plant and museum are visible from the highway; 502/781-7973 or 800/53-VETTE. Daily 8–5, extended hours in summer. $8 adults, $4.50 children, $6 seniors. (1 hour)

✸ **Riverview (Hobson House)**—A grand brick home dating from 1872, Riverview is located just west of Bowling Green. An award-

Riverview/Hobson House

Kentucky Dept. of Travel Development

winning interpretive tour presenting the perspective of Victorian servants is offered. Because this home was built after the Civil War, the servants at Riverview, although they were all African American, were paid employees.

Details: 1100 W. Main, 502/843-5565. Feb–Dec Tue–Sat 10–4, Sun 1–4. $3.50 adults, $1.50 students, children under 6 free, or $6 per family. (1 hour)

Bowling Green Walking Tours—The Landmark Association sponsors tours of four significant historic areas beginning around the old (dating from 1798) center of town, Fountain Square Park.

Details: 912H State St., 502/782-0037. Tours with a knowledgeable guide are by appointment only. $3–$5 per person. (2 hours)

Civil War Heritage Trail—Bowling Green was the crossroads of many troops from both sides in the early years of the war. Many soldiers stopped in for meals at the Shaker Village at South Union. In late 1861 Bowling Green became the Confederate capital of Kentucky. A driving tour of the area can be obtained at the Bowling Green Visitors Center.

Details: 352 Three Springs Rd., exit 22 on I-65; 502/782-0800. Mon–Fri 8–5, also open weekends 9–5 in summer. The self-guided driving tour brochure is free, but some sights charge admission. (3 hours)

CAVE COUNTRY SIGHTSEEING HIGHLIGHTS

✪✪✪ **Mammoth Cave**—Rediscovered by frontier-era Kentuckians around 1800, this series of caves, which snakes underground for about 350 miles, was named for its sheer size. Evidence exists of extensive use by nomadic bands of Archaic Indians, which decreased as agriculture was later developed by the Woodland and Mississippian peoples. Park rangers offer a number of fine explanatory tours covering a wide range of topics, from geology to history to biology. At least four tours are offered daily year-round (the cave remains at 54 degrees so dress accordingly), while others can be arranged by advance reservation. Caving trips can also be arranged. Reservations are highly recommended during the busy period of June through August and can be made up to five months in advance. Mammoth Cave offers a wide range of park concessions, from lodging, camping, and dining to boat excursions and horseback riding. For information, write or call the park.

Details: Mammoth Cave National Park, Mammoth Cave, KY 42259; exit 48 or 53 from I-65. Park information: 502/758-2328. Tour reservations (Destinet): 800/967-2283. Open daily. Admission to park is free, cave tours $3–$35 per person. (2 hours)

☆ **American Cave Museum and Hidden River Cave**—The cave habitat is presented here in both artificial and real forms. A favorite with kids is the guided nature walk into Hidden River, which had to be closed to mass tourism about 40 years ago. The museum and walk, projects of the American Cave Conservation Association, present a clear environmental message that parents will appreciate.
Details: 119 E. Main St., Horse Cave; 502/786-1466. Daily 9–5. $6 adults. (1½ hours)

☆ **Horse Cave Theatre**—At this well-known regional theater it is often possible to see three plays in two days. Recent offerings include *All the King's Men*, Robert Penn Warren's classic based on the life of Louisiana governor Huey Long; and *The Dancers of Canaan*, a new play with authentic Shaker music.
Details: 109 Main St., Horse Cave; 800/342-2177. Jun–Oct Tue-Sat evening performances, weekend matinees. $15-$17.

FITNESS AND RECREATION

The gently rolling terrain and paved country roads make Bowling Green perfect biking territory. Call the **Bowling Green League of Bicyclists** (502/781-2729) for maps of Shakertown and Mammoth Cave. If indoor workouts are more your style, Bowling Green has a new **YMCA** (1056 Lover's Ln., 502/782-2810) with gymnasium, indoor pool, and racquetball courts.

Mammoth Cave National Park offers a wonderland of outdoor activity for the whole family. For information and to make reservations for guided hikes, cave adventures, or a trip on the Miss Green riverboat (April–October, $5), call park information at 502/758-2243. Outfitters authorized by the park for outings on the Green River are **Green River Canoeing** (502/597-2031), whose self-guided and professionally guided trips range from $15 to $90; and **Barren River Canoeing** (502/796-1979), who will arrange self-guided outings for $25 to $35.

Fishing within the park does not require a license. A trail ride can be arranged through park concessionaire **Double J Stables** (Hwy. 800,

BOWLING GREEN AND
MAMMOTH CAVE

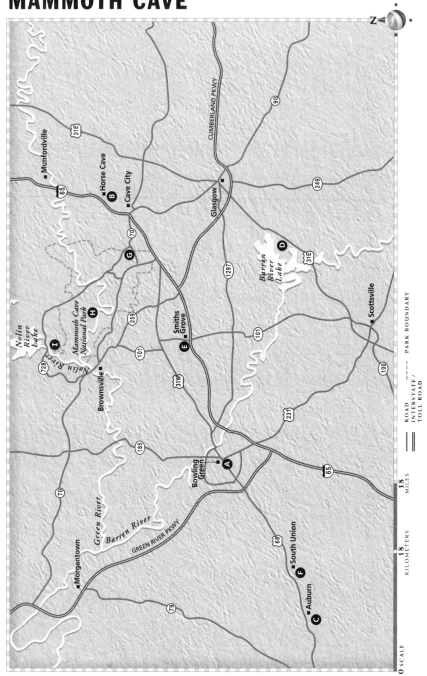

Food

- Ⓐ Al Baker's Courtyard Cafe
- Ⓑ Bookstore and Café
- Ⓐ Bread and Bagels Bakery
- Ⓐ 440 Main Restaurant and Bar
- Ⓑ Hal's Restaurant
- Ⓐ Parakeet Café
- Ⓐ Smokey's BBQ
- Ⓒ Yoder's Bakery

Lodging

- Ⓓ Barren River Lake State Resort Park
- Ⓔ Bryce Inn
- Ⓔ Cave Spring Farm
- Ⓒ Federal Grove B&B

Lodging (continued)

- Ⓐ News Inn of Bowling Green
- Ⓕ Shaker Tavern
- Ⓐ University Plaza Hotel
- Ⓔ Victorian House
- Ⓖ Wayfarer B&B
- Ⓑ Wigwam Village #2
- Ⓗ Woodland Cottages

Camping

- Ⓓ Barren River Lake State Resort Park
- Ⓗ Double J Stables & Campground
- Ⓗ Mammoth Cave National Park
- Ⓘ Nolin River Lake State Park

Note: Items with the same letter are located in the same town or area.

502/286-8167 or 502/730-HRSE) for $15 per person. One of the park's campgrounds has facilities for overnight horse-boarding if you book an extended trail ride. **Barren River Lake State Resort Park** (Hwy. 31, Lucas; 502/646-2151 or 800/325-0057), with 10,000 acres of water, has a marina and a golf course and is surrounded by a **Kentucky Wildlife Management Area** (502/842-0056). **Nolin River Lake** (Hwy. 728 to Hwy. 1827, 502/286-4240) is a 5,800-acre lake directly north of Mammoth Cave. Waterskiing and fishing are two of the major activities here.

FOOD

In Bowling Green, **Bread and Bagels Bakery** (871 Broadway, 502/781-1473) features baked-from-scratch breads. **Yoder's Bakery** (Hwy. 68), in the Mennonite community near Auburn, is acclaimed by locals.

Downtown Bowling Green's **Parakeet Café** (522 Morris Alley, 502/781-1538), a local favorite open for lunch and dinner, has moved around the corner from its original location on the square. Nearby is **Al Baker's Courtyard Cafe** (alley between Main and Fountain Square Park, 502/793-0106). Also downtown in a historic building is **440 Main Restaurant and Bar** (440 Main, 502/793-0450). Just east of downtown is **Smokey's BBQ** (Hwy. 31, Bowling Green; 502/781-1712). It's a perfect place to grab a sandwich for the road.

In Horse Cave, try the **Bookstore and Café** (111 Water St., 502/786-3084), a country-cooking restaurant lined with shelves of for-sale and not-for-sale books. **Hal's Restaurant** (Hwy. 31W, 502/786-4949) is a plain, family-style establishment open early every day for breakfast, lunch, and dinner, and featuring catfish on Fridays and fried chicken on Sundays.

LODGING

There are many historic bed-and-breakfast accommodations in the area surrounding Bowling Green. My first choice is the **Shaker Tavern** (Hwy. 73, South Union; 502/542-6801). Built in 1869 by the Shakers to accommodate visitors who arrived by train, the tavern has four guest rooms. The only meal served at present is breakfast. Several miles further west on Highway 68 in Auburn is **Federal Grove B&B** (502/542-6106), which was built circa 1886 and features four guest rooms with private baths. Twelve miles north of Bowling Green is the community of Smiths Grove, which features at least nine antique stores. Bed-and-breakfasts here include **Victorian House** (130 Main St., Smiths Grove; 502/563-9403), which has four guest rooms with private baths; and **Cave Spring Farm** (567 Rocky Hill Rd., Smiths Grove; 502/563-6941), with two rooms with private baths. The small, locally owned **Bryce Inn** (exit 38 off I-65, Smiths Grove; 502/563-5141) has 25 rooms and a pool.

Bowling Green has a number of national chain motels, many of which are located off I-65 at exit 22. The **News Inn of Bowling Green** (800/443-3701) is locally owned and offers complimentary breakfast, and the **University Plaza Hotel** (502/745-0088), which joins the convention center, has 219 rooms and is the newest and nicest in town.

To fully experience Mammoth Cave National Park, stay overnight at one of the rustic **Woodland Cottages** (available May–October).

They are within easy walking distance of the cave mouth so you can take advantage of evening and early morning activities at the park. The park also offers a hotel and a motor lodge available year round at reasonable rates. June through August are the busiest months, so try to make reservations (502/758-2225, fax 502/758-2301) before April if you will be there during the prime season.

Just outside the entrance to the park you will find a beautiful old white house with a crafts shop and the folk-style Floyd Collins Museum (open daily 9–5, $2) on the ground floor and the **Wayfarer B&B** (1240 Old Mammoth Cave Rd., 502/773-3366) upstairs. (Floyd Collins was a local man who became lost in the cave in 1925, attracting national attention. An outdoor drama based on his story is performed at the Green River Amphitheater during the summer months—see Nightlife, below.) **Barren River Lake State Resort Park** in Lucas (800/325-0057) offers an alternative to staying in Mammoth Cave National Park. Barren River Lake has a lodge with 51 rooms and 22 lakeside cottages, RV hookups, golf course, tennis courts, and horseback riding. Another fun option is **Wigwam Village #2** (601 N. Dixie Hwy., Cave City; 502/773-3381). The rooms are individual concrete wigwams. Don't miss it.

CAMPING

Mammoth Cave National Park offers primitive year-round camping for $5. Three other campgrounds are open March through November, and one accommodates horses (502/758-2251). The **Double J Stables & Campground** (502/286-8167) is the concessionaire for horseback riding in the park. **Barren River Lake State Resort Park** (800/325-0057) has RV hookups, and **Nolin River Lake State Park** (502/286-4240) allows primitive camping from April through December.

NIGHTLIFE

Ask at the **Shaker Museum** (502/542-4167) for a schedule of their occasional interpretive activities, including holiday dinners and musical performances. In Bowling Green, the **Capitol Arts Center** (416 E. Main St., 502/782-ARTS) offers not only theater performances but also nationally known music and performing arts groups; and the **Phoenix Theatre** (Morris Alley, 502/781-6233) puts on a fine yearly play series. **O'Pawley's Pub** (915 College St., 502/842-6349) is the venue for live music in Bowling Green.

For outstanding live theater, call the **Horse Cave Theater** (800/342-2177) in Horse Cave, which features both the works of new playwrights and classic dramatic productions. Families will enjoy the experience of outdoor theater at **Green River Amphitheatre** (Brownsville, 800/624-8687) north of Mammoth Cave National Park, where the *Floyd Collins Story* runs from June to September.

HELPFUL HINT

Listen to **WKYU** for excellent public radio (88.9) that serves all of western Kentucky and ties into the statewide public radio network. Some of the most exceptional programming on Kentucky Public Radio comes from the eastern Kentucky town of Whitesburg, home of Appalshop (see Chapter 7), a nonprofit entity that promotes Appalachian culture.

13

HENDERSON AND OWENSBORO

Henderson and Owensboro are located on the northern border of western Kentucky along the Ohio River. These two towns, approximately 30 miles apart, were and still are ports for the exportation of Kentucky goods to the outside world. Henderson, whose wealth came from tobacco, has a row of old brick mansions downtown on Main Street to testify to its former prominence. Henderson's downtown Central Park comes complete with a gazebo, conjuring visions of Sunday promenades at the turn of the century. In Owensboro, Kentucky's third largest city, one can still watch barges laden with coal moving down the swift river towards the Mississippi.

Henderson's most famous citizen was John James Audubon, who owned a gristmill near the river. In addition to that historic commemorative site, there is a museum complete with a collection of his works and personal artifacts, as well as a bird habitat in the state park that bears his name.

Both Henderson and Owensboro are cities on the move. They are well kept and are so proud of their history that they hold festivals celebrating their musical and culinary heritage: Henderson's W. C. Handy Blues and Barbecue Festival and Bluegrass in Central Park are annual events, as is the International Bar-B-Q Festival in Owensboro. ◪

HENDERSON

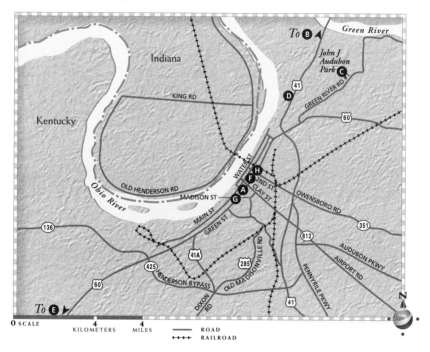

Sights

- **A** Central Park
- **B** Ellis Park
- **C** John J. Audubon Museum and Nature Center
- **D** River Park/Walk
- **E** Sloughs Wildlife Management Area

Food

- **F** Colby's
- **A** Mezzaluna Garden Cafe
- **G** The Mill

Food *(continued)*

- **A** Planters Coffeehouse
- **F** Wolf's Tavern

Lodging

- **C** Audubon State Park
- **H** L&N B&B

Camping

- **C** Audubon State Park
- **E** Sloughs Wildlife Management Area

Note: Items with the same letter are located in the same area.

A PERFECT DAY IN HENDERSON AND OWENSBORO

After touring the International Bluegrass Museum and watching the river traffic pass by from Owensboro's Riverpark Center, stop in at the museum of art to see the Kentucky craft collection. Then grab a sandwich at Moonlite BBQ on the way out of town, departing on Highway 60 for a drive through beautiful Kentucky farmlands to Henderson. Take a self-guided walking tour of historic downtown. Visit the Audubon gristmill and the fine museum at John James Audubon State Park before setting out on a sunset bird-watching walk in Sloughs Wildlife Management Area. Dine and spend the night in the historic downtown area, listening for the strains of W. C. Handy's music as you take an after-dinner walk in Central Park.

HENDERSON SIGHTSEEING HIGHLIGHTS

★★★ **John James Audubon Museum and Nature Center**—The museum is in a beautiful old stone building, with a new hands-on learning center that features a wild bird habitat. The museum includes works of art and artifacts related to one of the town's best-known citizens as well as interactive displays designed to bring visitors as close as possible to Audubon's inspiration.
   Details: John James Audubon State Park, Hwy. 41N. Museum: 502/827-1893; State Park: 502/826-2247. Daily 10–5. $4. (1 hour)

★★ **Sloughs Wildlife Management Area**—This 10,000-acre waterfowl refuge includes wetlands, fields, and woodlands. It is the largest Kentucky roosting ground for the great blue heron. Both hunting and camping are allowed in designated areas.
   Details: Hwy. 268, Henderson; 502/827-2673. Daily. Admission is free. (1 hour)

★ **Central Park**—This park, located downtown within a block of the Ohio River, was built in 1797. It is the oldest city park west of the Allegheny Mountains. *(15 minutes)*

★ **Ellis Park**—This thoroughbred racetrack is one of the largest in the United States. Live racing takes place here from late June to early September, but—as at Kentucky's other tracks—you can watch and bet on simulcast races taking place elsewhere in the state as well.

OWENSBORO

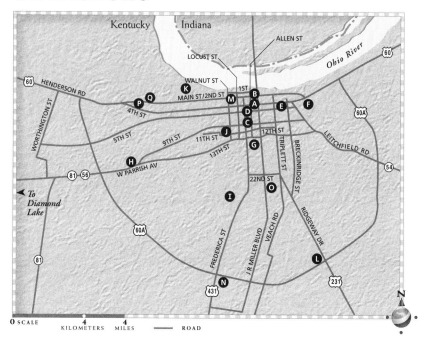

Sights

- **A** Andria's Homestyle Candies
- **B** International Bluegrass Music Association and Museum
- **A** Owensboro Area Museum of Science and History
- **C** Owensboro Museum of Fine Art
- **D** Raines Drive-Thru Shoe Hospital
- **B** Riverpark Center

Food

- **D** Barney's
- **D** Colby's Fine Food and Spirits
- **B** Famous Bistro
- **E** Gem Café

Food *(continued)*

- **F** George's BBQ
- **G** Jay Dee's
- **H** Moonlite Bar-B-Q Inn
- **I** Old Hickory BBQ Inn
- **J** Trotter's Restaurant and Lounge

Lodging

- **K** Cadillac Motel
- **L** Days Inn
- **M** Executive Inn Rivermont
- **N** Hampton Inn
- **O** Helton House
- **P** Holiday Inn
- **Q** Weatherberry

Note: Items with the same letter are located in the same area.

Details: Hwy. 41, Henderson; 800/333-8110. Post times Tue–Fri 3 p.m., weekends and holidays 1 p.m. $2 per person general admission.

Henderson Visitors Center—This center is located in a log cabin. Stop in and pick up a self-guided walking tour through Henderson's beautiful old downtown streets.
Details: 2961 Hwy. 41N, 502/826-3128. Mon–Fri 9–5. (15 minutes)

River Park/Walk—This one-mile jogging and exercise trail is located in Atkinson Park near the Ohio River boat ramps. The park has a playground and picnic area, as well as a swimming pool and golf course.
Details: Atkinson Park, 1801 N. Elm; 502/831-1200. (30 minutes)

OWENSBORO SIGHTSEEING HIGHLIGHTS

✩✩ **Owensboro Area Museum of Science and History**—Relocated in spring 1995 to a large former clothing store, this eclectic museum's exhibits include natural history, local and regional history, exploratory science displays for children, and a good gift and book shop.
Details: 220 Daviess St., 502/687-2732. Tue–Sat 10–5, Sun 1–4. Admission is free. (1 hour)

✩✩ **Owensboro Museum of Fine Art**—This museum is housed in a restored Carnegie Library building attached to the Civil War–era John Hampden Smith Mansion and bound together by a new addition on the back. It features changing exhibits and a Kentucky folk art collection. The permanent installation of stained-glass windows from a now-demolished Catholic church bears witness to the German Catholic heritage of this and nearby river cities, such as Louisville and Cincinnati.
Details: 901 Frederica St., 502/685-3181. Tue–Fri 10–4, weekends 1–4. $2 adults, $1 children under 12. (1 hour)

✩✩ **Riverpark Center**—This performance hall and culture center offers great views of the J. R. Miller Bridge and Yellow Bank Island. It features the Owensboro Symphony's season performances, touring dance and theater companies, local and regional theater, a "First Night" community New Year's Eve celebration, and a variety of programs for children. The **International Bluegrass Music Association and Museum** is also headquartered here. In addition to its September

International Bluegrass Music Association FanFest, which brought over 10,000 visitors annually until it was moved to Louisville last year, the IBMA sponsors a free bluegrass jam at the center on the first Thursday evening of every month from seven to ten.

Details: 101 Daviess St.; Riverpark Center Box Office: 502/687-ARTS. International Bluegrass Association Museum: 502/926-7891. Wed–Sun 1–4 and by appointment. $2 adults, $1 seniors and students, children under 6 free. (1 hour)

Andria's Homestyle Candies—This tiny candy factory, founded in 1910, specializes in Kentucky Bourbon Candy. The candy makes a great take-home gift and can be shipped anywhere in the United States.

Details: 217 Allen St., 502/684-3733. Mon–Fri 9–5:30, Sat 10–3:30. (30 minutes)

Raines Drive-Thru Shoe Hospital—This is surely a one-of-a-kind attraction. The hospital is still "operating," and you'll find its classic neon sign downtown on Frederica Street.

Details: 333 Frederica St., 502/683-9933. Mon–Fri 8–5:30. (15 minutes)

FITNESS AND RECREATION

Taking a walking tour of downtown Henderson (pick up a printed self-guided historical tour at the visitors center)—including **Central Park**, the **Audubon Gristmill** site, and the **River Park/Walk**—is a great way to stretch your legs. At the end of the walk you'll find **Atkinson Park**, which has a swimming pool and golf course. **John James Audubon State Park** has both tennis courts and a golf course, as well as hiking and fishing areas. **Sloughs Wildlife Management Area**, about six miles west of town, not only has abundant hiking and walking trails but allows hunting and fishing.

In Owensboro hike the nature trails or play a round of golf at **Ben Hawes State Park** (Hwy. 60, four miles west of town; 502/684-9808); walk the elevated wetlands trails at **Panther Creek Park** (Hwy. 81S to Wayne Bridge Rd. W.; 502/281-5346); or go out to **Yellow Creek Park** (Hwy. 144, off 60E; 502/281-5346), which has a climbable fire tower, to see more of the region's flat landscape. **Owensboro's Department of Parks and Recreation** (502/687-8700) operates 20 parks with tennis courts and other features, as well as the enclosed **Owensboro Ice Arena** (502/687-8720), open October through March. There's also a YMCA (900 Kentucky Pkwy., 502/926-9622).

FOOD

For morning coffee and a light lunch in downtown Henderson, try **Planters Coffeehouse** (130 N. Main, 502/830-0927). Both lunch and dinner are served at **Mezzaluna Garden Cafe** (104 N. Water St., 502/826-9401), a pleasant spot located on the river; and at **Wolf's Tavern** (31 N. Green; 502/826-5221), which serves hearty sandwiches and steaks in a historic building a couple of blocks from the center of town. Don't miss **The Mill** (528 S. Main, 502/826-8012). This one-time mill, now filled with antiques, serves lunch and dinner in a delightful atmosphere. **Colby's** (136 Second, 502/826-4235), an Owensboro's favorite, has just opened a second restaurant in a historic downtown location that was once an old hotel.

A favorite spot for breakfast in the downtown Owensboro area is the **Gem Cafe** (1006 E. Fourth, 502/926-9025), which also serves a good plate lunch. The **Famous Bistro** (102 W. Second, 502/686-8202), formerly the Famous Deli, has added pasta dishes to its bill of Greek-style sandwiches, and is now serving dinner. A few blocks away, still in downtown, you can't help but notice **Colby's Fine Food and Spirits** (202 W. Third; 502/685-4329) in a handsome old corner brick building. The interior is wood and tile, and the menu includes fresh fish and beef entrées. **Barney's** (420 Frederica, 502/683-2263) has a cozy ambiance and home-cooked food.

In the midtown area, **Jay Dee's** (1420 Breckenridge, 502/683-9419) serves home-cooked meals for breakfast and lunch, as well as homemade pie. **Trotter's Restaurant and Lounge** (1100 Walnut St., 502/685-2771), located in the renovated Cigar Factory complex, serves a variety of daily specials and salads and is a local favorite for lunch or a leisurely dinner.

Owensboro bills itself as the barbecue capital of the world and must have invented the designation "bar-b-q inn," where you can dine indoors in comfort with a range of side items to accompany what has traditionally been considered merely picnic fare. The **Moonlite Bar-B-Q Inn** (2840 W. Parrish, 502/684-8143) on the west side of town is a major tourist attraction because it is downright wonderful. This large restaurant, owned by three generations of the same family, has a cozy feel and is always packed with locals. It is famous for its spicy mutton barbecue, although beef, pork, and chicken are also available. Try the mutton—it tastes like lamb and is served sliced or chopped. A smaller restaurant, going back five generations and offering substantially the same menu, is **Old Hickory BBQ Inn** (Frederica St. and 25th, 502/926-9000). It's located in midtown on the exact site where Pappy Foreman, a local blacksmith, first started cooking mutton over the fire in 1918. **George's BBQ** (1346 E. Fourth St., 502/926-9276), on the east side, is another local favorite that also packs in quite a crowd for breakfast.

LODGING

In Henderson stay at the **L&N B&B** (327 N. Main St., 502/831-1100) in the historic district next to the old railroad trestle. **John James Audubon State Park** (Hwy. 41 N., 502/826-2247) has five one-bedroom cabins and one two-bedroom cabin available year round. Henderson has several national chain motels, all of which are located at the edge of town on Highway 41 North.

In Owensboro, the huge **Executive Inn Rivermont** (Second St., on Executive Blvd.; 502/926-8000 or 800/626-1936) backs up to the Ohio River for the best view in town. This is a convention center–type hotel with more than 500 rooms, indoor and outdoor pools, and reasonable rates, even if they are the highest in town. The Executive Inn has a large lounge featuring big-name country and rhythm and blues acts; check with the hotel management for schedules in advance and inquire about weekend packages including show tickets. The substantial weekend buffet breakfast here is also a good buy.

The **Cadillac Motel** (1311 W. Second St., 502/684-2343) has 40 rooms and is locally owned. Other hotels in the area include **Holiday Inn**, **Hampton Inn**, and **Days Inn**, all of which are located out near the Highway 60 bypass. Bed-and-breakfast choices in Owensboro include **Weatherberry** (2731 W. Second St., a bit west of town; 502/684-8760), an 1840s house with three guest rooms with private baths; and **Helton House** (102 E. 23rd St., 502/926-7117), which has three guest rooms, one of which is a two-room suite.

CAMPING

In Henderson, **John James Audubon State Park** (Hwy. 41N, 502/826-2247) has 70 sites with amenities but no RV hookups. Sites are offered on a first-come, first-served basis. **Sloughs Wildlife Management Area** (Hwy. 268, 502/826-3128) offers primitive camping only.

FESTIVALS

Both towns are big on festivals, and visitors might well want to plan accordingly. In these relatively small cities, the festival atmosphere will add just the right spice to your trip along Kentucky's northern riverfront.

Henderson has three cultural heritage events of interest to out-of-town visitors. The **W. C. Handy Blues and Barbecue Festival** (for information, visit the festival's Web site at www.handyblues.org; contact the Henderson Visitors Bureau, 502/826-3128; or call the Henderson Music Preservation Society, 502/827-1852), which brings in big-name entertainers to concert venues citywide, takes place annually in June. Handy, who married Hendersonian Elizabeth Price, lived here for 10 years in the 1850s while he traveled the minstrel show circuit. The festival, which lasts a whole week, takes place all over town, with music mostly at Audubon Mill Park and barbecue cooking contests mostly at Central (also known as Sunset) Park. The contests are officially "sanctioned" preliminaries to the Memphis-in-May barbecue contest, and include categories for chicken, mutton, pork shoulder, pork ribs, and whole hog. **Bluegrass in the Park**, held in Audubon Mill Park, takes place in August. Either the Henderson Area Arts Alliance (502/826-5916) or the visitors bureau (502/826-3128) can fill in this year's schedule for you. The **Big River Arts & Crafts Festival** (502/926-4433) which takes place in early October is one of the largest crafts fairs in Kentucky with more than 300 exhibitors and as many as 40,000 visitors. It is held in John James Audubon State Park.

In Owensboro, the Parks and Recreation Department (502/687-8700) sponsors the annual **Summer Fest**, which includes a big Fourth of July celebration at the riverfront. A group of civic boosters have started an annual **First Night (New Year's Eve) Festival** with the assistance of the Owensboro Tourist Commission (800/489-1131). Best known of all, however, is Owensboro's **International Bar-B-Q Festival** (502/926-6938), which happens in mid-May at the riverfront and includes competitive teams with names like Blessed Mother, Our Lady of Lourdes, St. Pius X, Precious Blood, and the Telephone Workers. What a photo op! You can get in the serving line and eat your fill for less than $10. The **International Bluegrass Music Association FanFest** (888/GET-IBMA) has moved its biggest event of the year to Louisville, but Owensboro is holding its own **Bluegrass Blast** in September at English Park, overlooking the Ohio River. It should come as no big surprise that the locals turn out in droves for the sounds of fast-paced string bands and plaintive vocalizing once you realize that Bill Monroe, the father of it all, was born just 35 miles down the road in the tiny town of Rosine, Kentucky.

NIGHTLIFE

When there's no live blues or bluegrass festival action in town, Henderson culture aficionados rely on the **Henderson Fine Arts Center** (2660 S. Green, 502/850-5324), located on the campus of Henderson Community College, for a lively schedule of music, dance, and theater events.

The **Riverpark Center for the Arts** is the place to hear the Owensboro Symphony Orchestra, except when they perform outside on special occasions like the Fourth of July riverfront spectacular. The center also features touring musical theater, popular music concerts, and a variety of other programming. The **Executive Inn Rivermont** (800/626-1936) books a regular schedule of music. The focus is on country and other big-name acts, but occasionally local swing, rock, or blues bands are invited to fill in.

14

WESTERN WATERLANDS

The far western portions of both Kentucky and Tennessee offer nature lovers the unforgettable experience of a vast wetlands ecosystem. The region allows historians and folk-culture aficionados to look at both past and present Mississippi river life. Reelfoot Lake, one of the largest lakes in the country at 15,000 acres, is located near the shared border of Kentucky and Tennessee, about 10 miles from the Mississippi River. The lake, which was formed by a cataclysmic earthquake in the winter of 1811 to 1812, is now a Tennessee state park offering facilities for fishing in spring, summer, and fall, and for eagle watching in the winter. For the curious visitor, local experts and interpretive museum displays in the nearby towns of Tiptonville and Samburg can provide a wealth of information about duck calling, stump-jumper boats, and the eventful history of Reelfoot Lake, dominion over which has been the subject of heated dispute since early in its history.

Journeying north along the Mississippi River, then inland 25 miles to historic Paducah—a town that is proudly restoring its heritage as a center of commerce at the confluence of the Tennessee and Ohio Rivers—takes one past the strategically critical Columbus-Belmont Civil War battle site, through fertile flat fields and Kentucky state wildlife preservation areas, and to an important Mississippian Indian ceremonial and trade center at Wickliffe Mounds. ◣

WESTERN WATERLANDS

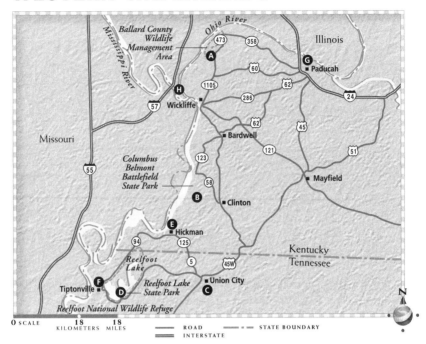

Sights
- **A** Ballard Public Wildlife Area
- **B** Columbus-Belmont State Park
- **C** Dixie Gun Works
- **D** Ellington Interpretive Museum
- **D** Reelfoot Lake
- **D** Reelfoot Lake State Park
- **E** Wickliffe Mounds

Food
- **D** Airpark Inn
- **F** Bluebank Resort
- **D** Boyette's Dining Room
- **G** Catfish House
- **H** Darrell Shemwell's BBQ
- **G** Jeremiah's

Food (continued)
- **G** Miss Rose Cafe
- **G** Peppermills Coffee Bar

Lodging
- **D** Airpark Inn
- **F** Bluebank Resort
- **F** Boyette's Resort
- **D** Spillway Motel
- **E** Wickcliffe Motel

Camping
- **B** Columbus-Belmont State Park
- **D** Reelfoot Airpark
- **D** Reelfoot Southend

Note: Items with the same letter are located in the same town or area.

A PERFECT DAY IN THE WESTERN WATERLANDS

Arrive at Reelfoot Lake State Park the night before in order to be in place for a 10 a.m. eagle-watching tour in winter or a 9 a.m. scenic boat cruise on the lake in summer. After experiencing the lake first-hand, learn more about its early history at the Ellington Museum at the park. For more local color, try the catfish at Boyette's Dining Room across the road. Drive north along Kentucky's "great river road" scenic highway for 40 miles paralleling the Mississippi River, stopping to view the bluffs at the Columbus-Belmont Civil War site and the excavated Mississippian Indian mounds at Wickliffe before arriving in Paducah's historic riverfront "upper town." End the day in Paducah, letting a carriage ride take you back into its glory days as an important nineteenth-century river and railroad town. Finally, wind down to a live blues performance at one of several downtown restaurants then settle in for the evening in the historic quarters of your choice.

REELFOOT LAKE AREA HISTORY

Obion County, where both the Obion (an Indian word meaning prongs or forks) River and Reelfoot Lake are located, was permanently settled only after the land was "purchased" from the Indians in the Jackson Purchase of 1818. Davy Crockett, while living in neighboring Gibson County, is said to have achieved his record hunt of 103 bears in Obion County. He represented the district in the U.S. Congress from 1827 to 1831 and from 1833 to 1835.

SIGHTSEEING HIGHLIGHTS

★★★ **Market House**—The center of commerce in Paducah's "upper town" was the Market House, an open-sided farmer's market originally built of logs in 1836. The current building, a brick classical revival–style structure, was erected in 1905. It is now home to the **Market House Museum**, the contemporary Yeiser Art Center, and the **Market House Theatre**. The museum, which concentrates on local history, includes the reconstructed 1877 interior of List Drugs, which once stood three blocks away. Special tribute is paid to Paducah's two favorite sons, Alben W. Barkley, vice president under Harry S. Truman; and humorist Irvin S. Cobb, who lived from 1876 to 1944. The Market House Theatre holds 250 for a six-show annual series by one of

Kentucky's fine regional theater groups. Call for a schedule of performances. The **Yeiser Arts Center**, founded in 1957, is both an art museum housing a nineteenth- and twentieth-century collection, and an arts center featuring exhibits of regional, national, and international contemporary artists.

Details: Museum: 200 Broadway, 502/443-7759. Mar–Dec Tue–Sat noon–4, Sun 1–4. $1.50 adults, 50¢ ages 6–17. Theater: 141 Kentucky Ave., 502/444-6828 or 888/MHT-PLAY. Box office open 10–5 Tue–Fri; plays scheduled Thu–Sat evenings, Sun matinees. $7–$9. Yeiser Arts Center: 200 Broadway, 502/442-2453. Feb–Dec Tue–Sat 10–4, Sun 1–4. $1 adults, children under 12 free. (3 hours)

✦✦✦ Museum of the American Quilter's Society

—Built in 1991, this amazing museum is home to a permanent collection of more than 200 quilts and also mounts temporary exhibits of regional quilts and related arts. The spacious galleries were specifically designed to display and light quilts of all periods and styles. A permanent collection of historical quilts is shown on a regular basis, as well as a collection of master quilts from the National Quilting Society and the Purchase Award winners from the 15-year-old AQS competition. A permanent display of stained glass based on contemporary quilt design adorns the front spaces of the museum, which hosts the ever-growing American Quilter's Society Quilt Show and Contest in late April. Workshops for quilters as well as community outreach activities for school children in surrounding states are held throughout the year. The museum has a well-stocked bookstore and a small gift shop of quilt-related items.

Details: 215 Jefferson St., 502/442-8856. Tue–Sat 10–5; Apr–Oct also open Sun–Mon 1–5. $5 adults, $3 students. (2 hours)

✦✦✦ Paducah

—This city was founded by explorer William Clark in 1827. As the story is told, Clark "purchased" older brother George Rogers Clark's 37,000-acre Revolutionary War land grant for $5 from his brother's estate, after returning from his famous expedition with Meriwether Lewis. Prior to Clark's arrival, the settlement was known as Pekin. Clark named his new town in honor of Chief Paduke, a leader of the Chickasaw. (A 1909 sculpture of Chief Paduke by classicist Lorado Taft can be seen at 19th and Jefferson Streets.) The younger Clark laid out a town 12 blocks square; he gave one block to the city which soon accommodated a courthouse, a jail, and a market house. The revitalized downtown historic district begins at the Market House

Square. Detailed historic self-guided walking tour brochures of both the original "upper town" and the later Victorian residential area known as "lower town" are available from the Paducah Convention and Visitors Bureau. Across the street from the visitors bureau is a massive concrete flood wall, a reminder of the constant threat of rising waters from the town's life force, the Ohio River. Paducah's civic spirit is expressed in visual storytelling, with murals depicting city history to be found on the flood wall interior and on several buildings along Broadway.

Details: Paducah Convention and Visitors Bureau, 128 Broadway; 502/443-8783 or 800/PADUCAH. Mon–Sat 9–5. (1½ hours)

✯✯✯ **Reelfoot Lake**—Reelfoot is rumored in local legend to have gotten its name from Chickasaw chieftain Reelfoot, who kidnapped a Choctaw maiden and brought her back to his Chickasaw home territory near the Mississippi. The story goes that the earth swallowed Reelfoot and his warriors, and water covered their burial ground. (The Indian lore obviously staked its claim long before the legend of Paul Bunyan attempted to explain the lake as one of Babe's footprints.)

© Mary Entrekin

Reelfoot Lake

Reelfoot Lake State Park is an American bald eagle nesting site during the winter months. Rangers offer guided eagle-watching tours December through mid-March at 10 a.m. daily, and guided cruises on the lake during summer months. The visitors center at Reelfoot includes the **Ellington Interpretive Museum**, which displays information and artifacts of the natural history and culture of the area and includes an earthquake simulator. Reelfoot Park is the only Tennessee state park with a landing strip. Across the street from the park is Dale Calhoun's Boat House, a trove of local fishing information. The Park has both the Spillway Lakeside Motel and the Airpark Lodge and Restaurant, as well as camping at Airpark and Southend campgrounds.

Details: Tiptonville (between Hwys. 22 and 78); 901/253-7756. Summer 8 a.m.–10 p.m., until dusk in winter. Admission is free. For guided-tour reservations call the visitors center, 901/253-9652. Eagle-watching tour $3, daily lake cruises $5–$7. (3 hours minimum)

✿✿ **Columbus-Belmont State Park**—This park commemorates the Civil War battles for the western frontier that took place in late 1861 and early 1862, when the Confederates had nearly 19,000 troops stationed on both sides of the river. Dubbed the "Gibraltar of the West" by the confident rebels, this location on the Mississippi River afforded them the opportunity to try and block the strategic waterway by using a six-ton anchor and heavy metal chain stretched across the river on pontoons. The Federal soldiers, led by General Ulysses S. Grant in his first foray as commander, burned the Belmont encampment and managed to overtake Columbus. The anchor and part of the chain are now on view at the Columbus-side park. A museum, containing both Indian and Civil War artifacts, is located in the park. Picnic areas and a hiking trail located on the bluffs overlook the river and earthen bunkers built by the Confederates.

Details: Hwy. 80, Columbus; 502/677-2327. May–Sept daily 9–5, Apr and Oct weekends only. Admission to park is free, museum 50¢. (30 minutes)

✿✿ **Wickliffe Mounds**—Located at the joining of the Ohio and Mississippi Rivers, Wickliffe Mounds was a ceremonial and trade site for the Mississippian Indians, who inhabited this area from around a.d. 800 to 1350. The mounds—located on a rise safe from flood waters, and surrounded by fertile river-bottom land—have been excavated, and several of them are covered by wooden buildings in which visitors may walk. Displays of artifacts and explanations of lifestyles and customs surround the earthen archaeological site. While the site itself is essentially masked from view, it is interesting as a study in the methods of archaeology and for the fascinating collection of finds, including potsherds, animal effigies, spear points and tips, and a number of flat "chuckey" disks for playing a ceremonial game thought to settle disputes between neighboring tribes. Murray State University now operates an interpretive site here, which holds workshops on such topics as native American herbal medicine, basketry, flintware, and pottery, as well as the basics of archaeology.

Details: 94 Green St. (Hwy. 60/62), Wickliffe; 502/335-3681. Mar–Nov daily 9–4:30. $3.50 adults, $2.50 ages 6–11, $3.25 seniors. The site is wheelchair accessible. (1½ hours)

✯ **Center for Maritime Education at Paducah**—This unique facility, run by the Seamen's Church Institute (headquartered in New York City), is used to train riverboat pilots and others who navigate inland waterways. The architecture of the building is itself boat-like—sleek, with white railings, and the flood stages of the Ohio River marked on it with metal plaques. Seeing the water levels so displayed is a potent reminder of the importance of the instruction that goes on in the four interactive simulated pilothouses above. Visitors can observe from a deck overlooking the classrooms.

Details: 129 South Water St., 502/575-1005. Mon–Fri 8–3. Admission is free, but only by advance reservation. (1 hour)

✯ **Paducah River Heritage Museum**—The four rivers (Mississippi, Ohio, Tennessee, Cumberland) region, as it is called, begs for a celebration of its natural and cultural history, as well as the industry and technology that have made it an important nexus of transportation between South and North. Centered in Paducah's oldest preserved structure, the Federal Bank, the museum features interactive media exhibits and historical memorabilia.

Details: 117 South Water St., 502/575-9958. Call for hours and admission costs. (1½ hours)

✯ **Union City**—Obion county's largest town, Union City got its name from the crossing of the Mobile & Ohio and the Nashville & Northwestern railroads in 1854. The area of small farms around Union City is among the highest producing in the state for corn, wheat, and apples. On Saturday mornings you can still go to the Farmer's Market when it opens at seven. The annual Fall Festival, sponsored by the Chamber of Commerce (901/885-0211) in September, celebrates the harvest with a variety of events for the whole community, including white bean and barbecue cook-offs; a "fishing rodeo;" and the Round House reunion, which re-creates the Bluebank Round House music-making of the 1950s and 1960s at Reelfoot Lake.

Details: Union City Chamber of Commerce: 901/885-0211

Ballard Public Wildlife Area—Located in the curve of the Mississippi River northwest of Paducah near the town of Monkey's Eyebrow, Ballard Public Wildlife Area has an observation tower for watching migrating and native birds and animals. A word of warning: Supervised waterfowl hunting is allowed at many of these Kentucky wildlife areas. The Kentucky Department of Fish and Wildlife Resources sells a wildlife viewing guide for $10.

Details: Kentucky Department of Fish and Wildlife Resources: Hwy. 358, 502/564-4336. (2 hours)

Dixie Gun Works—The Dixie Gun Works began in 1954 as a supplier of antique muzzle-loading guns and parts. It now features an antique car museum, a display of small antique tools, and an 1850 log gun shop.

Details: Hwy. 51, Union City; 901/885-0211. Mon–Fri 8–5, Sat 8–noon. Admission is free. (30 minutes)

Paducah Steamboat Dock at Shultz Waterfront Park—The dock is now port for three Mississippi River luxury steamers—the *Mississippi Queen*, the *Delta Queen*, and the *American Queen*—as well as the *Niagara Prince* cruise ship and the *RiverBarge Explorer*, all of which ply different routes up and down the Mississippi, Ohio, Tennessee, and Cumberland Rivers. Believe it or not, there is also a Grand Traverse excursion that carries RVs on a barge.

Details: Paducah Convention and Visitors Bureau: 900/PADUCAH. (15 minutes)

Players Bluegrass Downs—Players functions as a thoroughbred racing track in October and November, and as a simulcast, intertrack betting facility the rest of the year for both Kentucky and nationwide races. During the weeks of the live race meets at Players, visitors can stop by and watch morning workouts from eight to ten every day but Monday.

Details: 32nd and Park Ave., Paducah; 502/444-7117 or 800/ 755-1244. Admission to practice track is free. (2 hours)

FITNESS AND RECREATION

Boating, fishing, hiking, and swimming are all available at **Reelfoot Lake State Park**, as are hiking trails and paths at **Columbus-Belmont State Park** and **Kentucky Public Wildlife Areas**. Running suggests itself as a popular form of recreation in and around this flat country-side. From Reelfoot Lake south, you'll find the 177-mile **Mississippi River Bike Trail**, a relatively flat ride which has been mapped and marked with green and white MRT signs. For a brochure, write to: MRT, 7777 Walnut Grove Road, Box 27, Memphis, Tennessee 38120 (901/753-1400). Bicycling information for the Paducah area can be obtained by writing to: Bike World, 848 Joe Clifton Drive, Paducah, Kentucky 42001 (502/442-0751). Paducah's **Paxton Park Golf Course** (502/444-9514) is an 18-hole public course. **Noble Park** (2915 Park Ave., Paducah; 502/444-8539) has tennis courts and a public pool open from mid-June through August. Located 21 miles from Paducah are the magnificent forests, prairies, and lakes of the Tennessee Valley Authority's 170,000-acre **Land Between the Lakes National Recreation Area** (502/924-2000 or 800/LBL-7077; internet: www.lbl.org). Boating, hiking, biking, and more are available in this non-commercial sanctuary, which has visitor facilities but no overnight accommodations other than campgrounds.

FOOD

Reelfoot Lake State Park **Airpark Inn** (Hwy. 21, Tiptonville; 901/253-7756) provides breakfast, lunch, and dinner year round. As with all food at state park lodges in Tennessee, it's moderately priced local cuisine and is often quite good. Across the road from the park is **Boyette's Dining Room** (Hwy. 21, Tiptonville; 901/253-7307), a locally popular restaurant that has been serving all-you-can-eat catfish dinners with white beans, slaw, and onion rings since 1921. They also have sandwiches, crappie (a popular local lake fish), and fried chicken. The walls are lined with old photographs and the place fairly creaks with memories; it's an institution not to be missed. Nearby is the very nice **Bluebank Resort** (Hwy. 21, Tiptonville; 901/253-8976), which serves a scrumptious "fisherman's breakfast" of country ham, eggs, apples, potatoes, grits, and biscuits.

PADUCAH

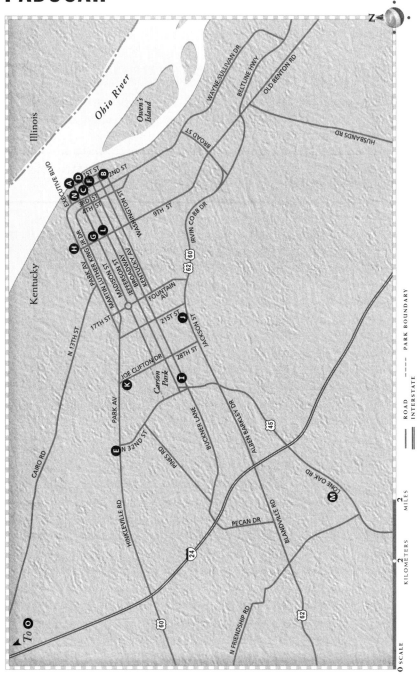

N

ROAD
INTERSTATE
PARK BOUNDARY

0 SCALE
KILOMETERS
MILES

Sights

Ⓐ Center for Maritime Education

Ⓑ Market House Museum

Ⓑ Market House Theater

Ⓒ Museum of the American Quilter's Society

Ⓐ Paducah River Heritage Museum

Ⓓ Paducah Steamboat Dock at Shultz Waterfront Park

Ⓔ Players Bluegrass Downs

Ⓑ Yeiser Arts Center

Food

Ⓕ C. C. Cohen

Ⓕ Cynthia's

Ⓖ Ninth Street House

Food (continued)

Ⓗ Oldtown Restaurant and Bar

Ⓘ Prices Bar-B-Q

Ⓙ Skinhead's

Ⓚ Starnes

Lodging

Ⓚ 1857 B&B

Ⓛ 1868 B&B

Ⓜ Denton's

Ⓝ Executive Inn Riverfront

Ⓛ Fisher Mansion

Ⓟ Paducah Harbor Plaza

Camping

Ⓞ Land Between the Lakes

Note: Items with the same letter are located in the same area.

Paducah offers a number of fine restaurants, most of which are in historic buildings. In the "lower town" area, the **Oldtown Restaurant and Bar** (701 Park Ave., 502/442-9616) used to be a stagecoach stop and tavern; and **Ninth Street House**, located in a 1886 Victorian (323 N. Ninth St., 502/442-9019), has a trained chef who prepares "new American cuisine" specialties in a romantic restaurant that has one of the city's longest-standing reputations for fine food. In the "upper town" (downtown), **C. C. Cohen** (101–105 Market House Square, 502/442-6391) is in an old store at Second and Market Streets. The atmosphere is fern-bar lively and the menu—heavy on oysters, shrimp, and snapper—has touches of New Orleans. **Cynthia's Ristorante** (127 Market Square, 502/443-3319) is chef-owned and boasts a menu that changes weekly. Located on two floors of what was a downtown store, Cynthia's decor features a nice melding of antique and contemporary design, with an open kitchen on the second floor. Fresh seafood, unusual gourmet treatments, and fine service make this one of Paducah's top restaurants. Several doors down is the **Moss Rose Cafe** (119 Market House Square, 502/575-4828), an oyster bar and grill that has live blues nightly. Across the square is Max's, with a wood-fired pizza oven whose fragrance wafts over the entire street, and a delightful outdoor courtyard for enjoying drinks and appetizers. Less upscale choices downtown include the **Catfish House** (303 Broadway, 502/441-7428), a brightly lit former department store turned restaurant where fried catfish comes with white beans, coleslaw, and hush puppies, and there is homemade pie for dessert. This place packs them in for lunch, which starts at 10:30 a.m.; and dinner, which ends whenever the last customer is finished. A block closer to the river is **Jeremiah's** (225 Broadway, 502/443-3991), a cozy brew pub and restaurant. This popular spot serves four handcrafted beers, steamed mussels, grilled seafood and steaks, and . . . grilled frogs' legs.

Don't miss **Skinhead's** (1020 S. 21st St., 502/442-6471) if you're on the outskirts of town. This local institution specializes in great breakfasts at low prices. Also on the edge of town is **Peppermills Coffee Bar** (2817 Lone Oak Rd., 502/534-0546), which serves delicious coffee drinks and low-fat muffins.

Barbecue, western Kentucky–style barbecue, is close kin to northwest Tennessee's hot pepper, vinegar, and tomato-sauced and hickory-smoked, chopped pork shoulder. **Prices Bar-B-Q** (3001 Broadway, 502/444-9256) has been in business for 50 years; and **Starnes** (1008 Joe Clifton Dr., 502/444-9555) also cooks beef and mutton and bottles its sauce for sale.

Across the Mississippi River from Wickliffe, in Cairo, Illinois, is **Darrell Shemwell's BBQ** (1102 Washington Ave., 618/734-0165) a tiny restaurant that has been operating in the same location since 1946. Sandwiches of sliced pork, beef, or turkey are served on white toast. The meat is smoky, moist, and delicious with a secret vinegar/mustard sauce. Shemwell's serves breakfast as well.

LODGING

Reelfoot Lake State Park (Hwy. 21, Tiptonville; 901/253-7756 or 800/250-8617) has modern facilities and moderate rates at the **Airpark Inn** and the **Spillway Motel**. Many rooms have kitchenettes and can be rented by the week. Across the road from the park, **Boyette's**

Resort (Hwy. 21, Tiptonville; 901/253-6523) has cabins for rent. **Bluebank Resort** (Hwy. 21, 901/253-8976) has a motel with 31 units as well as a new marina facility (901/538-2156) with cabins and a lodge looking out over the lake.

Between Reelfoot and Paducah you'll find the modest 19-unit **Wickliffe Motel** (Hwy. 60, Wickliffe; 502/335-3121), whose dining room advertises "quails."

Paducah is the place to stay, with a huge resort-type hotel planted right on the riverbank and a number of bed-and-breakfasts housed in historic structures. The **Executive Inn Riverfront** (One Executive Blvd., 502/443-8000 or 800/866-3636) is located outside the flood wall, with office and guest rooms beginning on the second level. The architecture may be plain, but the prices are moderate and the staff is accommodating. Ask for a room with a balcony overlooking the river and don't be surprised to hear tugboat blasts and bargemen's voices early in the morning. In "upper town," the **1857 B&B** (127 Market House Square, 502/444-3960 or 800/264-5607) is a three-story brick building with three bedrooms sharing one bath on one floor, and a suite with a private bath on the second floor. Also in the neighborhood is the five-story turn-of-the-century **Paducah Harbor Plaza** (201 Broadway, 502/442-2968 or 800/719-7799). The Plaza was at one time known as the Hotel Belvedere, which, in its day, welcomed distinguished steamboat and railroad travelers for overnight stays on the main square of downtown. Guests now breakfast in the old hotel's second-floor dining room. At present this bed-and-breakfast has four guest rooms with shared baths. About 15 blocks away in "lower town" are the **1868 B&B** (914 Jefferson St., 502/444-6801), a charming, high-gabled wooden bungalow with three guest rooms; and, just across the street, the **Fisher Mansion** (901 Jefferson, 502/443-0716), a beautifully renovated Victorian house. Each of the four guest rooms has a private bath, and the former ballroom on the top floor has been converted into a fully private honeymoon suite. East of town near I-24 is **Denton's** (2550 Lone Oak Rd., 502/554-1626 or 800/788-1626), a clean, locally owned, 34-room motel with suites with kitchenettes.

CAMPING

Reelfoot Lake State Park (Hwy. 21, Tiptonville; 901/253-7756 or 800/250-8617) has campgrounds at two different locations: the **Airpark**, which is open year-round; and the **Southend**, which is closed December through March. As with all Tennessee state parks, no reservations are taken for campgrounds and prices are very reasonable. **Columbus-Belmont State Park** (Hwy. 80, Columbus; 502/677-2327), located 36 miles south of Paducah, has both hookups and primitive camping. It is open April through October. **Land Between the Lakes** (21 miles east of Paducah on I-24, 502/924-2000 or 800/LBL-7077) has six primitive camping areas open year round, and three campgrounds with hookups open March through November. This national recreation area is operated by the Tennessee Valley and does take reservations.

NIGHTLIFE

Paducah has a variety of evening offerings. **Annie's Horse-Drawn Carriages** (Second and Broadway, 618/524-3272) will take you out into the historic city for a nominal fee. If you are a contemporary country music or rhythm and blues fan, check with the **Executive Inn Rivermont** (800/866-3636) to see who's playing while you are in town. Tickets for Rivermont shows range from $12 to $48 for big-name acts like Percy Sledge and Willie Nelson. The **Market House Theatre** (888/MHT-PLAY) offers six contemporary plays per year at $7 to $9 a seat; **Working Artists** (428–430 Broadway, 502/441-7844) is a coffeehouse with live music, poetry, and performances on Friday and Saturday evenings; and there's free blues after dinner at many of the downtown restaurants, including **C. C. Cohen** and **Moss Rose Cafe**.

15
MEMPHIS

High on the bluffs overlooking the Mississippi River stands the city of Memphis. Once a mid-fifteenth-century Mississippian Indian site known as Chucalissa, it is now a town of about 1 million inhabitants. Memphis calls itself the home of the blues and the birthplace of rock 'n' roll. The city can back both claims—W. C. Handy wrote "Memphis Blues" here in 1909 as a campaign song for E. H. "Boss" Crump, and Sun Recording Studios nurtured the mid-1950s boogie-woogie blues style that Elvis Presley promoted with "Hound Dog" and "Don't Be Cruel" into a worldwide music mania.

Once a gathering place for former slaves after the Civil War, Memphis seems destined to have played a major part in the twentieth-century drama of American race relations. Today the Lorraine Motel, where Martin Luther King was shot in 1968, has been preserved as part of the National Civil Rights Museum, located within a few blocks of W. C. Handy's famous Beale Street neighborhood. Several blocks away, Front Street faces the river and is still "Cotton Row," a site of active commerce as bales of cotton arrive from points south in late summer, just as they have for generations. The famous downtown Peabody Hotel, where visitors can marvel at the opulence that cotton money built, has been restored to its former splendor, as has the Orpheum Theater, where one can hear Opera Memphis just a stone's throw from the all-night music on restored Beale Street. ◪

MEMPHIS

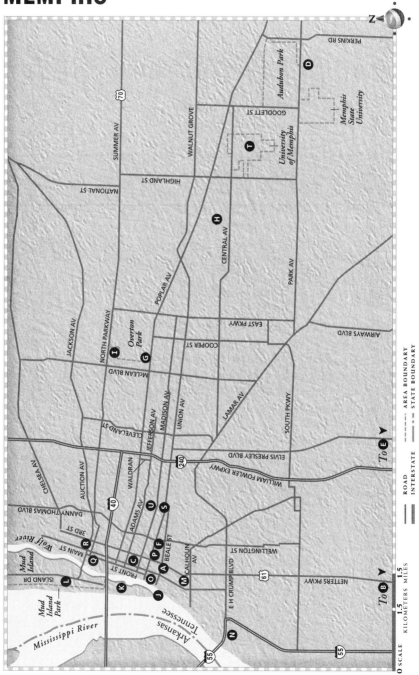

Sights

- Ⓐ Beale Street
- Ⓑ Chucalissa
- Ⓒ Cotton Row and Main Street Trolley
- Ⓓ Dixon Gallery and Gardens
- Ⓔ Graceland
- Ⓕ Hunt-Phelan House
- Ⓖ Memphis Brooks Museum of Art
- Ⓗ Memphis Pink Palace Museum and Planetarium
- Ⓘ Memphis Zoo
- Ⓙ Mississippi Riverfront

- Ⓚ Mississippi River Museum
- Ⓛ Mud Island Museum Park
- Ⓜ National Civil Rights Museum
- Ⓝ National Ornamental Metal Museum
- Ⓞ Orpheum Theater
- Ⓟ Peabody Hotel
- Ⓠ The Pyramid
- Ⓡ Slavehaven, the Burkle Estate
- Ⓢ Sun Studio
- Ⓣ University of Memphis Art Museum
- Ⓤ Victorian Village

A PERFECT DAY IN MEMPHIS

Overton Park is a great place for an early morning walk or jog, especially before the heat of a summer's day arrives. After coffee and conversation (Memphians are friendly and helpful folks) at Otherlands Coffee Bar on Cooper, get over to Sun Studios for a tour, stopping in afterward around the corner at Marshall Arts (artist's studio cooperative) Gallery for the latest in cutting-edge visual art. Visit the back-to-back Memphis Brooks Museum of Art and Memphis College of Art and have lunch at the Brooks' Brushmark Restaurant whose patio seating overlooks Overton Park. Head downtown for a tour of the National Civil Rights Museum then continue south down historic Main Street to the National Ornamental Metals Museum. Located on a high bluff, the west-facing gardens offer a nice sunset view overlooking the Mississippi. Stop for drinks in the cocktail lounge of the Peabody Hotel for great people-watching and a glimpse of the famous ducks that live on the roof. Dine across the street at Automatic Slim's Tonga Club, and ask at the bar where to go for Memphis nightlife.

MORE MEMPHIS HISTORY

Before the Europeans arrived in the person of Hernando DeSoto in 1541, Mississippian-period Indians dwelt near the modern city on the shores of the powerful wide brown river, called by the Chickasaw, "Father of the Waters." The restored fifteenth-century village of Chucalissa, a Choctaw word meaning "abandoned house," is located just south of the city and can be visited today. The French founded Fort Assumption in 1739 on the high bluffs overlooking the river in the same location as the current city. Modern Memphis was founded by Andrew Jackson's close friend Judge John Overton of Nashville in 1819, after the Chickasaw Indian treaty of 1818 ceded control of West Tennessee to the United States. Overton named it for the ancient Egyptian city whose name meant "place of good abode." River trade made Memphis prosperous, and the city's capture was a boon to the Federal forces in 1862.

SIGHTSEEING OVERVIEW

If you want to get a feel for the breadth of Memphis, take Poplar Avenue—one of the city's main east-west arteries—into town from the I-240 loop. Poplar, which dead-ends at the river, runs from suburban neighborhoods and prosperous shopping centers to less-affluent commercial areas, past mid-town's Overton Park and its historic neighborhoods, through the centralized medical center area, and right into the River City.

SIGHTSEEING HIGHLIGHTS

★★★ **Beale Street**—Ike Turner once said that you could find "anything you were looking for" on Beale Street. This famous street is close to downtown Memphis and within walking distance of the Peabody Hotel. There are lots of touristy music clubs and restaurants on Beale now, including one owned by the reigning godfather of the blues, B.B. King. Friday night is "wristband night," when the street is closed and visitors pay a $10 flat fee for admission to all clubs. If your timing is right, you might catch a performance at the New Daisy Theater (901/525-8979) to get a sense of the old ambiance of Beale. W. C. Handy's Home has been made into a museum. The Center for Southern Folklore, a nonprofit institution dedicated to the preservation of Southern folk culture and expression, has a storefront location where you can watch *If Beale Street Could Talk*, a multimedia presentation about historic Beale Street; and pick up a printed walking tour. Don't miss A. Schwab's Dry Goods (163 Beale), in business since 1876, for a souvenir stop (closed Sundays).

Details: Center for Southern Folklore: 209 Beale St., 901/525-3655. Mon–Thu 10 a.m.–11 p.m., Fri–Sat 10 a.m.–2 a.m., Sun 11–11. $5 donation requested. W.C. Handy Home: 352 Fourth, 901/522-1556. Mon–Sat 10–5, Sun 1–5. $2 adults, $1 students. (1–2 hours)

★★★ **Chucalissa**—A restored fifteenth-century Choctaw Indian village, this site includes mounds and a plaza, as well as exhibits on southeastern Indians. It is managed by the Department of Anthropology at the University of Memphis, and includes a working excavation display.

Details: 1987 Indian Village Dr. (Third St. south to Winchester Rd., right on Mitchell), Memphis; 901/785-3160. Tue–Sat 9–4:30. $3 adults, $2 students. (1 hour)

★★★ **Graceland**—Walking through the faded decor of Elvis's "mansion" with a freshly combed young tour guide, spending time in the gaudy "trophy room" of Elvis excess, standing at the memorial garden and reading the sentiments on floral arrangements that arrive in quantity on a daily basis, and finally being deposited at the huge commercial operation across the street, is enough to make one weep for the failure of innocence and the corruption of the American Dream. The 20-minute film that begins your visit is quite good. Using lots of old footage, it chronicles the incredible appeal of the young Elvis. Entrance to the visitors center and gift shop is free. There are separate charges for all other parts of the complex, including the house, airplane, automobile, and museums. Tours are offered in seven languages, and Elvis now "lives" online at www.elvispresley.com.

Details: 3734 Elvis Presley Blvd. (Hwy. 51 south), Memphis; 901/332-3322 or 800/238-2000. Daily 9–5. Mansion only: $10 adults, $5 ages 7–12, $9 seniors. All-inclusive: $18.50 adults, $11 ages 7–12, $16.65 seniors. Parking is $2. (1½ –3 hours)

★★★ **Memphis Brooks Museum of Art**—Housed here are collections ranging from classical to contemporary art and a portion of the Kress collection of Italian Renaissance masterpieces. The museum's fascinating new postmodern facade, which joins a classical revival building and a 1960s addition, was designed by the architecture firm Skidmore, Owings, and Merrill. The museum mounts important temporary exhibitions in their extensive changing galleries, and there is a continuous schedule of films, lectures, and family workshops throughout the year. The Brushmark Restaurant presents a seasonal menu daily for lunch and on some Thursday evenings when the museum stays open until eight.

Details: Overton Park, Memphis; 901/722-3500. Tue–Fri 9–4, Sat 9–5, Sun 11:30–5. Admission is free, except for special exhibits. (1½ hours)

✰✰✰ **National Civil Rights Museum**—This unusual building is located on the site of the Lorraine Motel, where Martin Luther King Jr. was assassinated in 1968. The museum features artifacts and re-creations of notable Civil Rights events such as lunch-counter sit-ins and bus boycotts. The full-scale interactive exhibits are designed to make visitors feel as if they are experiencing these dramatic moments for themselves. The museum also sponsors educational programs.

Details: 450 Mulberry St., Memphis; 901/521-9699. Mon, Wed, Fri, Sat 9–5; Thu 9–8, Sun 1–5; extended hours in summer. $6 adults, $5 students, $4 ages 4–17. (1½ hours)

✰✰ **Memphis Pink Palace Museum and Planetarium**—A hybrid history and natural history museum, the Pink Palace is located in a palatial pinkish stone home that once belonged to the owner of Piggly Wiggly grocery stores. The museum is now home to an eclectic range of permanent and changing exhibits and includes the Sharpe Planetarium and IMAX theater.

Details: 3050 Central, Memphis; 901/320-6320. Mon–Wed 9–4, Thu 9–8, Fri–Sat 9–9, Sun noon–5; extended hours in summer. Museum or Imax theater only: $6 adults, $5.50 seniors, $4.50 ages 3–12. Planetarium only: $3.50 adults, $3 children and seniors. Inquire about combo ticket prices. (1½ hours)

✰✰ **Memphis Zoo**—This popular attraction, located in mid-town Memphis, was founded in 1906. The zoo has just undergone a hugely expensive renovation that has rendered it an appropriate habitat for endangered and exotic species. Exhibits such as *Animals of the Night*, *Primate Canyon*, and *Madagascar* feature state-of-the-art construction, display, and protection methods. Take a look at the zoo on the Internet before you go: www.memphiszoo.org.

Details: *2000 Galloway (Overton Park), Memphis; 901/276-WILD or 800/288-8763. Daily 9–5. $7 adults, $4.50 ages 3–11, $5.50 seniors, parking $2, Mon afternoon free. (2 hours)*

✹✹ **National Ornamental Metal Museum**—Located on a bluff overlooking the Mississippi River at the south end of town, this is my favorite undiscovered museum in Tennessee. Not only does it feature a permanent collection of decorative and utilitarian objects made of metal, but it has a regular schedule of changing exhibits that includes some of the finest metalwork being done today. The facilities include a gift shop with unusual handmade items, and an outdoor working blacksmith shop. The last time I was there the grounds were filled with metal sculptures entered in a creative barbecue-cooker competition.

Details: *374 Metal Museum Dr. (at I-55 Bridge, Crump Ave., exit 12C), Memphis; 901/774-6380. Tue–Sat 10–5, Sun noon–5. $3 adults, $2 students and seniors, children under 6 free. (1½ hours)*

✹✹ **Orpheum Theater**—This theater is a beautifully restored 1928 vaudeville playhouse. The schedule at the Orpheum includes both music and musical theater productions. Check to see if Opera Memphis is performing here while you are in town; they create excellent original theatrical productions in addition to the traditional operatic fare. Call for the schedule of performances and to inquire about tours of the building.

Details: *203 S. Main (intersection of Main and Beale), Memphis; 901/525-7800 (general information) or 901/525-3000 (box office).*

✹✹ **Peabody Hotel**—Memphis's historically elegant 1880s hotel features an ornate, sparkling, gilded interior which lends an air of excitement to just sitting in the lobby bar while watching the well-heeled clientele. Promptly at 11 a.m. daily a small cadre of ducks is paraded off an elevator and around the lobby to the central fountain to the march music of John Philip Sousa; at 5 p.m. they are returned to their rooftop home. Children will be delighted by this freebie, whose Boston counterpart was chronicled in Robert J. McCloskey's children's classic *Make Way for Ducklings*.

Details: *149 Union St., Memphis; 901/529-4000 or 800/PEA-BODY. (30 minutes)*

★★ **Sun Studio**—Still an active recording studio, this is the spot where musicians can feel the vibes of their famous predecessors like Elvis, Carl Perkins, Johnny Cash, Roy Orbison, and Jerry Lee Lewis. It's open daily for tours with a gallery/gift shop and café.
Details: 706 Union, Memphis; 901/521-0664. Daily 10–6. $7.85 adults, children under 12 free. (1½ hours)

★ **Cotton Row and Main Street Trolley**—Take in Front Street's Cotton Row and hop on the restored Main Street Trolley line to get a feel for old Memphis for only 50 cents. The trolley serves an area extending from the Pyramid to the National Civil Rights Museum.
Details: 574 N. Main, Memphis; 901/274-6282. Operates daily until midnight, Sun until 6. 50 cents, 25 cents seniors and handicapped, $2 all day.

★ **Dixon Gallery and Gardens**—This museum, which houses a noted collection of Impressionist art, is located in the Dixon Mansion and surrounded by seasonally landscaped gardens. The museum has nice galleries in an adjacent wing for changing exhibits of fine and decorative arts. The gardens are open Mondays for half the regular admission price.
Details: 4339 Park Ave., Memphis; 901/761-5250. Tue–Sat 10–5, Sun 1–5. $5 adults, $3 students, $4 seniors, $1 ages 3–12. (1½ hours)

★ **Mississippi Riverfront**—The Mississippi Riverfront area has captured the imagination of local officials and is currently being redeveloped. The face-lifting originally began in 1982 with a monument to the river: **Mud Island Museum Park**. Marking the northern boundary of downtown's riverfront footage is the **Pyramid**, a new 32-story glass indoor sports arena. Stroll or walk the riverfront area, and take the monorail to Mud Island to visit the **Mississippi River Museum** and see an interpretive outdoor scale model of the river.
Details: 125 North Front St., Memphis; 901/576-7241 or 800/507-6507. Tue–Sun 10–4:30, summer daily 10–8. Admission to grounds $4 adults; $3 seniors, handicapped, and ages 4–11. Admission to all attractions $8 adults; $6 seniors, handicapped, and ages 4–11. (1–2 hours)

★ **Slavehaven, the Burkle Estate**—Slavehaven, built by German immigrant Jacob Burkle in 1849, served as a way station on the Underground Railroad. A tour of the house reveals secret tunnels and trapdoors. On display are artifacts that tell the story of the slave era.

Details: 826 N. Second St., Memphis; 901/527-3427 (Heritage Tours). Mon–Sat 10–4; advance reservations required. $5 adults, $3 students. (1 hour)

✤ **University of Memphis Art Museum**—The museum, which houses permanent collections of Egyptian and West African art, also features an outstanding yearly schedule of contemporary exhibits. The museum is located in the Music and Arts Complex of the university. It often hosts lectures and receptions.

Details: 3750 Norriswood, Memphis; 901/678-2224. Mon–Fri 9–5. Admission is free. (1 hour)

✤ **Victorian Village**—Several of the homes in an area along Adams Avenue have been restored to period splendor and are now open to the public. The Woodruff-Fontaine House is an 1870 French-style dwelling that features changing exhibits of textiles, clothing, and antique furniture. The three-story, 25-room Mallory-Neely House is furnished in high-Victorian style with stained-glass windows, faux finishes, and stencil painting. The tiny clapboard Magevney House, built circa 1835, was a middle-class residence owned by an early Irish immigrant schoolteacher.

Details: Woodruff-Fontaine House: 680 Adams, 901/526-1469. Mon–Sat 10–3:30, Sun 1–3:30. $5 adults, $3 students, $4 seniors. Mallory-Neely House: 652 Adams, 901/523-1484. Mar–Dec Tue–Sat 10–4, Sun 1–4. $4 adults, $3 students. Magevney House: 198 Adams, 901/526-4464. Mar–Dec Tue–Fri 10–2, Sat 10–4; extended hours in summer. (3 hours)

Hunt-Phelan House—This white-columned brick home, designed by Robert Mills, architect of the Washington Monument and portions of the White House, was built circa 1830. Residents of this staunchly Old South house vacated their home when the city was occupied by Union forces in June 1862. It became Grant's headquarters for some months, was used as a Federal hospital, then after the war became the site of a Freedmen's Bureau school. It was later returned to the family, who brought back a lot of the original furnishings and spent a number of years repairing and restoring the house.

Details: 553 Beale, Memphis; 901/344-3166 or 800/350-9009. Mon–Sat 10–4, Sun noon–4; extended hours in summer; Jan–Mar and Sept–Dec closed Tue–Wed. $10 adults, $9 students, seniors; $6 ages 5–12. (1 hour)

FITNESS AND RECREATION

In Memphis you need places to cool off in the summer. The downtown **Fogelman YMCA** (245 Madison, 901/527-9622) has an old indoor pool, and most of the downtown hotels (including the Peabody) have indoor fitness facilities with pools. Many suburban hotels (and the Union Street Holiday Inn) have outdoor pools. There is also a pool at **Mud Island**, and access is included in the general admission fee. The Memphis Park Commission (901/454-5200) operates a number of public swimming pools and tennis courts around town.

On cool mornings or evenings going to a park is popular with Memphians. **Overton Park**, in midtown, makes a great place to bike, walk, or run. There is also a public golf course in the park (901/725-9905). The **Lichterman Nature Center** (5992 Quince, 901/767-7322) has a three-mile trail and a 10-acre lake, and offers guided nature walks and wildlife programs on weekends. It's primarily an environmental education center and wildlife sanctuary. **Memphis Botanic Garden** (750 Cherry Rd., 901/685-1566) has 96 acres of woodlands, lakes, and display gardens open year round.

Bicyclists or runners might wish to call the **Memphis Hightailers** (901/386-9356) or **Memphis Runners Track Club** (901/534-6782) to see what organized rides or runs are on tap during your visit to Memphis.

There are two state parks in the Memphis area, both of which offer recreational facilities. **Meeman-Shelby** (901/876-5215), 15 miles north of the city, has swimming, boating, horseback riding, and hiking. It's free and open daily until 10 p.m. **T. O. Fuller State Park** (901/543-7581), which includes the Chucalissa Archeological Museum within its boundaries, has an 18-hole golf course and a swimming pool.

FOOD

Memphis calls itself the pork-barbecue capital of the world, but, with nearly 100 barbecue restaurants, it may be the barbecue capital of the world. The Memphis in May World Championship Cooking Contest and the Mid-South Fair every fall feature competitive barbecue pits. Chopped pork and slabs of ribs, served with a sweet, thick sauce, are what I think of as Memphis barbecue. Recommendations for Memphis' best are a tough call, for everyone you ask has their own favorite and there are many neighborhood eateries that see few outside customers.

All over town you will find **TOPS**. The atmosphere is nothing special, and the pork sandwiches are on the greasy side, but it's the real thing—barbecue cooked in an on-the-premises pit—and will do in a pinch. **Corky's BBQ** (5259 Poplar, 901/685-9771) ships its tender ribs around the country and its crusty pork sandwiches are excellent. The **Bar-B-Q Shop** (1782 Madison, 901/272-1277), an unpretentious lunchroom, offers yummy pulled pork, brisket, ribs, and all the trimmings—including beer. A top local favorite is another 1950s-style hangout called the **Pig 'n' Whistle**. It has two locations (7144 Winchester, 901/754-4400; 2740 Bartlett Rd., 901/386-3300). Made famous in a John Hiatt song, the **Rendezvous** (52 S. Second, 901/523-2746) serves an unusual "dry" (the sweet and tangy spices are rubbed in) slab of ribs. The restaurant is large, but its basement atmosphere is cozy and its tourist business is substantial, so you might want to call ahead.

Downtown choices for an inexpensive breakfast include the **Arcade** (540 South Main, 901/526-5757), a dinette featured in Mystery Train that also makes great pizzas the rest of the day; and **Cafe Expresso** (149 Union, in the Peabody Hotel; 901/529-4000). Lunch can also be found downtown for a very reasonable price at the **Little Tea Shop** (69 Monroe, 901/525-6000), Memphis' oldest restaurant, established in 1910, which serves Southern-style plate lunches. The **Cupboard Too** (149 Madison, 901/527-9111) was voted the number-one restaurant for home-cooked food by Memphis magazine. Also downtown, **Automatic Slim's Tonga Club** (83 South Second, 901/525-7948) serves fresh, lively cuisine at moderate prices for lunch or dinner in a very hip atmosphere.

For breakfast in midtown try **Brother Juniper's College Inn** (3519 Walker, near the University of Memphis; 901/324-0144) or grab a fresh-baked scone at **Otherlands Coffee Bar** (641 S. Cooper, 901/278-4994). Moderately priced lunches are available at **Café Ole** (959 S. Cooper, 901/275-1504), a friendly place that serves imaginative neo-Mexican dishes; **Wild Oats** (1801 Union, 901/752-4823), a health food store that serves a help-yourself lunch and provides a peaceful dining area in which to enjoy it; and **Saigon Le** (51 North Cleveland, 901/276-5326), a simple dining room with very good Vietnamese food. The **Brushmark Restaurant** (Memphis Brooks Museum, 901/722-3555) is a fine upscale lunch spot where diners may eat outside on a deck facing Overton Park when the weather permits. For a nice midtown dinner, choose **La Montagne** (3550 Park, 901/458-1060) for gourmet vegetarian specialties in a cozy atmosphere; or **Café Society** (212 N.

MEMPHIS

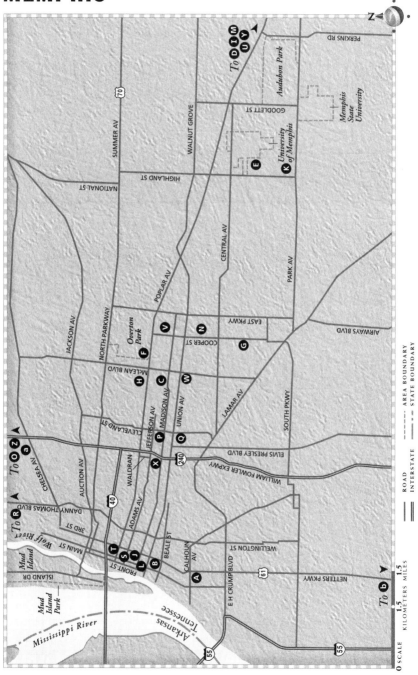

Food

- 🅐 Arcade
- 🅑 Automatic Slim's Tonga Club
- 🅒 Bar-B-Q Shop
- 🅓 Belmont Bar and Grille
- 🅔 Brother Juniper's College Inn
- 🅕 Brushmark Restaurant
- 🅖 Cafe Expresso
- 🅖 Café Ole
- 🅗 Café Society
- 🅘 Corky's BBQ
- 🅙 Cupboard Too
- 🅚 La Montagne
- 🅛 Little Tea Shop
- 🅜 Lulu Grille
- 🅝 Otherlands Coffee Bar
- 🅞 Pig 'n' Whistle
- 🅟 Rendezvous
- 🅟 Saigon Le

Food (continued)

- 🅠 TOPS
- 🅡 Wild Oats

Lodging

- 🅢 Comfort Inn Downtown
- 🅣 Crowne Plaza
- 🅤 East Memphis Hilton
- 🅥 French Quarter Suites
- 🅦 Holiday Inn Midtown
- 🅧 Lowenstein-Long House
- 🅟 Peabody Hotel
- 🅨 Ridgeway Inn
- 🅩 Talbot Heirs Guest House

Camping

- 🅩 Fort Pillow
- ⓐ Meeman-Shelby State Park
- ⓑ T. O. Fuller

Note: Items with the same letter are located in the same town or area.

Evergreen, 901/727-2177), a charming and friendly spot that serves delicious nouvelle cuisine.

In East Memphis for supper? The fine **Lulu Grille** (565 Erin Dr., 901/763-3677) and the **Belmont Bar and Grille** (4970 Poplar, 901/767-0305), whose specialty is the steak sandwich, are neighborhood restaurants with faithful followings.

LODGING

Famous beyond reason but quite nice, the **Peabody Hotel** (149 Union, 800/PEABODY) is Memphis' only historic luxury hotel. Other downtown hotels include the riverfront **Crowne Plaza** (250 N. Main, 901/527-7300 or 800/2-CROWNE), one of the first luxury Holiday Inns in the country since that company started in Memphis. The **Comfort Inn Downtown** (100 North Front, 901/526-0583 or 800/228-5150) has double rooms with a river view for only $80 to $90. A tempting choice for those who'd like to stay downtown but avoid the hotel route is to book a suite or studio at **Talbot Heirs Guest House** (99 South Second, 901/527-9772). These one- or two-room lodgings have full kitchens and lots of amenities including a room-delivered continental breakfast. The $150-and-up price tag might be worth the convenience.

In midtown the less pricey **Holiday Inn Midtown** (1837 Union, 901/278-4100 or 800/HOLIDAY) is convenient and quiet. The **French Quarter Suites** (2144 Madison, 901/428-4000 or 800/843-0353), another good choice, comes with higher rates, so ask about weekend specials. **Lowenstein-Long House** (217 N. Waldran Blvd., 901/527-7174) is an unusual, moderately priced bed-and-breakfast on the edge of midtown. This historic house, furnished with antiques, is adequate but not fancy. It also has hostel accommodations on the premises, so breakfast is a self-service affair.

Out east near I-240 and Poplar are a number of modern hotels whose rooms fall into the $100-per-night range. Try the nice **Ridgeway Inn** (5679 Poplar, 901/766-4000 or 800/822-3360), whose restaurant Café Expresso is a good, moderately priced choice for all three meals; or the **East Memphis Hilton** (5069 Sanderlin, 901/767-6666 or 800/445-8667).

CAMPING

Memphis is a big, spread-out city. It would not occur to me to want to camp here. For the more dedicated camper, however, there are two state parks (call 800/421-6683 to inquire about any Tennessee state park) with facilities in the vicinity: **T. O. Fuller** (901/543-7581) to the south of town has camping; and **Meeman-Shelby State Park** (901/876-5215), 15 miles north, has cabins. **Fort Pillow** (901/738-5581), 50 miles north, also has campsites.

NIGHTLIFE

Before you arrive in Memphis check the *Memphis Flyer*, alternative weekly listings on the internet at www.memphisflyer.com. When you get to town pick up the real thing as you'll find a good listing of assorted happenings and a section on night life. The daily *Memphis Commercial Appeal* is another good source. If you are a dyed-in-the-wool blues fan, listen to local radio station **WEVL** (FM 90) for information regarding the Memphis scene. This grassroots-flavored station is run by volunteers. Listening in will help you understand why Memphis is the blues capital of the world.

Memphis nightlife runs the gamut from so-smoky-you-can't-stand-it blues bars to open-mic literary evenings to fine local theater, ballet, and opera. The nightclubs on Beale are now, for the most part, sanitized and popularized versions of the real thing. Not to be ignored, however, is **B. B. King's Blues Club** (901/524-KING), which features a stellar lineup nearly every night. The "King of Beale" stops in every now and again. For other top clubs you'll have to inquire in the right places, for they are mostly hidden in neighborhoods around town.

Professional theater performances are regularly scheduled at **Playhouse on the Square** (midtown: 51 South Cooper, 901/726-4656). **Opera Memphis** (901/678-2706), a fine local group, performs at the Orpheum Theater. **Theatre Memphis** (630 Perkins Extended, 901/682-8323), **Ballet Memphis** (4569 Summer, 901/763-0139), and the **Memphis Symphony Orchestra** (3100 Walnut Grove Rd., 901/324-3627) all mount regular-season schedules. The **Germantown Performing Arts Center** (1801 Exeter Rd., 901/757-7256) presents prominent touring music, dance, and theater events. Call to see what is playing during your visit.

Poetry readings and coffeehouse musical performances are held at Davis-Kidd, Bookstar, Barnes & Noble, and Borders bookstores, and can be found in conjunction with the **Blues City Cultural Center** (901/942-7707), which also mounts grassroots community theatrical performances on occasion. The **New Daisy** (330 Beale, 901/525-8979) also presents blues and rock performances. Lest you think Memphians groove only on blues and jazz, check out the variety on **Newby's** bill (539 South Highland, 901/452-8408); or the large, high-energy dance club **Six One Six** (600 Marshall, 901/526-6552), which features rave nights, disco nights, and national rock music acts. There is a lively alternative rock scene in Memphis (the home of ARDENT studios) so look for local heroes like Mudboy and the Neutrons among the club listings or stop by **The Map Room** (107 Madison, 901/525-1286) for live jazz or art-rock.

Memphis is definitely a sports-oriented town. A new AAA baseball stadium for the **Memphis Red Birds** (901/523-2449) will soon stand next to downtown, while the flashy **Pyramid Arena** (901/521-9675) makes a terrific place to take in University of Memphis Tigers basketball (901/678-2231) and other events. The **Memphis Riverkings** (901/278-9009) hold the ice at the Mid-South Coliseum.

Think a trip to Memphis wouldn't be complete without a ride on the mighty Mississippi? You can book a 90-minute cruise on the *Memphis Queen* (901/527-5694 or 800/221-6197) for less than $10 and see for yourself

GALLERIES

Memphis has a number of fine nonprofit and commercial art galleries. A partial list includes: **Clough Hanson Gallery** (Rhodes College, 2000 North Pkwy., 901/843-3442), **Cooper Street Gallery** (964 South Cooper, 901/272-7053), **Marshall Arts/Delta Axis** (639 Marshall St., 901/522-9483), **Lisa Kurts Gallery** (766 South White Station Rd., 901/683-6200), **Albers Fine Art** (1102 Brookfield, 901/683-2256), and **Ledbetter Lusk Gallery** (4540 Poplar, 901/767-3800).

Scenic Route: Highway 64 to Savannah

State Highway 64 runs across the southern part of Tennessee, roughly paralleling the border, from Memphis to Monteagle. Because this is truly the road less traveled, much of it is far from any interstate highway. There are many small, very Southern-seeming towns along the way that have remained much as they were in the nineteenth century. The scenic route at the end of Chapter 4 is centered in the area where Highway 64 ends. The route described here remains within West Tennessee, bounded on the east by the Tennessee River and on the west by the Mississippi River.

Headed east out of Memphis on Highway 64/100, you'll be on the "barbecue road;" watch for smoke rising behind small general stores and country eating establishments. About an hour outside of Memphis, where 64 and 100 split at **Whiteville**, there is a wonderful Mennonite bakery. If you follow Highway 100—which deviates toward the northeast—for 13 miles you'll come to **Chickasaw State Park** (901/989-5141), an area of high timberland reclamation in the 1930s by the Civilian Conservation Corps. The park has a lake, cabins with fireplaces, horseback riding, and a campground with hookups. Another 15 or so miles northeast is **Pinson Mounds State Archeological Park** (901/988-5614). A Woodland Indian ceremonial and burial site dating back earlier than A.D. 500, Pinson contains 12 mounds; Saul's Mound, at 72 feet tall, is the second tallest in the country. Administered by the Tennessee Department of Conservation, Pinson Mounds and its interpretive museum are worth going out of your way to see. About 10 miles north of Pinson on I-40 is Jackson, the largest city between Memphis and Nashville.

Jackson, named in honor of Battle of New Orleans hero Andrew Jackson when it was founded in 1821, also claims its own local heroes: Casey Jones, Carl Perkins, and Sonny Boy Williamson. You'll find the **Casey Jones Museum and Restaurant Complex and Carl Perkins' Suedes** restaurant in Jackson, along with a strip of national chain motels and restaurants. If you are lucky enough to arrive in June you might get to set up your own lawn chairs and taste the homemade barbecue at the **Shannon Street Bluesfest**, held at the West Tennessee Farmer's Market, which honors Sonny Boy Williamson. Call the Jackson Convention and Visitors Bureau (901/425-8333) for the exact dates.

From Jackson take Route 18 south for 30 miles (the southeasterly Highway 64 fork at Whiteville will also get you there) to **Bolivar**, an antebellum town that seems to literally rise from the cotton fields.

This was plantation country, and the early 1800s brick residences in this charming town are the epitome of the Old South. The courthouse square is intact, and the 1849 **Magnolia Manor** (901/658-6700), now a bed-and-breakfast, is in the town's historic district. At Selmer, 23 miles east on Highway 64, you can visit the **Hockaday Broom Company** (901/645-4823), run by Jack Martin, the great-grandson of the founder. Call to let him know you are coming.

Shiloh National Military Park (901/689-5696) is on the Tennessee River just southwest of Savannah, and can be reached by Route 142 from Selmer or by staying on Highway 64 and turning south on Route 22 before you reach Savannah. The eight-day Battle of Shiloh in April of 1862 engaged a number of famous generals and had an enormous casualty count: 24,000 soldiers or one-fifth of the Union men and one-fourth of the Confederate force. The battle was a major loss for the Confederates, who relinquished control of important supply lines along the Tennessee River and West Tennessee. The visitors center shows a film explaining the complexly orchestrated battle, and the nine-mile driving tour of the battlefield has explanatory markers along the way.

HIGHWAY 64 TO SAVANNAH

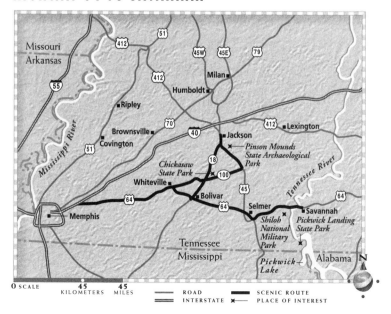

South of Shiloh is the enormous **Pickwick Lake**, created in 1935 by a massive dam on the Tennessee River. **Pickwick Landing State Resort Park** (901/689-3135), which is a very popular vacation spot for Tennesseans and Alabamians, has a modern lodge and cabins and offers boating, swimming, golf, and camping. East of Shiloh is Savannah, whose "Historic Trail" tells the stories of local American Indians and of those who passed this way on the Trail of Tears. Where it runs along the river, it tells also about the ferry run by Alex Haley's grandfather and points out Civil War sites. The **Tennessee River Museum** (800/552-3866), operated by the Chamber of Commerce, is open daily.

From Savannah you can continue across the southern part of the state on Highway 64 through the picturesque towns of Waynesboro, Lawrenceburg, Pulaski, Fayetteville, and Winchester, until you reach Monteagle, a favorite mountain retreat and summer chautauqua for many Tennesseans. Or you can head north to Nashville on the scenic **Natchez Trace Parkway**, which intersects Highway 64 about 25 miles east of Savannah. This two-lane National Park Service road, which runs for 450 miles from Nashville to Natchez, bears interpretive markers describing its history and importance even before it was first documented as an Indian trail by French explorers in 1733. For information, call 800/305-7417. ◼

APPENDIX

METRIC CONVERSION CHART

1 U.S. gallon = approximately 4 liters
1 liter = about 1 quart
1 Canadian gallon = approximately 4.5 liters

1 pound = approximately $\frac{1}{2}$ kilogram
1 kilogram = about 2 pounds

1 foot = approximately $\frac{1}{3}$ meter
1 meter = about 1 yard
1 yard = a little less than a meter
1 mile = approximately 1.6 kilometers
1 kilometer = about $\frac{2}{3}$ mile

90°F = about 30°C
20°C = approximately 70°F

Planning Map: Kentucky/Tennessee

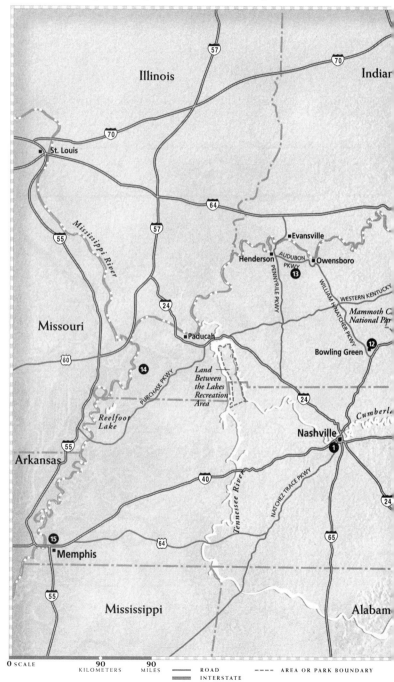

Illinois

Indian

St. Louis

Missouri

Evansville

Henderson

Owensboro

AUDUBON PKWY

PENNYRILE PKWY

WILLIAM HNATCHER PKWY

WESTERN KENTUCKY

Mammoth C
National Par

Paducah

Bowling Green

Mississippi River

PURCHASE PKWY

Land
Between
the Lakes
Recreation
Area

Reelfoot
Lake

Nashville

Cumberle

Arkansas

Tennessee River

NATCHEZ TRACE PKWY

Memphis

Mississippi

Alabam

O SCALE | **90** KILOMETERS | **90** MILES | ROAD | AREA OR PARK BOUNDARY | INTERSTATE

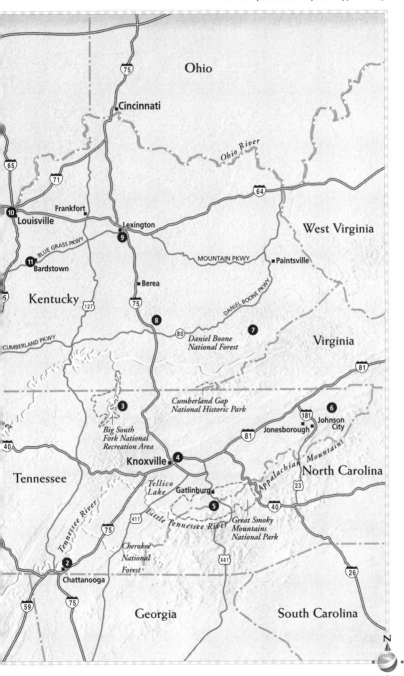

INDEX

Map Index

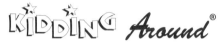

Cater to Your Interests on Your Next Vacation

**The 100 Best Small Art Towns in America
3rd edition**
Discover Creative Communities, Fresh Air, and
Affordable Living
U.S. $16.95, Canada $24.95

**The Big Book of Adventure Travel
2nd edition**
Profiles more than 400 great escapes to all corners
of the world
U.S. $17.95, Canada $25.50

Cross-Country Ski Vacations
A Guide to the Best Resorts, Lodges, and Groomed
Trails in North America
U.S. $15.95, Canada $22.50

Gene Kilgore's Ranch Vacations, 5th edition
The Complete Guide to Guest Resorts, Fly-Fishing,
and Cross-Country Skiing Ranches
U.S. $22.95, Canada $35.50

Indian America, 4th edition
A traveler's companion to more than 300 Indian
tribes in the United States
U.S. $18.95, Canada $26.75

Saddle Up!
A Guide to Planning the Perfect Horseback
Vacation
U.S. $14.95, Canada $20.95

Watch It Made in the U.S.A., 2nd edition
A Visitor's Guide to the Companies That Make Your
Favorite Products
U.S. $17.95, Canada $25.50

The World Awaits
A Comprehensive Guide to Extended Backpack
Travel
U.S. $16.95, Canada $23.95

**JMP travel guides are available
at your favorite bookstores.
For a FREE catalog or to place a
mail order, call: 800-888-7504.**

John Muir Publications ◆ P.O. Box 613 ◆ Santa Fe, NM 87504

Clark Thomas

ABOUT THE AUTHOR

Susan Knowles has been active in the Middle Tennessee arts community for more than 20 years. She has held curatorial positions at the Country Music Hall of Fame and the Cheekwood Museum of Art and has directed art gallery programs for the Metro Nashville Arts Commission, Middle Tennessee State University, and the Nashville International Airport. As an independent curator, Knowles directed the Tennessee exhibit for the National Museum of Women in the Arts and coproduced an interactive project called "Southern Voices: English in the American South" for the Tennessee Humanities Council.

Knowles lives on a small farm two hours east of Nashville with her husband, artist Andrew Saftel. She is the author of *CitySmart: Nashville* (John Muir Publications, 1999) and writes regularly for *Art Papers, Number*, and *Nashville CitySearch*.